A Confederate Legend

MERCER
UNIVERSITY PRESS

Endowed by
TOM WATSON BROWN
and
THE WATSON-BROWN FOUNDATION, INC.

A Confederate Legend

SERGEANT BERRY BENSON IN WAR AND PEACE

Edward J. Cashin

MERCER UNIVERSITY PRESS
MACON, GEORGIA

MUP/764

© 2008 Edward J. Cashin
Published by
Mercer University Press
1400 Coleman Avenue
Macon, Georgia 31207

First Edition.

Books published by Mercer University Press are printed on acid free paper that
meets the requirements of American National Standard for Information
Sciences—Permanence of Paper for Printed Library Materials.

Library of Congress Cataloging-in-Publication Data

Cashin, Edward J., 1927-2007
A Confederate legend : Sergeant Berry Benson in war and peace / Edward
J.
Cashin. -- 1st ed.
p. cm.
Includes bibliographical references and index.
ISBN-13: 978-0-88146-118-3 (hardback : alk. paper)
ISBN-10: 0-88146-118-0 (hardback : alk. paper)
1. Benson, Berry, 1843-1923. 2. Confederate States of America.
Army—Biography. 3. Scouts (Reconnaissance)—Confederate States of
America—Biography. 4. United States—History—Civil War, 1861-
1865—Scouts and scouting. 5. Shooters of firearms—Confederate States of
America—Biography. 6. United States—History—Civil War, 1861-
1865—Prisoners and prisons. 7. Prisoners of war—New York
(State)—Elmira—Biography. 8. Elmira Prison (Elmira, N.Y.) 9. United
States—History—Civil War, 1861-1865—Campaigns. 10. Augusta
(Ga.)—Biography. I. Title.
E467.1.B46C37 2008
973.7'82092—dc22
[B]
2008015724

Contents

Preface

Historian James M. McPherson set out to discover why men fought in the Civil War by reading letters soldiers wrote home. Before he finished, he had read 25,000 personal letters and 249 diaries. He learned that men on both sides fought for their conception of liberty, for home and family, out of a sense of duty, for the sheer love of adventure, and "for one's public reputation, one's image in the eyes of his peers."[1] Berry Benson's war journal is not among those listed in McPherson's bibliography, nor is his name cited in the text, but the historian might have come to the same conclusions—less scientifically but also less tediously—by reading the single manuscript.

Other findings listed by McPherson are also illustrated in Benson's journal: the surprising literacy of the Civil War soldier, the recourse to religion in impending peril, the sustaining influence of support from home and the demoralizing effect of the withdrawal of such support, the power of leadership by example, the intangible mystique of the flag, the adrenalin of battle followed by lassitude and even illness, the contempt for skulkers, and the settled certainty of belonging to "a band of brothers." "The boys," Berry Benson wrote, "that's what we all called the others, 'the boys,' and when at home, held by a wound, or on furlough, soon a kind of home-sickness took possession of one, and he wanted to get back to camp and see the boys, as badly as he had wanted to get home."[2]

---

[1] James M. McPherson, *For Cause and Comrades: Why Men Fought in the Civil War* (New York: Oxford University Press, 1997) 23.

[2] Berry Benson, "The War Book, Reminiscences of Berry Greenwood Benson, CSA," (Typescript prepared by Charles G. Benson, Ida Jane ["Jeanie"] Benson, and Olive Benson), Special Collections, Reese Library, Augusta State University, Augusta GA; hereafter cited as "War Book"), 117. A copy of the typescript is also held by the Southern Historical Collection at the University of North Carolina, Chapel Hill, in its Berry Benson Papers, ms. 2636. Two of the original manuscript diaries (ms. 326)

So typical in many ways, Berry Benson remained unique. He could be awed by the clarity of the moon as he marched into battle at Chancellorsville; he could go to sleep during the fighting at the Bloody Angle at Spotsylvania. While spying out an enemy camp, he thought he might steal a Yankee colonel's horse—and did so. While escaping from a prison camp and still in Union territory, he hopped a ride on a train carrying provisions for the Union army, and sat atop a car chatting companionably with a Union soldier. Arrested in another spying foray, he reprimanded one of his captors for using bad language. The term "happy warrior" might have been coined for Berry Benson.

Berry Benson's devotion to the flag of the Confederacy contains a lesson for those who still argue about the meaning of the flag. Some wonder whether a flag associated with slavery should be honored at all. Georgia legislators gave a pejorative meaning to the Confederate battle flag by incorporating it into the state emblem as an act of defiance against integration. For Berry Benson, the flag stood for home and family. It meant living up to one's best. It represented the men he most admired. He vested in it, consciously or otherwise, his own standards of honor, courage, and decency. "A red flag," he wrote, "(there will be those who say),—a red rag tied to a stick, and that is all! And yet—that red rag, crossed with blue, with white stars sprinkled on the cross within, tied to a slim, barked pine sapling, with leather thongs cut from a soldier's shoe, this rough red rag my soul loved with a lover's love."[3] There was no racial hatred or regional bitterness in his veneration of the flag. He disassociated himself from the later attempt of the Ku Klux Klan to enlist the flag in the cause of prejudice. There was no hate in his heritage.

---

are located in the Hargrett Rare Book & Manuscript Library at the University of Georgia in Athens.
[3] Susan Williams Benson, ed., *Berry Benson's Civil War Book: Memoirs of a Confederate Scout and Sharpshooter* (Athens: University of Georgia Press, 1962) 24. Susan Benson was the wife of Charles Benson and the daughter-in-law of Berry Benson.

McPherson found slavery cited as an issue in only twenty percent of the letters written by Southern soldiers. Berry mentioned it not at all. If anything, he took slavery for granted as a fact of life. His father owned two household slaves whom Berry and his brother Blackwood regarded as dependent family members. Neither brother had any objection to the Confederacy's last-minute plan to induct slaves into the army, except that it showed that the cause of Southern independence was in desperate straits.

Growing up in Augusta, I heard the name Berry Benson spoken with respect and affection. My grandfather, Thomas J. O'Leary, worked with Berry Benson as an accountant at John P. King Mill. William D. O'Leary, my "Uncle Bill," when he was a scoutmaster, went off on Boy Scout hikes led by Berry Benson. We all knew that Benson was a Civil War hero, and that his image stood atop the lofty Confederate Monument on Broad Street representing the enlisted men of the Confederacy. I did not know that his post-war activities also set him apart and deserved recognition. My decision to look more closely at Benson's career came after reading Steve Oney's brilliantly thorough study of the Leo Frank case, *And the Dead Shall Rise: The Murder of Mary Phagan and the Lynching of Leo Frank.* When it seemed that all of Georgia was caught up in an ugly wave of anti-Semitism, Berry Benson argued for Frank's innocence. His statements were printed in newspapers around the country and contributed to a national movement to save Frank from the gallows. A lynch mob frustrated justice, but Georgia's image in this sordid affair is better because Berry Benson and a few fellow Georgians spoke up for the right. I am grateful to Steve Oney for sharing with me his research on Benson's relationship with Frank.

Two of the original diaries that formed the basis of Berry Benson's war journal are in the Hargrett Collection at the University of Georgia. Benson's son Charles made four typescripts of the journal itself, which was apparently written around 1875. He titled the manuscript "Berry Benson's War Book," because that was how the Benson family referred to it. One copy of the War Book is in the Southern Historical Collection at the University of North Carolina at Chapel Hill; another is in the Special Collections at the Reese Library, Augusta State University. In the same depository, there are separate files containing papers of Berry Benson's children, Jeanie, Arthur, and Charles.

Charles Benson's daughter Frances, now Mrs. Harold Thompson of Starkville, Mississippi, graciously allowed me to examine the boxes of family papers in her possession. In opening one fragile letter from Berry to his wife Jeanie, a dried, crushed rose fell out, a touching indication of his love for her. A trove of other papers belongs to Arthur Dupre, Berry Benson's great-grandson. Professor Dupre, now on the faculty of Rutgers University, bears a striking physical resemblance to Berry Benson, and like his great-grandfather, has a facility for mathematics and pursues a wide range of interests. I appreciate his hospitality to my wife and me on our visit to Newark, New Jersey, and for letting me borrow valuable family material. Most of Benson's post-war letters are in the Southern Historical Collection. Some of his are among the Leo Frank Papers at the Atlanta History Center.

Berry Benson would be surprised that he is remembered so fondly and with such esteem almost a century after his death. Each year, on the anniversary of his birth, members of the Sergeant Berry Greenwood Benson Camp, Sons of Confederate Veterans, and of the Berry Benson Chapter, Daughters of the Confederacy, conduct a ceremonial ritual at the Benson gravesite in Sunset Hill Cemetery, North Augusta, South Carolina. Boys and girls of the Jeanie Benson chapter Children of the Confederacy participate. There are recitations and songs in the time-honored tradition. Women dressed in period attire remind the spectator that customs and attitudes change very slowly. A squad of men in Civil War uniforms fire antique muskets three times in salute. The old soldier would not have expected such attention, but he would have been pleased by it.

I am indebted to several of Georgia's most prominent Civil War historians who have read the manuscript. They include Emory Thomas, biographer of Robert E. Lee; Anne Bailey, whose Civil War books include *War and Ruin: William T. Sherman and the Savannah Campaign*; Russell Brown, biographer of Augusta native General W. H. T. Walker; William Bragg, author of *Joe Brown's Army: The Georgia State Line, 1862–1865* among others; and C. L. "Chip" Bragg, biographer of another Augustan, General Marcellus A. Stovall. James C. Cobb, holder of the Spalding Distinguished Professor of History Chair at the University of Georgia, and author of *Away Down South: A History of Southern Identity*, commented generously on the text. So did Steve Oney, already mentioned as author of *And the Dead Shall Rise: The Murder of Mary Phagan and the Lynching of Leo Frank*. Finally, I thank the distinguished film documentarian, Ken Burns, who read a synopsis of the book and agreed that Berry Benson's story deserved telling. As always, I appreciate the willing support of the staff of ASU's Reese Library and Media Center, particularly John J. O'Shea and Carol Waggoner-Angelton of special collections.

PUBLISHER'S NOTE

Edward J. Cashin passed away just after submitting his final version of this manuscript. The family of Mr. Cashin was enthusiastic in the publication of this book. Considered by many as the Dean of Georgia Historians, Mr. Cashin was as popular with the general audience as he was with the academic community. He was widely published and had written two books published my Mercer University Press. His presence is sorely missed.

The book could not have been completed without the assistance of William Harris Bragg. A Civil War scholar in his own right, Mr. Bragg assisted in reading the proofs and in preparing the index. The Press wishes to thank him for his work and his time given generously in Mr. Cashin's memory.

Berry Benson

Berry Benson, C.V.C. poster

Augusta Confederate Monument, 1895
(photo take for the sculptor)

The Benson boys

Benson block on Bay Street, Augusta

Benson home

Benson home

Cecrops Malone

Charley Benson

Charles and Lewis Benson

Ingraham Hasell

Jeannie Benson

Melvin Conklin

Mary Phagan

Olive Benson

J. M. Womak

Blackwood K. Benson
(photo taken soon after the war)

French orphan girl

French orphan boy

Gun salute, Berry Benson anniversary

Berry Benson grave marker

John Fox Maull and family

*Elmira Prison escapees at veterans' convention: l-r Berry Benson, George G. Jackson,
[_____] Purifoy, William H. Templin, Wash. B. Traweek*

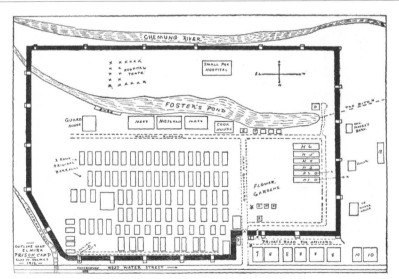

(A) Main entrance to prison camp; (B) Officers' private entrance to camp; (D) Dead house, where bodies were prepared for burial; (E) Officer of the day and guard tending main gate; (H) The six new hospital barracks; (P) Officers' tents; (R) Commandant's office; (S) Sulter's store; (T) Mess house of the 16 police sergeants; (X) Tunnel outlet from Hospital No. 1; (Z) Unfinished tunnel from Hospital No. 2; (7) House for off duty guards; (8) Officer's quarters; (9) Colonel Moore's living quarters (10) Officers' quarters; (13) Barracks of 16th V. R. C.; The famous tunnel is shown near northeast corner of camp. Observatory seen on left, located on opposite side of Water Street.

Elmira prison camp

Fairfax County Jail

Fort Moultrie, 1863

Olgethorpe Infantry

Lewis on pony

"Destroying R.R."

"Turning the Flapjack"

"JACKSON OR A RABBIT!"

"Jackson or a Rabbit!"

SNOW FIGHT.

"Snow Fight"

Berry Benson and escort at parade

Berry Benson leading parade, 1920

Berry Benson gathering mushrooms

Berry Benson gathering mushrooms

Berry Benson reenactment

Savannah, 1864

"Shettland Pony"

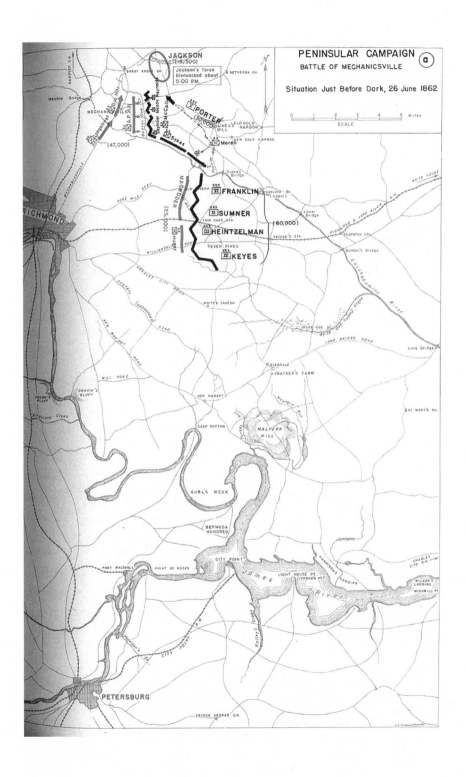

PENINSULAR CAMPAIGN (a)
BATTLE OF MECHANICSVILLE

Situation Just Before Dark, 26 June 1862

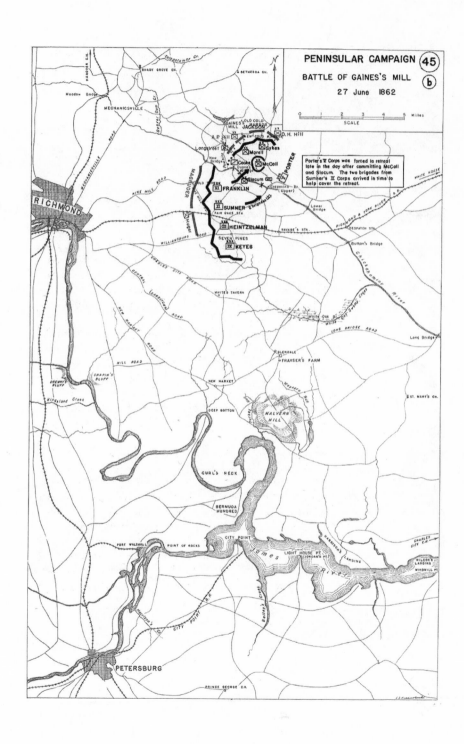

PENINSULAR CAMPAIGN (45)
BATTLE OF GAINES'S MILL (b)
27 June 1862

Porter's V Corps was forced to retreat late in the day after committing McCall and Slocum. The two brigades from Sumner's II Corps arrived in time to help cover the retreat.

SECOND BULL RUN
CAMPAIGN
Situation Night of 26 Aug 1862

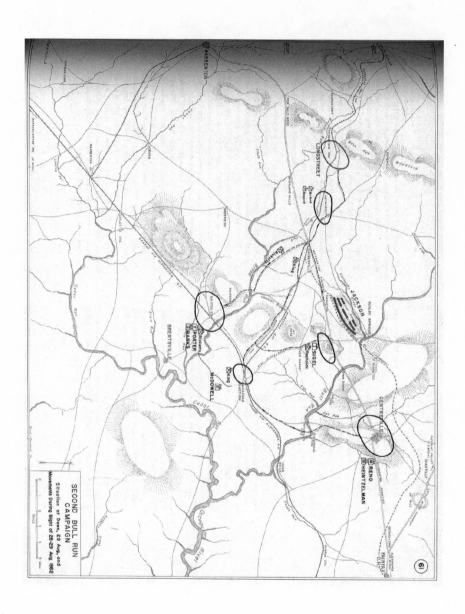

SECOND BULL RUN
CAMPAIGN
Situation at Dawn, 29 Aug, and
Movements During Night of 28-29 Aug 1862

61

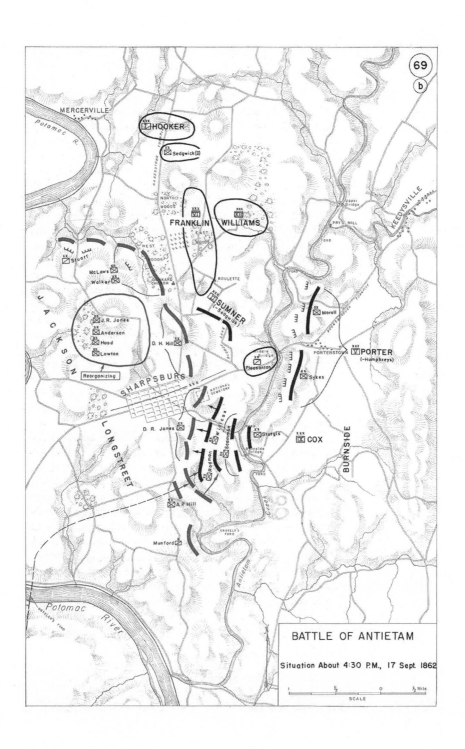

MERCERVILLE

Potomac R.

KEEDYSVILLE

HOOKER

Sedgwick (II)

NORTH WOODS

FRANKLIN   WILLIAMS

VI   XII

Upper Bridge

PRY'S MILL

EAST WOODS

FORD

WEST WOODS

Stuart

McLaws

Walker

DUNKARD CHURCH

ROULETTE

FORD

SUMNER
(-Sedgwick)

J.R. Jones

Anderson

Hood

Lawton

D. H. Hill

Morell

Middle Bridge

PORTERSTOWN   PORTER
(-Humphreys)

Pleasonton

Sykes

Reorganizing

SHARPSBURG

NATIONAL CEMETERY

D. R. Jones

Willcox

Scammon   Sturgis

Rodman   Burnside Bridge   COX

A. P. Hill

FORD

BURNSIDE

SNAVELY'S FORD

Munford

Antietam Creek

Potomac River

battery road

BATTLE OF ANTIETAM

Situation About 4:30 P.M., 17 Sept. 1862

SCALE

JACKSON

LONGSTREET

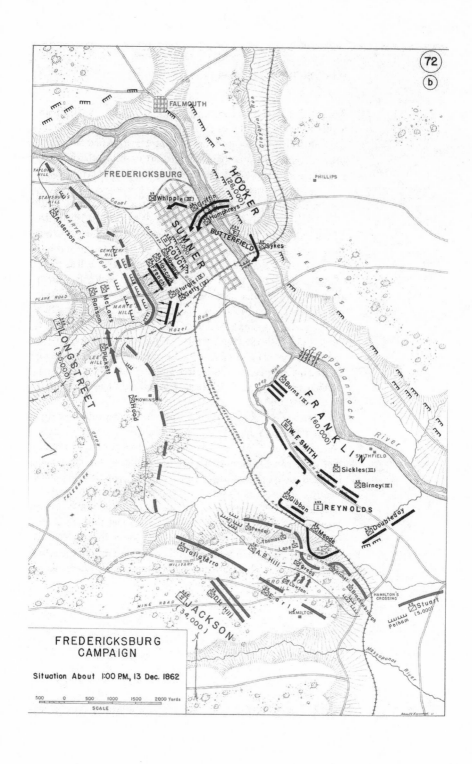

FALMOUTH

FREDERICKSBURG

PHILLIPS

TAYLOR HILL

STANSBURY'S HILL

HOOKER (26,000)

Whipple (III)

Griffin

Humphreys

SUMNER (27,000)

BUTTERFIELD

Anderson

CEMETERY HILL

McLaws

COUCH

Howard

French

Hancock

Sturgis (IX)

Getty (IX)

Sykes

PLANK ROAD

MARYE HILL

Ransom

Hazel Run

LONGSTREET (35,000)

LEE HILL

Pickett

HOWINSON

Burns (IX)

FRANKLIN (60,000)

W.F.SMITH

SMITHFIELD

Sickles (III)

Birney (III)

Gibbon

REYNOLDS

Doubleday

Pender

Thomas

Meade

Taliaferro

A. B. Hill

Lane

Gregg

Archer

D.H. Hill

Early

Lawton

JACKSON (34,000)

HAMILTON

HAMILTON'S CROSSING

Brockenbrough

Stuart (5,000)

Pelham

Massaponax River

FREDERICKSBURG CAMPAIGN

Situation About 1:00 P.M., 13 Dec. 1862

500   0   500   1000   1500   2000 Yards

SCALE

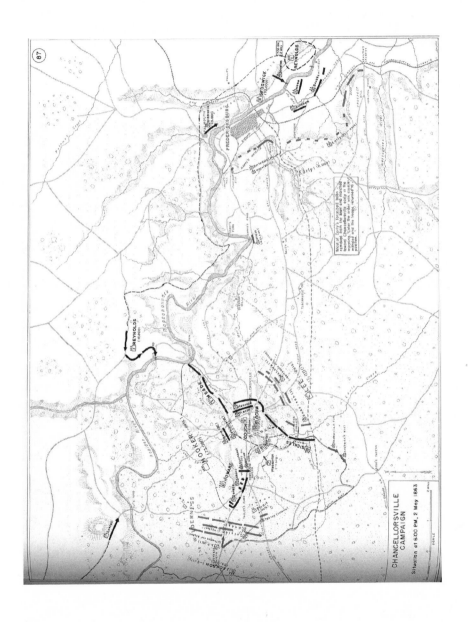

**CHANCELLORSVILLE
CAMPAIGN**

Situation at 6:00 PM, 2 May 1863

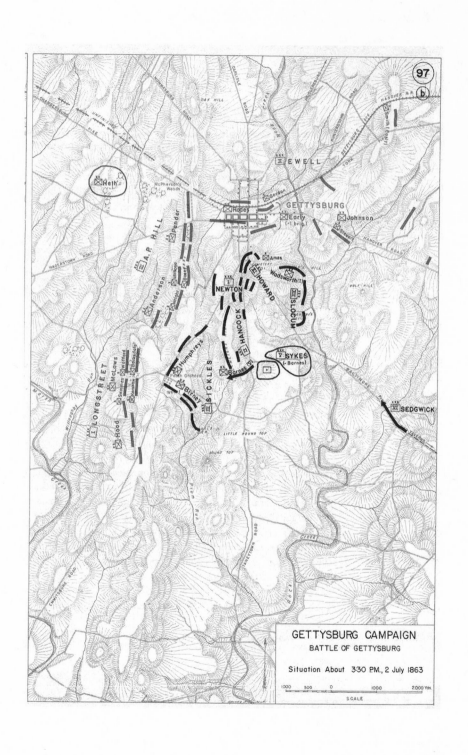

GETTYSBURG CAMPAIGN
BATTLE OF GETTYSBURG

Situation About 3:30 P.M., 2 July 1863

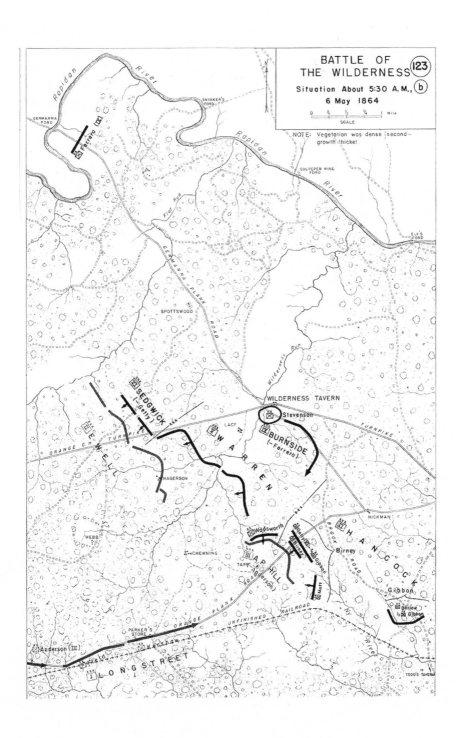

BATTLE OF
THE WILDERNESS 123
Situation About 5:30 A.M., b
6 May 1864

0 ¼ ½ ¾ 1 Mile
SCALE

NOTE: Vegetation was dense second-
growth thicket.

Rapidan River

GERMANNA FORD

Ferrero [IX]

SKINKER'S FORD

Flat Run

Rapidan River

CULPEPER MINE FORD

GERMANNA PLANK ROAD

ELY'S FORD

SPOTTSWOOD

Wilderness Run

SEDGWICK [VI]
(-Getty)

WILDERNESS TAVERN

Stevenson

TURNPIKE

EWELL

ORANGE C.H. TURNPIKE

LACY

WARREN

BURNSIDE [IX]
(-Ferrero)

HAGERSON

WADSWORTH

HICKMAN

BROCK ROAD

HANCOCK

WEBB

CHEWNING

Birney

A.P. HILL
TAPP
(-Anderson)

Gibbon

Mott

ANDERSON

ORANGE PLANK ROAD

UNFINISHED RAILROAD

PARKER'S STORE

Ni River

Carroll
Gibbon

Anderson [III]

Field

Kershaw

LONGSTREET [I]

TO TODD'S TAVERN

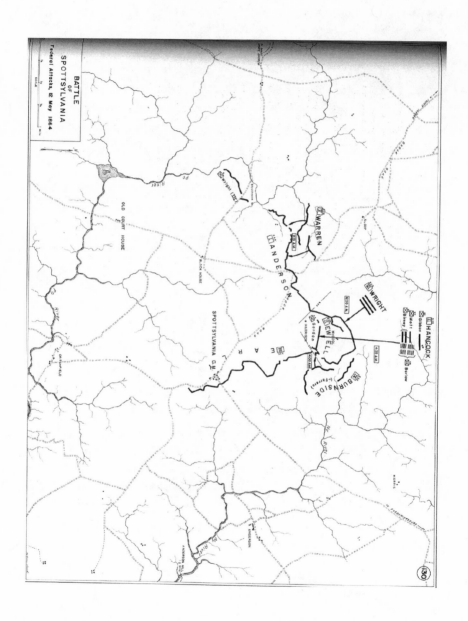

BATTLE
OF
SPOTTSYLVANIA

Federal Attacks, 12 May 1864

SCALE
0   ½   1
MI.

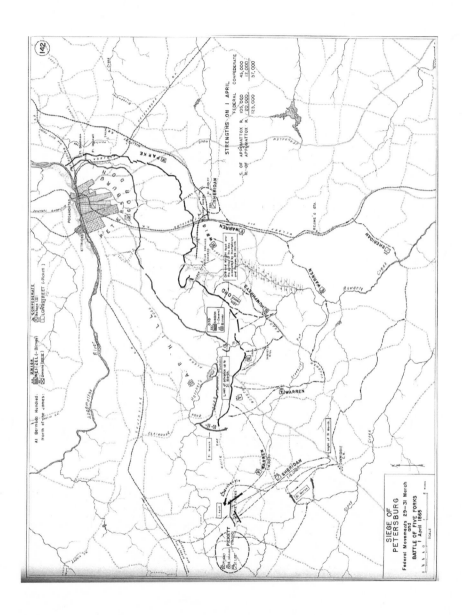

SIEGE OF
PETERSBURG
Federal Movements 29-31 March
and
BATTLE OF FIVE FORKS
1 April 1865

SCALE

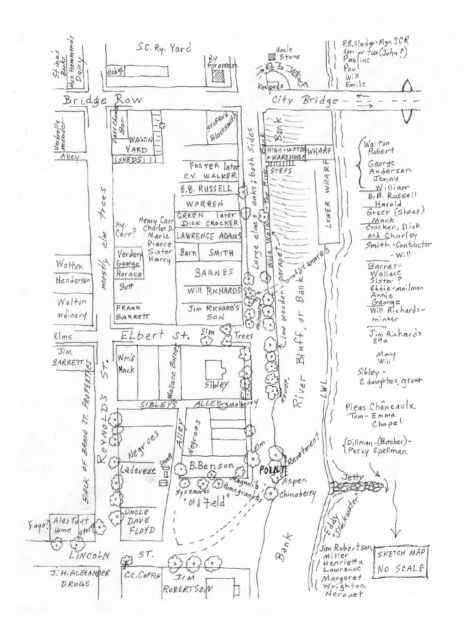

SC. Ry. Yard

Uncle
Stone

Rd. to Wharf
Keepers

P.R. Sledge - Mgr. SCR
Son or two (John?)
Pauline
Paul
Will
Emile

Stine's Bakery
Mrs. Hammond's Dairy

Sledge

Ry.
Foreman

Bridge Row   City Bridge →

Umbrella Mender
Alley

Last Chance Bar

WAGON
YARD

SHEDS

Stofford
Blacksmith

Bank

HIGH-WATER
+ WAREHOUSE

WHARF

STEPS

LOWER WHARF

Walton
Robert

George
Anderson
Jenny
    William
B.B. Russell
    Harold
Greer (shoes)
    Mack
Crocker, Dick
and Charley
Smith - Contractor
    - Will

FOSTER later
C.V. WALKER

B.B. RUSSELL

WARREN

mostly elm trees

Hy.
Carr?

Henry Carr
Charles D.
Marie
Pierre
Sister
Harry

GREEN later
DICK CROCKER

LAWRENCE ADAMS

Verdery
George
Horace
Butt

Barn   SMITH

BARNES

Will RICHARDS

Large elms + oaks; both sides

Wide Walk

The River

low wooden parapet

Barnes-
Wallace?
Sister ?
Eddie - mailman
Annie
George
Will Richards -
minter

Walton
Henderson

Walton
ordinary

FRANK
BARRETT

JIM RICHARD'S
SON

sycamores

River Bluff, or Bank

Jim Richards
Etta

May
Will

Elms

JIM
BARRETT

Elbert St.

Elm   Trees

Wm's
Mack

Sibley

Reynolds St.

BACK OF BROAD ST. PROPERTIES

Wallace Barnes

Revet.

LWL

Sibley -
2 daughters, grown

Pleas Chêneaulx
Tom - Emma
Chapel

Dillman - (Butcher) -
Percy Spellman

SIBLEY'S   ALLEY   Mulberry

Negroes

Alley   Negroes

Elm

Ladeveze

Stone

B. Benson

POINTE

Magnolia

Revetment

Jetty

Fayo?

Alex Tant
Home

Store

UNCLE
DAVE
FLOYD

sycamores   Pomegranates

"Old Field"

Aspen   Chinaberry

Bank

Eddy
"Slackwater"

LINCOLN   ST.

J.H. ALEXANDER
DRUGS

C.C. COFFIN

JIM
ROBERTSON

Jim Robertson
Miller
Henrietta
Lawrence
Margaret
Wrighton
Nerouet

SKETCH MAP
NO SCALE

Growing up in Hamburg

"These were my golden schooldays."

Berry Benson was peculiar. It was a common saying among his friends that he was "peculiar" and this was truer than most who said it thought. In a world of selfishness, he was unselfish. Surrounded by craft and duplicity, he was honest. Amid deceit, he was truthful in thought and act. There was no sham in his nature. There was no malice in his heart. He lived his creed. As a soldier he was valiant. As a citizen he was loyal. As a friend, he was constant. He yearned for knowledge. He loved the beautiful. He knew no guile. He was clean in word and thought.... A gentle and knightly soul is gone from among us.[1]

Those were the sentiments written on the occasion of Berry Benson's death on New Year's Day, 1923, by one who knew him well, his friend and pallbearer, Theodore Oertel. In just a little more than a month, Berry Benson would have lived eighty years. Few men have a life filled with such adventure; few have relished life as much. His character took shape in antebellum Hamburg, South Carolina, and Augusta, Georgia, twin cities straddling the Savannah River, in the era of optimism enjoyed by Southerners before events made optimism an anachronism.

The child was father to the man. Berry's earliest memories were of romps through the countryside and the joy of discovery of nature's good things. Berry Greenwood Benson was born on 9 February 1843, in Hamburg, South Carolina, to A. Madison (Mat) and Nancy

---

[1] *Augusta Chronicle*, 3 January 1923.

Harmon Benson. Their town, Hamburg, was the brainchild of a German immigrant named Henry Shultz. Shultz built the first successful bridge across the Savannah River, made a fortune, and sold the bridge to Augusta businessmen. When the buyers went bankrupt, an Augusta bank seized Shultz's bridge, the collateral put up by the purchasers. Blaming Augustans for the "theft" of his bridge, Shultz retaliated by founding the town of Hamburg in 1822 on the South Carolina side of the bridge and became famous in the process. When the great Lafayette came to Augusta in 1825, he kept the city dignitaries waiting while he called upon Henry Shultz in Hamburg. For a while, Shultz and his instant town prospered as commercial rivals to Augusta. The South Carolina Railroad made Hamburg famous by linking it with Charleston in 1833, advertising it as the longest railroad in the world at the time.[2]

Henry Shultz still lived on the hill bearing his name when Berry Benson came into the world. Shultz kept a park open for picnickers. The Bensons lived at the bottom of the hill, and enjoyed the picnics. Berry grew into his teens in the house at the bottom of the hill, "a good friend and companion of mine that old hill was," he recalled. Low-lying Hamburg suffered worse than Augusta did when a massive flood swept down the Savannah River in 1852. Fortunately, the Bensons lived on the second floor, and they stepped into a boat from the upstairs window, and waited on Shultz Hill for the waters to recede. The floods and competition from Augusta hastened the decline of Hamburg.[3]

---

[2] For Henry Shultz and Hamburg, see Edward J. Cashin, *The Story of Augusta* (Augusta GA: Richmond County Board of Education, 1980) 71–74.

[3] Berry Benson, "The War Book, Reminiscences of Berry Greenwood Benson, CSA," (Typescript prepared by Charles G. Benson, Ida Jane ["Jeanie"] Benson, and Olive Benson), Special Collections, Reese Library, Augusta State University, Augusta GA; hereafter cited as "War Book"), 11. A copy of the typescript is also held by the Southern Historical Collection at the University of North Carolina, Chapel Hill, in its Berry Benson Papers, ms. 2636. Two original manuscript diaries (ms. 326) are located in the Hargrett Rare Book & Manuscript Library at the University of Georgia in Athens.

Berry's companion in his boyhood escapades was his brother, Blackwood Ketcham, two years younger than Berry. A third brother, Bradford Harmon, born in 1848, was too young to be considered a playmate by his older brothers. In 1849, Mat Benson left the family to find gold in California. Mat kept a letter six-year-old Berry wrote and assumed that Nancy had written it for her son. But Berry wrote it himself, copying his mother's style. It read, "Dear Father, We are all well to day. Yesterday and to day is so verry [*sic*] cool that it appears like winter is returning again, and I wonder if you will return with it? Mother says if you do not she will make a little tent in the woods and live upon roots."[4] Mat returned in a year and a half no richer but with a fondness for California that he expressed by naming their next child "California." Callie was born on 5 December 1851. The last surviving child, Elizabeth Bradley, came into the world on 1 July 1854.

The people of Hamburg shared their founder's bias against the more prosperous town across the river. For one thing, the promoters of the South Carolina Railroad had hoped that their line would cross Georgia and tap the resources of the West. However, the Augusta authorities refused to allow the railroad to enter their city. Adding injury to insult, the Georgians borrowed the Carolina idea and built their own line from Augusta westward. Not until the frustrated Carolinians threatened to bypass Georgia completely and build through North Carolina did the gentlemen of Augusta relent and allow the South Carolina Railroad to build a bridge across the Savannah River. Small boys began crossing the bridge before it was finished, among them young Berry Benson. When Hamburg boys met Augusta boys on the bridge, they exchanged taunts and sometimes exchanged projectiles.

The bridge was the scene of Berry's first battle. The Augusta boys started it. A crowd of them crossed to the Hamburg side,

---

[4] Benson, "War Book," 10.

stepping carefully with the river clearly in view between the ties. At the end of the bridge they stood on enemy soil and set up a clamor that quickly attracted the attention of the Hamburg boys who were just leaving school. Berry and his mates determined to defend their territory, and armed themselves with rocks. With a yell, they dashed toward the Augusta invaders. Berry learned then a lesson in military strategy that proved true in the war to come. A gallant charge while holding your fire will rout a less resolute foe. So the Augusta boys retreated to the middle of the bridge, their boundary line, and there began to hurl iron taps left by the workmen. The Hamburg boys had the advantage; they could throw the taps back at the Augustans, and they had an endless supply of rocks carried up by Blackwood and the smaller boys. The fight ended when one of the hurled taps broke an Augusta boy's leg.[5]

Soon, however, the Benson boys had to cross over to Augusta when Mr. David Griffin closed his school in Hamburg and moved to the North. Berry and Blackwood then attended Houghton Institute, a free school endowed by a wealthy Augusta merchant. When Mr. Griffin decided to return South and open a school in Augusta, Berry and Blackwood happily transferred to his school. Somewhat to his surprise, Berry discovered that the Augusta boys, his former enemies, were not so bad.[6]

From his twelfth year to his sixteenth, Berry crossed and recrossed the bridge to Griffin's school on the corner of Ellis and Seventh Streets. An assumption in the old South held that, though people may have come into the world in a certain kind of equality, they soon divided into classes on the basis of their brains and abilities. Only a talented few, prodded by their parents and their own ambition, went beyond the basic grammar school level of instruction, and many did not have even that because the public school system did not exist in the antebellum South. Berry and Blackwood had to get

---

[5] Ibid., 14–16.
[6] Ibid., 23.

up early to hike three miles to Griffin's school in order to be there by nine in the morning. At one o'clock came a two-hour break for dinner. (The mid-day meal was traditionally "dinner" the evening meal "supper.") At first, the Benson boys brought their lunch to school, but as they grew older they preferred to go home by way of the dangerous railroad bridge rather than the Shultz Bridge. It was dangerous because they could see the river between the spaces between the ties, because they tried to walk on the rails, and especially because a train might come and catch them in the covered bridge. They had to be back at school from three to five in the afternoon. The twelve-mile daily trek proved to be good training for later when they marched in Stonewall Jackson's "foot cavalry."

Expectations in Griffin's School seem impossibly high by modern standards. The same would be true in Mr. Joseph Derry's school a decade later when young Woodrow Wilson and Joseph R. Lamar learned their lessons. Berry had to learn Latin, Greek, and French, as well as history, geography, and grammar. Unlike most students, he liked grammar, with its parsing of sentences into nouns, verbs, and the rest. Mr. Griffin enlivened the class by allowing each student to correct the parsing done by any other student, and even of the teacher himself. Once, Berry noticed a mistake by a fellow scholar. When nobody challenged it, Berry raised his hand to do so. A spirited debate followed. Finally, Mr. Griffin allowed the class to vote. Everyone voted against Berry. Then Mr. Griffin delivered the verdict, "I think Berry is right."[7]

If parsing was fun, mathematics was a delight. Berry began a lifelong fascination with numbers and number games. He generally won all the spelling bees, except once when he deliberately missed so his current sweetheart could win. He enjoyed the botany classes, especially when they would go on field trips identifying plants. Sometimes Mr. Griffin would keep them after dark to give lessons in

---

[7] Ibid., 24.

astronomy that became occasions for flirtation. In fact, Berry excelled at everything in school, marbles included. Mr. Griffin, a good sport, challenged Berry to a game of marbles, and was soundly defeated. Martin Calvin, a classmate of Berry's and later principal of Houghton Institute and the first superintendent of post-war public schools in Richmond County, had this to say of Berry: "I recall Berry Benson the boy at school, first in conduct, first in Latin, therefore first in English, first in Greek and in mathematics, first in the boyish sports of the day."[8] To be first in so many categories was no small achievement in a school with a hundred students.

Berry read books for improvement and books for fun. He especially liked the stories of derring-do. He read Harrison Ainsworth's 1839 novel *Jack Sheppard* based on a real life thief of that name who was hanged at Tyburn on 16 November 1724, but not until he had become a hero to London's underworld for his daring and a brand of gallantry. Jack Sheppard escaped from Newgate prison three times by various ingenious means, becoming more famous each time. He dressed like a beggar to listen to ballads sung about him. He aspired to be a gentleman, and he stole clothes to dress the part—then stole money to treat his hangers-on to drinks. Even on his way to execution, Sheppard sought ways to escape. Berry relished the stories of escape. He read Ainsworth's novel about the highwayman Dick Turpin and his horse Black Bess. The real Dick Turpin was a ne'er-do-well, but the storied Turpin became a folk hero like Robin Hood. Berry read about "Sixteen String Jack," who dressed like a dandy, with sixteen silken strings tying his breeches to his knees and a satin waistcoat laced with silver. He was tried and acquitted for highway robbery six times, but he was sentenced to death on the seventh charge. He faced the gallows at Tyburn in 1774 at the age of twenty-four. Berry enjoyed reading about Claude Duval, born in France, but who achieved notoriety as a highwayman in

---

[8] *Augusta Chronicle*, 7 July 1902.

England. His success in robbing travelers matched his success with the women. He too met his fate on the gallows at Tyburn on 21 January 1670. On his gravestone in the Covent Garden church is the inscription, "Here lies Du Vall [*sic*]; reader, if male thou art / Look to thy purse; if female, to thy heart." Berry's strict moral code would not allow the liberties of the Dick Turpins and Claude Duvals, but the stories challenged him to take risks, and in the great war ahead of him, there would be opportunity for derring-do.[9]

Berry recalled his boyhood time as a golden era. On Saturdays, he and Blackwood hunted and fished, or hiked through the woods with Berry attempting to recognize the plants he read about in botany books. They picked blackberries and muscadines and peddled them house to house in Augusta for pocket change. On warm summer days they would swim in Brook's Pond or in Horse Creek. These apprentice highwaymen were not above raiding orchards for peaches. Hiking, swimming, and foraging skills proved extremely useful later.

Grief punctuated the happy time when Nancy Benson died on 12 February 1857, just after Berry's fourteenth birthday. She died in childbirth, as did her baby. The loss devastated Berry. She had been his first teacher and remained his best friend. He had habitually confided in her for everything, and would report his daily doings as a matter of routine and close with a goodnight kiss. Her love and good opinion of him gave him the sense of self-worth that became part of his character. For many nights his tears wet his pillow.[10] But life went on.

There had been another dark moment in the young boy's life. When he was seven-years-old and Mat Benson had gone to California, Nancy Benson took her children to her parents' house in the country near Greenville, South Carolina. Berry's grandfather was pleasant enough when sober, but when in drink, he turned mean to

---

[9] Berry mentions such childhood heroes in "War Book," 359.
[10] Benson, "War Book," 37.

the point of being homicidal. On the occasions when he returned home driving his wagon erratically, his wife would hide knives, guns, and anything dangerous, and call upon a strong young slave named Anthony to stand by. Once, Berry saw a horrifying sight. His drunken grandparent found an axe, and began to chase after a slave woman who had given him no provocation whatever. He swung the axe in a stroke that would have cleaved her if she had not run. Instead, it sliced into her back. Anthony managed to wrest the axe away and subdue the crazed man. Berry watched his grandmother bathe the wounded back of the woman. He then resolved never to touch liquor, and he never did.[11]

But, Berry had a happy disposition, and a general air of optimism pervaded that part of the South. Augusta enjoyed a boom as the result of its new canal and factories. Georgia political leaders Alexander Stephens and Howell Cobb had helped avert a sectional crisis in 1850. When Berry reached his fourteenth birthday, the question of slavery in the western territories cast a shadow over the bright prospects of the future. Berry's father owned two slaves, and Berry accepted slavery as part of the natural order of things. Both Berry and Blackwood asked to be remembered to the servants in their wartime letters home. By Berry's seventeenth year the issue of slavery in territories dominated political discussion, and Berry heard some politicians talk of war with the North.

The war talk in 1860 caused David Griffin to close his school and move to Illinois. He had become a father figure to Berry, and he called Berry "his boy." Griffin admitted that Berry had learned everything Griffin could teach him, and advised, "Follow a vocation that involves mathematics, for that is your forte."[12] They embraced and parted. Within the year, Berry received the sad news that his mentor and teacher had died.

---

[11] Berry Benson to Mrs. R. L. Miller, n.d., Benson Family Papers, in private collection of Arthur Dupre, Newark NJ.

[12] Benson, "War Book," 39.

Berry later recalled the names of his schoolmates who died in the war. Pete Ransom died at Gettysburg. Jim Robinson died in Maryland, leading a charge with the regimental colors in his hand. Caspar Gardner, John Cheeseborough, Brooks Matheny, Henry Rhodes, Henry Gray, Milbourne Carter, William Miller, Sampson Butler, were all killed in battle. Perhaps there were others, also, but those he remembered.[13] The graduating class of 1860 was dreadfully winnowed by war.

So, at seventeen, Berry had completed his formal education and went to work for his father, an accountant with the cotton firm of S. D. Heard and Simpson. Berry discovered that he actually liked bookkeeping, and he was good at it, just as Mr. Griffin had predicted. He and his father ate their lunches together in the warehouse behind the office, a cotton bale as their table. When Mat Benson went to Charleston on business, he took Berry along. They did some sightseeing, visiting Fort Moultrie on Sullivan's Island with its grave of the famous Seminole chieftain Osceola. Berry could not have predicted that within a few months, he would be standing guard on the same island, defending the independent state of South Carolina.[14]

---

[13] Ibid., 24–25.
[14] Ibid., 21.

CHAPTER 2

Fort Sumter

"A jerk at the lanyard, and I had fired my first hostile shot—64 pounds of solid iron."

More than any other state in the South, South Carolina boiled with talk of secession. Frustrated twice by its sister states when it threatened secession, once over the tariff in 1832, and the second over Clay's Compromise Bill in 1850, now in 1860 it needed only a spark to set off an explosion. Lincoln's election struck that spark. The only national party left was the Democratic, and that party came apart at its convention held that summer in Charleston, where cooler heads did not prevail. One wing of the party nominated Stephen Douglas who advocated leaving the issue of slavery in territories to the resident voters. The more radical wing named John Breckinridge and ran on a demand for a guarantee of slavery in territories. The more moderate-minded adopted a platform that would leave the issue to Congress and supported John Bell. Abraham Lincoln ran on a platform that included the elimination of slavery in territories.

During the election campaign, emotions ran high, especially in South Carolina. Prosperous Augusta was more cautious than declining Hamburg, as Georgia was in comparison to South Carolina. All over the Palmetto State men copied the cockades worn during the Nullification Crisis in 1832 (palmetto leaves pinned to turned-up hat brims), formed companies of Minute Men, and drilled, many using broomsticks instead of guns. Seventeen-year-old Berry and fifteen-year-old Blackwood drilled as enthusiastically as anyone. Across the river, Augustans, who traditionally distrusted Carolina, looked askance at the martial displays. While Carolina appeared to be unanimously for Breckinridge, Augusta voted for Douglas, Bell, and Breckinridge in that order.[1]

In the end, it did not matter what Augusta did, or what Georgia did. The Carolina legislature remained in session, waiting election results. With the announcement of the electoral vote, the legislators declared themselves a convention, and on 20 December 1860, proclaimed South Carolina an independent state. For weeks, South Carolina stood defiant and alone. Berry Benson noted that "We were going to whip all the other thirty states of the union if necessary."[2]

The Hamburg company of Minute Men, thirty strong, offered their services to Governor Francis Pickens who lived in nearby Edgefield. That town had its own contingent, the Edgefield Rifles. Berry felt a thrill when the Rifles came marching into Hamburg to board the train for Charleston, with a band playing and a flag displaying the inscription, "Give us a place in the picture near the flashing of the guns." Berry was probably one of the few cheering people there who realized that the riflemen seemed to want to be killed. "It was then I first began to realize that war was to mean something more than flags and music and cheers," he recalled.[3]

On 7 January 1861, the companies boarded the train for Charleston. If she were still alive Nancy Benson might have objected to her two teenagers going off to war, but Mat Benson gave the boys his blessing and a little money. Two days later, the companies, along with others from across the state, were mustered in for six months.

---

[1] Berry Benson, "The War Book, Reminiscences of Berry Greenwood Benson, CSA," (Typescript prepared by Charles G. Benson, Ida Jane ["Jeanie"] Benson, and Olive Benson), Special Collections, Reese Library, Augusta State University, Augusta GA; hereafter cited as "War Book"), 41. A copy of the typescript is also held by the Southern Historical Collection at the University of North Carolina, Chapel Hill, in its Berry Benson Papers, ms. 2636. The original manuscript diary (ms. 326) is located in the Hargrett Rare Book & Manuscript Library at the University of Georgia in Athens; *Augusta Chronicle*, 9 November 1860; Edward J. Cashin, *The Story of Augusta* (Augusta GA: Richmond County Board of Education, 1980) 115.
[2] "Berry Benson Sets Record Straight," *Augusta Chronicle*, 6 December 1913.
[3] Benson, "War Book," 44; *Augusta Chronicle*, 6 December 1913.

Berry thought that should be long enough to resolve the matter without actual warfare. These first recruits formed the 1st Carolina Regiment, commanded by Colonel Maxcy Gregg, an erudite gentleman from Columbia, South Carolina, who had many abilities and one disability—he was almost deaf. Berry and Blackwood enjoyed playing soldier in that exciting time, especially when pretty ladies came out to watch their parades. They drilled five times a day. Less enjoyable was sentry duty during the winter nights on windswept Sullivan's Island.[4]

Major Robert Anderson, U.S.A., had removed his command from Fort Moultrie on Sullivan's Island to the vacant and still unfinished Fort Sumter on its man-made island out in the harbor. The South Carolina authorities thought that they had an understanding with the Buchanan administration to observe the status quo, and they considered this move to Sumter a provocative act. President James Buchanan, in an unusually decisive mood, decided to support Anderson's continued occupation of the fort, and therefore dispatched much-needed supplies in the ship *Star of the West*. On 9 January 1861, the supply ship attempted to steam into Charleston harbor. A battery on Morris Island, guarding Charleston harbor, fired at the ship, and its commander prudently turned back.[5] On that same day, Berry Benson and his friends were being mustered in for a six-month service.

By 4 February 1861, the lower tier of Southern states had seceded, and they joined South Carolina in forming the Confederate States of America. Brigadier General P. G. T. Beauregard arrived in Charleston on 3 March to take command of the siege of Fort Sumter. When Abraham Lincoln assumed office on 4 March, he had to

---

[4] Benson, "War Book," 45.

[5] Events in Charleston harbor from December 1860 through April 1861 are detailed in US War Department, comp., *The War of the Rebellion: A Compilation of the Official Records of the Union and Confederate Armies*, 128 vols. (Washington DC: Government Printing Office, 1880–1901) ser. 1, vol. 1, p. 2, 10, 134–36.

decide whether to maintain or to abandon Fort Sumter. In other words, he had to agree to the principle of secession or disagree. If he disagreed, he had to do something about it. He decided to send a squadron to defend Fort Sumter.

Meanwhile, the South Carolina troops made use of February to build batteries on the points of land that encircled Sumter's little island. Berry's company left the comparative comfort of Sullivan's island for Morris Island, and set to work filling bags with sand, and piling the bags into fortifications. Captain Tom Lamar of the Edgefield Rifles picked eight men to man the eight-inch columbiad cannon. Berry felt honored to be among the chosen. Lamar would sight the gun; Berry would fire it. Other batteries took shape to the right and left of his "Edgefield Battery." The most impressive was that on Cummings Point, the nearest to Sumter. This was a slanting roof of iron rails supported by massive timbers, built so that shells would bounce off the rails. The idea would later be used to build ironclad ships like *The Merrimac.*

By 1 April 1861, a ring of cannon encircled Fort Sumter. Berry woke from sleep to the sound of guns on 3 April 1861. He ran to his battery to find the captain already there. In the first light of dawn, a schooner flying the United States flag glided boldly into the harbor. It had drawn fire from other batteries before Berry fired the Edgefield's sixty-four pound ball. He thrilled at the clear sight of the ball arching across the water, and skipping like the stones he threw on a pond as a lad, before it sank. He did not need a second shot. The unsuspecting captain, carrying a cargo of ice from Maine, had not heard the news that Charleston had suddenly become a foreign country. He hastened to haul down his flag in a sign of surrender.[6]

President Lincoln's relief squadron sailed from New York on 10 April 1861. On 11 April General Beauregard presented Major Anderson with a demand to surrender. Anderson replied that he did

---

[6] Benson, "War Book," 45–47.

not wish to surrender until his supplies were exhausted. He set 13 April as the likely date for his withdrawal. On that day the Union flotilla loomed upon the horizon and would be at the bar of the harbor by the following morning. At 3:20 A.M. Beauregard sent Anderson the message that bombardment would begin in an hour. At 4:30 A.M. a mortar at Fort Johnson on James Island fired the first shot of the war.[7]

Manning his gun at the Edgefield battery, Berry Benson marveled at the curving streaks of fire lighting the darkness of early dawn. For a time, Anderson did not respond. Then his gunners focused on the closest target, the Iron Battery at Cummings Point. Berry watched, fascinated, as the balls struck sparks on the iron roof and bounced off into the marsh behind. Colonel Lamar had been ordered to hold his fire, but when a stray ball came skipping across the water in his direction, he could restrain his crew no longer. So, Berry set off his second shot, and then countless others. The relentless Confederate barrage lasted all that day and into the night. The next morning smoke could be seen from fires in the fort started by "hot shots." The United States flag, visible through the smoke, suddenly came down. Berry's mates cheered. But with its shattered flagstaff repaired, it rose again. Confederates cheered again at the garrison's bravery. Around noon, his ammunition exhausted, Anderson surrendered. It was the 13 April, the day he had planned to give up the fort unless supplies arrived. Next day, his troops boarded the Union steamer *Isabel*, and the watching Confederates cheered again.[8]

Berry managed to obtain (though he didn't say how) a piece of the Sumter flagstaff.

The action at Sumter, and Lincoln's call for states to furnish troops to put down the rebellion, provoked the secession of another tier of states, including Virginia. The volunteers in Charleston had a

---

[7] Journal of Capt. J. G. Foster, *OR*, ser. 1, vol. 1, p. 16–25.
[8] Reports of Gen. P. T. Beauregard, *OR*, ser. 1, vol. 1, p. 29–35.

choice of going home or finishing out their six-month tour in Virginia. Of course, Berry and Blackwood opted for Virginia. North Carolina had not formally seceded as the Carolina troops went through the state, Berry noted that they had to travel through the United States on their way to Virginia. People turned out to cheer them as heroes of Fort Sumter. When they reached Richmond, the people vied with one another to lavish attention upon them. Crowds attended their drills at the fairgrounds. Storekeepers refused to take pay for items. Berry had to force a man to take his money for a pair of shoes. The man grudgingly agreed but forced a hunk of cheese upon Berry.[9] As the crowds of soldiers increased, the hospitality of the locals decreased.

Berry noted in his journal that on 23 May 1861 federal troops had occupied Alexandria, Virginia. Before this war ended he would become better acquainted with Alexandria as a prisoner there. The importance of the news at the moment lay in that the Confederate army now had an objective, namely to prevent the enemy from advancing further into Virginia. For that purpose Confederate general Joseph E. Johnston took up a strong position at Manassas Junction. Berry's 1st Regiment probed cautiously toward Alexandria, reaching Drainesville on 16 June 1861, only three miles from the Potomac. Here they could guard the railroad to Alexandria. Soon a train loaded with troops from Ohio on their way to Alexandria came into Berry's view from his vantage point on a hill. Confederate artillery smashed into the train. Berry could see men leaping from the cars and running in a panic. His regiment did not become engaged. So far, it was war at a distance, still something of a lark.[10]

Berry had his heart set on seeing the famous Potomac River, now the border between two countries. So he was keenly disappointed when the 1st Regiment received orders to fall back to Germantown where

---

[9] Benson, "War Book," 52–53.
[10] Ibid., 55.

the regiment would be disbanded, the men having completed their six-month enlistment. Perhaps he would never be as close to the river as now, he felt. What would happen if he just went to take a look? He told Blackwood of his plans, but nobody else. Alone, he went on his quest—one that might have got him shot as a deserter later in the war. As he neared the river, a troop of Confederate cavalry on patrol caught up with him. The officer was not satisfied with Berry's explanation that he just wanted to see the river. He put him under arrest. The guardhouse in this case was a tent, and the congenial Berry soon came outside and sat talking to the guard who did not seem to mind. A new guard approached and asked, "What am I supposed to guard?" The first guard pointed to this and that piece of equipment, but did not point to Berry. No sooner had the old guard walked away, than Berry sauntered off also. He expected trouble when he rejoined his regiment, but in the confusion attending the dissolution of the regiment on 2 July 1861, no one objected to his absence without leave.[11]

Among his fellow soldiers of the 1st Regiment were the Haskells, a remarkable family of brothers from Abbeville. Those brothers will become an important element in this narrative, second only to the Benson brothers. Langdon, Aleck, and William Haskell belonged to Captain James Perrin's company in Gregg's 1st Regiment. That company consisted almost entirely of sons of wealthy upcountry planters. Colonel Gregg selected Aleck to be on his staff. Three other Haskell brothers (Charles, John, and Joseph) enlisted after Sumter, and all attained distinction. Charles Haskell joined the staff of Colonel R. H. Anderson and remained on duty in Charleston. Later General Joseph E. Johnston asked John Haskell to join his staff, and John brought along his younger brother, Joseph.[12] The Benson brothers admired all the Haskells, but especially William.

---

[11] Ibid., 55–56.

[12] John Cheeves Haskell, *The Haskell Memoirs*, ed. Gilbert E. Govan and James W. Livingood (New York: G. P. Putnam's Sons, 1960) 110–11.

They saw in William the qualities of a born leader. Therefore, when he asked them if they would sign up for a company he intended to form, they readily agreed. After a visit home, they would meet William Haskell in Charleston on 31 July 1861 and sign up for the duration.

The Benson brothers came home to the accompaniment of praise and applause from friends and neighbors and to the embrace of their father, sisters Callie and Betty, and envious younger brother, Brad. Hamburg had not changed much, except that it seemed almost deserted. But, across the river Augusta hummed with activity. The hesitation of December had given way to the excitement attending Georgia's secession on 19 January 1961. When the federal garrison at the United States Arsenal on the Hill declined to surrender, Augusta very nearly became an earlier Sumter. Governor Joseph E. Brown called out the militia, and a thousand troops marched up Walton Way to attack the arsenal and presumably start a war, with martial music stirring them on. Captain Arnold Elzey reconsidered the matter, and prudently surrendered his eighty-man contingent. A white flag with a red star representing Georgia flew over the arsenal, and Governor Brown obtained 22,000 guns for his militia.[13]

From 1 April to 1 July, Augusta sent eleven companies off to war and would send thirty in all before it was over. Over two thousand local men served. Berry noticed the conspicuous absence of young men when he attended St. James Church on Greene Street. Augusta was proud of its generals, among them James Longstreet, Lafayette McLaws, Joseph Wheeler, William H. T. Walker, Ambrose R. Wright, and Edward Porter Alexander. Those names would soon be known all over the Confederacy.[14]

---

[13] *Augusta Chronicle*, 25 January 1861; Florence Fleming Corley, *Confederate City: Augusta, Georgia, 1860–1865* (1960; repr., Augusta GA: Richmond County Historical Society, 1995) 35–37.

[14] Corley, 39.

There were many changes. Georgia and South Carolina railroads met in the city, linking the eastern and western sectors of the Confederacy. Important statesmen and generals used Augusta as a base. There seemed to be a constant flow of troops through the town. A huge camp near the depot accommodated the transients, and the Ladies Lunch Association handed out picnic baskets to the men. The great Augusta Factory contributed cloth for uniforms. Women worked at the Arsenal manufacturing cartridges, balls, and munitions. Berry could not have known it, but Colonel George W. Rains had selected Augusta as the site of the Confederate Powder Works. Augustans thought of their city as the "Heart of the Confederacy." Mayor Robert May campaigned for the capital of the Confederacy to be located in his city.[15]

The news of the glorious victory at Manassas on 21 July seemed to assure a short war. Berry and Blackwood felt cheated that the Yankees had come out just when their regiment left Virginia. They were anxious to get back into action before the war ended. They said their goodbyes, and on a general wave of fervor, went off to meet Captain William T. Haskell.

---

[15] Ibid., 53–59.

CHAPTER 3

The Seven Days

"And all the while the din and the roar, and the pulse of artillery, and the cheers and the cries of Forward! Forward! and the grey smoke mixed with it all."

Captain William Haskell seemed glad to see the Bensons in Charleston. They went with him to Richmond and then to Suffolk, Virginia, where Colonel Maxcy Gregg organized his new 1st Regiment. Haskell had handpicked his company, and Berry and Blackwood felt honored to have been chosen. Haskell's officers included Lieutenants John G. Barnwell, Grimke Rhett, and Charles Pinckney Seabrook, all from old and distinguished South Carolina families. Berry respected them. The prevailing philosophy in the South of Berry's day was that nature divided persons into categories according to their natural talents. Thus society was provided with its clerks, manual laborers, preachers, and merchants. At the top were the natural rulers. This generally accepted philosophy prompted persons to pursue excellence in the quiet hope that they, too, might be among the leaders. Berry knew that Haskell, Barnwell, Rhett, and Pinckney Seabrook had already attained that envied status. In his heart, he hoped to be counted among them.

In the early days of organizing and training at Suffolk, Haskell showed himself to be a hard taskmaster. He insisted on perfection in drills and in the care of the camp. His men considered him the strictest officer in the regiment, and some grumblers complained that he acted like a martinet. There was no use complaining to his officers; they backed him completely. Soon, however, Haskell's H Company won the reputation of being the smartest-looking and best-drilled in the regiment. When Colonel Gregg called H Company his "model," the complaining stopped. Men from other companies derisively called them "models" until their officers began emulating Haskell.[1]

In one of these early days, Berry risked his future by daring to confront Haskell, endangering their incipient. friendship. The company elected Pinckney Seabrook to the lieutenancy, recognizing his abilities and not less, recognizing his name. Seabrook had held the rank of sergeant, so his promotion left a vacancy. Haskell could have allowed his company to elect their non-commissioned officers; instead, following a dress parade, he read out the names of the non-commissioned officers. Berry was pleased when Haskell named him corporal. He was only eighteen, younger than most of the company. The men expected the second ranking sergeant, a man named Miller, to be raised to the first rank, but to their surprise, Haskell promoted Corporal Mackay 1st Sergeant. "We were thunderstruck," Berry recorded. Haskell had usurped his authority, he thought. Fair was fair, the second-ranking sergeant Miller was a good man; he deserved the upgrade in rank. So, in his impetuous way, Berry went around the company collecting signatures to protest Haskell's decision. Boldly, Berry took the petition to Haskell, knowing that an officer, mean-spirited or overly conscious of rank, could strip him of his promotion. Nevertheless, Berry, on behalf of the men, asked the captain to reconsider in favor of Miller. Haskell might have stood on his dignity, but he calmly asked Berry to sit down and discuss the grievance. Miller was certainly a good man, but Mackay had the

---

[1] Berry Benson, "The War Book, Reminiscences of Berry Greenwood Benson, CSA," (Typescript prepared by Charles G. Benson, Ida Jane ["Jeanie"] Benson, and Olive Benson), Special Collections, Reese Library, Augusta State University, Augusta GA; hereafter cited as "War Book"), 59. A copy of the typescript is also held by the Southern Historical Collection at the University of North Carolina, Chapel Hill, in its Berry Benson Papers, ms. 2636. The original manuscript diary (ms. 326) is located in the Hargrett Rare Book & Manuscript Library at the University of Georgia in Athens.

qualities Haskell wanted. Yes, he had the authority to name non-commissioned officers, and he showed Berry his instructions.

Berry had no choice but to report back to the company. He might be satisfied, but they were not. They insisted that he take the grievance to Colonel Gregg. Berry knew that Captain William Haskell's brother, Aleck Haskell, was Gregg's favorite officer, and that he had no chance of success, but he dutifully carried the complaint to the colonel. And he carried back the colonel's polite refusal to consider the appeal.[2]

Berry felt obliged to make amends, and apologized to Haskell for the trouble. Haskell laughed it off, putting Berry at ease. As they talked they discovered mutual interests. They liked poetry. Haskell recited Tennyson's "The Poet's Song" by heart. Berry admired Tennyson; he mentioned that he liked Horace also. Coincidentally, Haskell had a copy of Horace's poems in Latin in his knapsack. Would Berry want to borrow it? Flattered that Haskell should assume that he knew Latin (a correct assumption as it happened), Berry accepted the offer.[3] Most of us likely marvel at these warriors who liked poetry and could read Latin. And we may wonder more that soldiers who couldn't read at all would shake their heads in admiration of their betters, instead of sniggling at pretensions of gentility.

In anticipation of winter, the men began to build better quarters for themselves. Each company constructed a long house, where the men met for inspection and for meals. The company divided into "messes" presided over by a non-commissioned officer, eight men to a mess. The men chose their own mess, and Berry felt flattered that so many competed for his. He liked people generally, and he particularly liked his mess-mates, referring to them as "birds of a feather." His group included Larkin, Box, Bail, Veitch, Youmans, Munnerlyn and, of course, Blackwood, only sixteen but fast learning

---

[2] Ibid., 171.
[3] Ibid., 144, 173.

the soldiers' trade. Larkin had the honor of carrying the regimental flag—and with it the likelihood of being the target of enemy fire. Red-haired Munnerlyn had a quick temper, but could not harbor a grudge. He became the target of practical jokes, perpetrated mostly by Veitch. Berry made sure his men ate well by hiring a young black man named Geoffrey to do the cooking. Berry hated cooking, and on the march, Bail cheerfully volunteered to do that chore. Of the eight men in the mess, three would be killed and five wounded.

In December 1861 Maxcy Gregg received promotion to brigadier general, with command of four regiments (the 12th, 13th, 14th, and Orr's Regiment of Rifles) in addition to his old regiment, the 1st. Colonel Daniel H. Hamilton assumed command of the 1st Regiment. He held inspections every Sunday, visiting each company in its long house. On one occasion he was late for inspection of Company H, and the men grew restless. "I wonder how long it will be before headquarters will be around," grumbled Private Bellot. "Headquarters is here now, sir," said an unsmiling colonel who had just entered. Thereafter he was Colonel "Headquarters Hamilton" to the men of his regiment.[4]

Berry's insatiable curiosity led him astray occasionally. On Christmas 1861 he decided to go exploring. He had heard about the Great Dismal Swamp, wondered about it, and now that his camp lay within a few miles of it, he decided to go have a look. He followed the railroad until coming to a canal that cut into the swamp. He borrowed a convenient boat that had no visible owner, and rowed down into a lake. Surrounded by forest, Berry sat silent in his boat, alive to the natural beauty, and utterly happy in his soul. Like a latter-day Bartram, he gathered plant specimens and moss, and put them in his knapsack. He watched fish splash and observed unfamiliar birds. A more prudent explorer would have left the Great Dismal

---

[4] Ibid., 68.

Swamp before darkness, but prudence was not among Berry's virtues. The black winter night fell before he rowed his boat to its original location. Then he got lost trying to find the railroad. Guessing his way, he fought through bushes and briars, knee deep in dank water. He somehow came out right. He reached camp after 9:00 and had missed the evening roll call. Captain Haskell might have done much worse that merely give him extra guard duty the next day.[5]

So the winter passed with the brigade quiet in its Suffolk camp. Along the Potomac, the federal army under General George McClellan grew ponderously large and strangely immobile. In February, Gregg ordered several companies of the 1st Regiment, including H Company, to go down to the Blackwater River to prevent Union gunboats from landing. The prospect of action excited the company. Haskell's Company led the march, and the Benson brothers led the company! When they came to the flooded river, neither Berry nor Blackwood had the faintest idea how deep it was. Without hesitation they waded in, as though they knew what they were doing. Fortunately, the water came no higher than their waists. After crossing, the men set up camp. They found themselves in a land of plenty, and requisitioned chickens, pigs, butter, eggs, milk, and fruit. The fact that they encountered no gunboats did not seem to matter; morale remained high.

In March the regiment went to Goldsborough, North Carolina, again to prevent rumors of a gunboat invasion. In fact all along the Southern seaboard, inland cities set up frantic cries about the imminence of a gunboat attack. The military authorities in Augusta, safely distant from the sea, stretched a giant chain across the Savannah River, and kept watch in expectation of a river attack. When the enemy failed to appear near Goldsborough, the regiment boarded the train for Guinea's Station near Fredericksburg, Virginia. Union cavalry patrolled along the course of the Potomac. Captain

---

[5] Ibid., 70–72.

Haskell decided to see if he could find one of those patrols. On 10 May 1862, he asked Berry if he wanted to go on a little adventure with him, knowing that Berry would leap at the chance. Haskell gave the password to the regimental pickets standing guard over the camp, so as not to be shot on returning. The two made their way quietly through the woods. Berry liked nothing more than a tramp through the woods, and the element of danger added a certain zest. Coming out into an open lane, the two followed along. Suddenly, they heard the sound of hoof beats approaching rapidly. Haskell and Berry dived into bushes on the side of the road, and watched as a troop of Union cavalry galloped by. His curiosity satisfied, Haskell decided to return to camp.[6]

At the end of May, the three regiments that had been guarding the coast rejoined Gregg's Brigade. Gregg now commanded the 1st, 12th, 13th, 14th, and Orr's Rifles. The Haskells were well represented with Aleck as Gregg's assistant adjutant general, and Langdon as aide-de-camp. Colonel Daniel "Headquarters" Hamilton had charge of the 1st, with Lieutenant Colonel A. M. Smith, and Major Edward McCrady. General Joseph E. Johnston recalled his scattered forces around Richmond to face the enormous threat posed by General McClellan's long-delayed but inexorable movement up the Peninsula between the Chickahominy and James Rivers with Richmond his objective. On Johnston's staff were two other Haskells, John Cheves and Joseph. Johnston put Gregg's Brigade under Major General Ambrose P. Hill.[7]

McClellan's main body of troops advanced south of the Chickahominy, and he threw a strong force across that river to circle around the northern approaches of Richmond. Johnston decided to attack McClellan frontally while the flooded Chickahominy prevented the northern wing of the Union army from rejoining the

---

[6] Ibid., 74–76.
[7] John Cheeves Haskell, *The Haskell Memoirs*, ed. Gilbert E. Govan and James W. Livingood (New York: G. P. Putnam's Sons, 1960) 6–7.

rest. The result was the Battle of Seven Pines on 31 May 1862. In heavy fighting, the Confederates forced the enemy to retreat, at a staggering cost of lives. More than half of the 14,000 casualties were Confederate. John Haskell acted as courier during the engagement. Joseph Haskell tended the seriously wounded General Johnston. With Johnston incapacitated, President Jefferson Davis named General Robert E. Lee commander of the Army of Virginia. Lee's fertile mind quickly seized upon a strategy. He would leave a token force under General John Bankhead Magruder south of the Chickahominy to face McClellan, and send three divisions north of the river to attack General FitzJohn Porter's troops near the village of Mechanicsville. Lee's ace card would be Stonewall Jackson's command that had so terrorized the Shenandoah Valley. While the divisions of A. P. Hill, D. H. Hill, and James Longstreet attacked Porter frontally, Jackson would come in on the Union left flank. The plan depended on timing, and on Magruder's histrionics. Magruder had delayed McClellan's march up the peninsula by setting up tree trunks as artillery; now he had to pretend that he was about to launch a major attack on a vastly superior force.[8]

Gregg's Brigade did not become engaged in the Battle of Seven Pines, and Berry and his mates chafed at their continued inaction as A. P. Hill camped near the Meadow Bridge of the Chickahominy, waiting for Jackson to come down. At every camp, pickets kept watch for a possible attack. Captain William Haskell asked Berry if he would like to prowl around and see if he could find the enemy. Berry would like nothing more, and he dashed off toward the river. A heavy rainstorm provided cover at first, but it suddenly let up as he neared the river, and there in plain view were Union soldiers loitering about on the other bank. Berry dived for cover, and followed a ravine down to the riverside. He watched the bluecoats cutting wood and going about the business of camp. There was no sign that they were on the

---

[8] Bruce Catton, *This Hallowed Ground: The Story of the Union Side of the Civil War* (New York: Doubleday and Company, Inc., 1956) 139.

move, or about to be. This was the intelligence Haskell
wanted—should he go back? Or, with the enemy in plain view,
should he risk a shot? He could not resist. He aimed his rifle, pulled
the trigger—and nothing! The rain had wet the powder. Crawling
back to report, he found Larkin waiting for him in a ditch. Haskell
had worried about Berry and sent Larkin to fetch him back.[9]

Berry's report may have influenced A. P. Hill's strategy, or it
may not have. Wartime intelligence was made up of such bits and
pieces of information. Knowing that Union troops camped across
Meadow Bridge, Hill sent L. O'B. Branch's Brigade seven miles
upriver, to cross there and then sweep away the enemy so that the
divisions of the two Hills and of Longstreet might cross unopposed.
The plan called for Branch to begin his operation on the north bank
when he heard of Jackson's approach. At 10:00 A.M. on 26 June 1862,
Branch learned of Jackson's near-arrival, and cleared the way for the
crossing. At 3:00 P.M. the same day, A. P. Hill ordered his brigades
across the river in the confidence that Jackson would be in position.
Hill had six brigades, those of Gregg, J. R. Anderson, Charles Field,
Dorsey Pender, and James Archer. Branch, of course, waited on the
other side. Ambrose Hill, a small, handsome man, who dressed like a
dandy and sat well on a horse, was a man of unproven ability and had
to make a crucial decision on the late afternoon of 26 June.
Intelligence failed when he most needed it. Longstreet and D. H.
Hill were not in place. Jackson was supposed to loom just over the
Mechanicsville hills. Hill decided to attack. He held Gregg's Brigade
in reserve and sent the others into a frontal assault on the enemy who
had strongly entrenched at Beaver Dam Creek. The battle raged
until 9:00 P.M., with Union General FitzJohn Porter stubbornly
holding his ground. In his report, Hill noted bitterly, "It was never

[9] Benson, "War Book," 76–77.

intended that my division alone should have sustained the shock of battle, but such was the case."[10]

At one point General Gregg dispatched Langdon Haskell (Aleck happened to be sick in Richmond) to ask General Hill if he should come up as a reinforcement, but Langdon could not find Hill in the confusion of battle. So Berry's 1st Regiment crouched on the ground and behind trees, seeking whatever protection they could find from the artillery shells and spent musket balls dropping about them. This business of sitting around while bullets and shrapnel tore through trees overhead, landing haphazardly, taxed the spirits of the men as much as if they had been in the fight. But they had not fought yet in the history of the regiment, so they could not yet compare. Their turn came next day at Gaines' Mill, the second of the Seven Days Battles. The regiment would never be the same after that bloody day.[11]

General Hill assigned Gregg's Brigade to lead the attack on 27 June, with Archer's Brigade on his right. Colonel Hamilton's 1st Regiment and Colonel Barnes's 12th led the brigade, with the 13th and Orr's Rifles as back up. Gregg held the 14th in reserve. The enemy had withdrawn from their previous lines. With Haskell's Company deployed in front as skirmishers, and Berry alongside Haskell, the men advanced resolutely over yesterday's battlefield, still littered with dead men and horses. Discarded knapsacks and equipment lay about. Some tents remained in place. Suddenly a withering storm of musketry opened upon the company. Haskell ordered his men to take cover behind boxes, barrels, or declivities in the ground. John Veitch, who crouched next to Berry, cried "I am

---

[10] Report of Maj. Gen. Ambrose P. Hill, 5 March 1862, in US Department, comp., *The War of the Rebellion: A Compilation of the Official Records of the Union and Confederate Armies*, 128 vols. (Washington DC: Government Printing Office, 1880–1901) ser. 1, vol. 11, pt. 2, p. 834–40; Catton, *This Hallowed Ground*, 140; J. F. J. Caldwell, *History of a Brigade of South Carolinians Known First as "Gregg's" and subsequently as "McGowan's Brigade"* (Philadelphia: King and Baird Printers, 1866) 14.

[11] Benson, "War Book," 78.

shot." Berry dragged him into a tent, gave him water, and heard his
last wish, "Give my sister my love and tell her I died for my country."
The rest of the regiment came up and took cover as best they could.
But some of the artillery fire came from the left, the north, where
there were no Yankees. Colonel Hamilton wrote that he was
"astonished" at discovering that Jackson's Division was shooting at
him. He dispatched a courier to inform Jackson of his mistake.[12]

When the entire brigade took position, Gregg ordered a charge
at the double quick. All along the front, men rose and ran forward,
voicing the high-pitched, frenzied "rebel yell." A. P. Hill called the
charge of Gregg's Brigade "the handsomest charge in a line I have
seen during the war."[13] The months of drill paid dividends. The
enemy gave up their strong position and retreated to a curving ridge
at Gaines' Mill near Cold Harbor, where entrenchments had been
prepared. The men of the 1st paused in the abandoned works to rest.
Someone found brandy among the medical stores, and Haskell
encouraged his men to take a drink; they deserved it. Berry and
Blackwood declined, likely the only ones to do so. Only a short rest,
then they pressed on, now with Branch's and Archer's brigades
extending Gregg's line to the right. The plan called for Longstreet to
come up the road paralleling the river and divert the enemy while
Hill and Jackson carried out the main offensive. Again, Jackson's
strange inactivity left Hill alone, so Longstreet had to launch a real
attack rather than act as a diversion.[14]

As Gregg resumed the offensive, the 1st and 12th again led the
way in line. A Union rear guard posted in a thicket of young pines
poured a damaging volley into the oncoming ranks, but delayed the
charge not at all. Gregg's men crashed through the thicket and fired

<hr/>

[12] Caldwell, *History of a Brigade*, 15–17; report of Brig. Gen. Maxcy Gregg, 6
August 1862, *OR*, ser. 1, vol. 11, pt. 2, p. 852–58.
[13] Report of Brig. Gen. Maxcy Gregg, 6 August 1862, *OR*, ser. 1, vol. 11, pt. 2, p.
836.
[14] Hill's report, 5 March 1862, *OR*, ser. 1, vol. 11, pt. 2, p. 836.

at the scattered enemy running up an incline to the protection of their entrenchments along the ridge. Their colorful Egyptian-like uniforms with baggy pants, vests, and red hats marked them as the famous New York Zouaves. As the Confederates emerged from the woods and reached a small stream at the bottom of the hill, a withering blast of artillery met them. They had to take advantage of the poor protection the terrain offered there in the open. Berry remembered that "bullets and shells came hot and fast with a terrible din of battle raging in front and on the right and left. What we had seen before was child's play." An officer lying next to Berry suddenly vomited blood, turned over, and died. A ball struck Berry a glancing blow on the shoulder; an exploding shell threw mud over him. Wounded men got up as best they could and straggled to the rear. Lieutenant Grimke Rhett, next to Captain William Haskell, received a mortal wound. Berry's messmate Box, who lay near Berry, rose to shoot and fell dead.[15]

Gregg ordered Orr's Rifles to charge the battery on the right that was inflicting the most damage. They carried the hill at a frightful cost in casualties. With the 1st and 12th Regiments pinned down and exhausted, Gregg sent in the 13th and ordered Hamilton's 1st Regiment to fall back. In the din of artillery and musketry, some did not hear the orders. Berry was one of those who did not, or chose not to hear. Here came Colonel Samuel McGowan's 14th on the double-quick, forming a line of battle. Berry ran with the foremost, men dropping on each side of him. At point-blank range the musket fire and the artillery created havoc in the oncoming line. The rush slackened on the very verge of success. "Half a minute more would have carried the crest," Berry remembered. But no troops could sustain such fire; grudgingly they drifted back down the hill, leaving comrades scattered on the bloody hillside.[16]

---

[15] Benson, "War Book," 80.
[16] Gregg's report, 6 August 1862, *OR*, ser. 1, vol. 11, pt. 2, p. 852–58.

In the confusion, Berry had become separated from his company. Now he searched among the wounded, calling for Haskell and for 1st Carolina. On all sides, men searched for their units, calling "10th Mississippi," "4th Alabama," "13th Georgia." Here was Larkin, his messmate. He, too, had joined the attack. A soldier named Rice answered Berry's call. He volunteered to take Berry and Larkin to Company H. They found their friends, and there lay Blackwood, bloody with a wound to his thigh and unable to walk. Berry stanched the flow of blood as well as he could, and he and Larkin stayed with Blackwood that night, with dead and wounded all about.[17]

Meanwhile, General Lee had finally arranged a coordinated assault by D. H. Hill, Longstreet, and Jackson at 7:00 P.M. that carried the hill. McClellan withdrew his troops to the south of the Chickahominy during the night.[18]

The next morning, Berry and Larkin made a stretcher of blankets and carried Blackwood to a farmhouse used as a field hospital. Wounded men occupied two full acres of land around the hospital. A team of doctors tended the most seriously hurt. Nothing but amputation would do for limbs smashed by minie-balls. With no anesthesia, speed with the saw might save the patient from death by shock. If a man survived the amputation, he had to face the possibility of gangrene. Thankfully, the bullet had missed Blackwood's bone, and passed through the fleshy part of the thigh. Berry put him on one of the wagons bound for the hospital in Richmond. Then Berry looked for and found the body of Lieutenant Grimke Rhett. He liked and admired Rhett, so now he took a scissors and cut a lock of hair as a memorial of their friendship. He still had the lock of hair years later.[19]

---

[17] Benson, "War Book," 81; Bruce Catton quoted from Benson's diary in *Terrible Swift Sword* (New York: Doubleday and Company, 1963) 131.

[18] Caldwell, *History of a Brigade*, 20.

[19] Benson, "War Book," 41, 82.

The battered 1st Regiment assembled within sight of the field hospital. Colonel Daniel "Headquarters" Hamilton might have chosen a better place to give his men a fighting speech. With a backdrop of surgeons working with their saws and a growing pile of dismembered legs and arms, the colonel declared, "One more glorious day like yesterday and our country is free." There could be no better testimony to the influence of tales of chivalry upon the men of that generation, than the colonel's description of the previous day's carnage as "glorious," and the fact that the men who had escaped death but might die tomorrow—that these listening men applauded the speech. Berry thought to himself, "Yes, ours is the victory; but if this is victory, what in God's name is defeat?" He commented to his journal that one thing that he admired about Captain Haskell was that he did not make such speeches.[20]

Later, Captain Haskell told Berry about the amazing adventure of his brother John, on the staff of General D. R. Jones after General Johnston's hospitalization. John was sick with the ailment that affected so many during that summer's heat, the "Chickahominy fever." But hearing the sound of guns on 27 July, he persuaded a doctor to supply him with opium pills, mounted his horse, and rode to join General John B. Magruder, whose division was demonstrating in front of the enemy while the main attack was being launched across the river. "There's a horse that can do it," John heard an officer say. Viewing the unfolding battle across the river, Magruder thought that Longstreet's right might be flanked by the enemy. He needed someone to warn Longstreet and asked John to do it. John swam his horse across the river and splashed through the shallows with a Yankee patrol hot on his heels. He outran them, found Longstreet, and delivered his message to Lee himself, who was with Longstreet. Longstreet asked Haskell to go find General J. R. Anderson and tell him to bring his brigade to the threatened point.

---

[20] Ibid., 82; "The Battle of Cold Harbor," *Augusta Chronicle*, 28 June 1914.

When John found Anderson, that general asked him to order General W. C. Whiting to attack. Off to Whiting dashed John. Once the message was delivered, Whiting asked John if he would mind leading the charge. Of course he would not mind such a request! At the head of three hundred men, still mounted and a target for enemy sharpshooters, John Haskell rode into the same murderous rifle and artillery fire that Berry and his mates endured on another sector of the front. John saw General George Pickett standing by his horse in a sheltered declivity "bewailing himself." Pickett called upon him to send for a litter because he had been seriously wounded. John quickly discovered that the injury was insignificant and informed Pickett that he was too busy; he despised Pickett thereafter. John resumed the charge, leading his men over a regiment lying prone. He snatched the colors from the ground, and prodded the colonel to get up and lead his men. Instead, the colonel, quivering with fright, raced to the rear. The men followed this strange leader as he galloped with the colors straight at the Union line. His horse bore him into the entrenchment and fell dead from several shots. A Union officer tried to wrest away the colors and John drove his sword through him. Then he dashed toward the battery that had played on them so furiously. John could see the gunner yank the lanyard that sent a cannon ball straight at him. The ball tore off his right arm at the shoulder. Somehow he managed to stagger back, still with the colors, using the staff as a prop. General Whiting found him and took him to the field hospital where he was bandaged and sent to Richmond. John Cheves Haskell had served five generals that day: Lee, Magruder, Longstreet, Anderson, and Whiting. Whiting described "the chivalrous daring of young Major Haskell" in his report: "His personal bearing in a most deadly fire, his example and directions, contributed not a little to the enthusiasm of the charge of the 3rd." In spite of his terrible wound, "he walked from the field as heroically as he had gone into the fire." John Haskell wrote his brother William not to worry; he would be out of the hospital soon. The Captain

remarked wryly to Berry that he thought John could write better with
his left hand than he could with his right.[21]

After the terrible battle of Gaines Mill or Cold Harbor,
McClellan backed his troops down the peninsula. Lee doggedly
followed him, every day attacking a strong position, losing men, and
attacking again: on 29 June, Savage Station; 30 June, Frazer's Farm;
and on 1 July, Malvern Hill. Here Lee suffered 5,300 of the 8,500
total casualties without dislodging the enemy. But McClellan
followed his old habit of dislodging himself and retired to safety of
his gunboats where he began the tedious business of embarking his
troops.[22]

Gregg's Brigade rested a day before crossing the river and
joining the pursuit. The brigade missed the fight at Savage Station
but caught up in time for Frazer's Farm. Longstreet's Division bore
the brunt of that battle, with A. P. Hill in support. Each day of
fighting and marching, the men had to endure the sweltering
summer heat. Men collapsed and were left by the road. Oddly,
Berry's clearest memory of those exhausting marches was that of a
baby. As his dirty, ragged line passed a house, a black nurse stood at
the gate, holding a baby. A murmur passed down the ranks, "Look at
the baby." The contrast between a field of dead and the promise of
new life struck a chord in these battle-hardened men.[23]

---

[21] John Cheves Haskell, *The Haskell Memoirs*, ed. Gilbert E. Govan and James W.
Livingood (New York: G. P. Putnam's Sons, 1960) 31–35; Benson, "War Book,"
171.

[22] Catton, *This Hallowed Ground*, 143–44.

[23] Caldwell, *History of a Brigade*, 22–24; Benson, "War Book," 87.

CHAPTER 4

Second Manassas

*"At close quarters, never more than a little strip of ground betwixt us,
all day the battle raged, fierce and bloody…"*

After Malvern Hill, Gregg's Brigade marched back through a
succession of battlegrounds. A horrible stench pervaded each one
from unburied and bloated horses, and from bodies of men buried in
too-shallow graves. Berry kept his blanket roll pressed to his nose,
and even then the odor made him gag. Near Richmond the brigade
set up camp at Laurel Hill. The brigade had lost a thousand
men—half the enlistment. It lived on an unhealthy diet of fried bacon
and half-cooked bread, and the men's dirty, sweat-soaked clothing
became a breeding ground for lice.[1]

Berry obtained permission to go see Blackwood in Byrd Island
Hospital in Richmond. Blackwood told his big brother not to worry;
the danger of gangrene had passed. The wound healed nicely.[2]

On 1 August, the men cleaned up as best they could and
marched into Richmond to board a train for Gordonville. General
Lee had decided on a bold tactic. Counting on McClellan's caution,
Lee would leave a token force guarding Richmond and take most of

---

[1] Berry Benson, "The War Book, Reminiscences of Berry Greenwood Benson,
CSA," (Typescript prepared by Charles G. Benson, Ida Jane ["Jeanie"] Benson, and
Olive Benson), Special Collections, Reese Library, Augusta State University, Augusta
GA; hereafter cited as "War Book"), 90. A copy of the typescript is also held by the
Southern Historical Collection at the University of North Carolina, Chapel Hill, in
its Berry Benson Papers, ms. 2636. The original manuscript diary (ms. 326) is located
in the Hargrett Rare Book & Manuscript Library at the University of Georgia in
Athens; J. F. J. Caldwell, *History of a Brigade of South Carolinians Known First as
"Gregg's" and subsequently as "McGowan's Brigade"* (Philadelphia: King and Baird
Printers, 1866) 25.

[2] Benson, "War Book," 93.

the army into northern Virginia to face the Union Army of the Potomac under General John Pope. Pope had terrified people of the region with bombastic proclamations about shooting anyone who helped the rebels. On the march, Jackson commanded his own "Stonewall Brigade," as well as Ewell's Brigade. Lee attached A. P. Hill's division to Jackson, giving him 30,000 men. Across the Rappahannock, Pope had twice that number. Even so, Jackson decided to attack him.

Though Jackson was the most secretive of generals, Berry and his mates knew that a major engagement loomed. Since the Seven Days, they had lost the careless confidence of invincibility. Groups gathered around campfires asked each other to give messages to loved ones in case of death. Many men read their Bibles. Berry carried the Bible that his mother had given him, and he loaned it to others of the company.[3]

As it happened, no one in Gregg's Brigade died in the Battle of Cedar Mountain on 9 August 1862. The brigade had the dubious honor of guarding the wagon train, in spite of Gregg's vehement protests, while the rest engaged a detached division of Pope's army under General Nathaniel Banks, whom Jackson had famously humiliated in his earlier Valley campaign. This time Banks repulsed the charge of the Stonewall Brigade and Jackson had to send in A. P. Hill to finish the job. The Battle of Cedar Mountain, really a minor skirmish in this great struggle, had the important effect of confusing General Pope and inspiring General Lee. Pope suddenly became cautious. Expecting an offensive directly across the Rappahannock, Pope guarded the likely fording places in the river. Lee, with his gambler's instinct, decided to send Jackson's Corps away to the west on a sixty-mile trek behind the Bull Run Mountains, through Thoroughfare Gap and in behind Pope's army. Jackson would bring on an engagement with Pope, while Lee with Longstreet's Division

---

[3] Ibid., 94.

would come up on the other side. The plan depended upon unusually careful coordination, and the Seven Days showed that coordination was not the Army of Northern Virginia's strong point. Lee needed to hurry with his operation, because the vanguard of McClellan's 100,000-man army had already joined Pope, giving that general 70,000, to Lee's divided army of 55,000.[4]

On 25 August 1862, Jackson issued orders to begin his soon-to-be legendary march, "with the utmost promptitude and without knapsacks." It seemed not to concern Jackson that the men would have nothing to eat and hardly time to rest. "From that day to this," Berry wrote, "not one of us has seen his knapsack."[5] Even before the march Berry had come down with a fever and in his weakened condition had trouble keeping up with his regiment. He had to stop now and then to rest, and then hurry on to join the regiment. The excitement of the quick march, of doing something both dramatic and important kept him going, as did the cheers of the ladies who came out to see the men march by. Without stopping, men would grab any proffered food or drink, with a quick "Thankee, Ma'am." When the column halted for the night, hungry men canvassed the entire neighborhood for something to eat, paying for it if need be, but gladly accepting if not.

On 26 August, the column marched through Salem. Who should step out from the sidewalk but Blackwood! Berry marveled that his brother could have found the company, and worried that the wound might rupture. On they marched together, one with fever, the other with a bad leg, through Thoroughfare Gap to Bristoe Station. The countryside was poorer and food harder to find. Men ate unripe corn. Some were reduced to picking corn out of horse dung, washing and eating it. They had to drink water when they found it, stagnant or not.[6]

---

[4] Caldwell, *History of a Brigade*, 26.
[5] Benson, "War Book," 95.
[6] Ibid., 101.

The half-famished men reached Manassas Junction on 27 August, and there like a mirage stood a train loaded with provisions. The Yankee guard was quickly sent flying, and the men fell upon all kinds of food and drink, though Jackson sequestered the liquor. They ate all they could, and with captured knapsacks, they loaded all the provisions they could carry. Men without shoes or shirts found plenty to choose from. Then they set fire to the train, and slept by the light of the burning cars.

Jackson, so far, had carried out Lee's orders to perfection. In the words of Colonel Samuel McGowan of Gregg's Brigade, Jackson "had completed a bold flank movement by which we crossed the Rappahannock, turned the right of the enemy, got entirely in his rear, and cut off his communications—seemingly without his knowledge."[7] The next move would be critical. Jackson had to find a defensive position, provoke the enemy to attack him, and hold his attention while Lee crept up unawares. Jackson selected a position along a ridge on the western fringe of the old Bull Run battlefield. Gregg's Brigade lined up a few yards behind a recent cut for a projected railroad. Gregg placed the 13th Regiment under Colonel O. E. Edwards on the right, anchored in a thicket. On its left Lieutenant Colonel Edward McCrady commanded the 1st, in the absence of Colonel Hamilton, ill since the Seven Days. Colonel Dixon Barnes's 12th Regiment came next. These three fronted the railroad cut, and beyond the cut men had a clear view of an open field ending in a thick woods. Slanting off behind a fence to the left was Colonel Samuel McGowan's 14th. Gregg and his staff, including Lieutenant Langdon Haskell, stood dismounted on the ridge behind the lines. Orr's Rifles, Colonel Foster Marshall, waited in reserve.[8]

---

[7] Report of Brig. Gen. Samuel McGowan, 9 February 1863, of operations of Gregg's Brigade, 16 August–2 September 1862, in US War Department, comp., *The War of the Rebellion: A Compilation of the Official Records of the Union and Confederate Armies*, 128 vols. (Washington DC: Government Printing Office, 1880–1901) ser. 1, vol. 12, pt. 2, p. 679.

[8] Caldwell, *History of a Brigade*, 34.

Pope had persuaded himself that Jackson was retreating, as any outnumbered military commander should, and scattered his troops in search of the Confederates. Following conflicting orders, one regiment marched in a circle entirely around a mountain with the mountain in clear view all day. General Franz Sigel with 11,000 men first located Jackson, and without waiting for the rest of the army to come up, advanced through the wooded area straight at the railroad cut.

Gregg sent Langdon Haskell to order his brother Captain William Haskell to take his company out into the woods and see what was causing the commotion there. Berry, Blackwood, and the men of Company H followed Haskell into the woods, creeping from tree to tree. They could see through the trees a massive line of bluecoats, stretching beyond sight on either side, smashing through the underbrush. Berry's mates began the Second Battle of Manassas by opening fire, and then retreating slowly, in pace with the methodical approach of the enemy. Emerging from the trees, the Union troops formed a battle line and approached the railroad cut. A furious volley at close range checked their advance and Gregg sent the 1st and 12th out in a counterattack. The men charged with high-pitched rebel yells and drove the enemy into the wood. A gap developed as the 1st slanted off to the right to avoid being flanked, and the 12th went off to the left for the same reason. Gregg dispatched Colonel Edwards's 13th Regiment to support McCrady's 1st. Edwards made a name for himself by his leadership, his clear voice directing the attack, urging his men on. Berry praised Captain Haskell for his cool bravery as he led his men. Colonel Marshall with Orr's Rifles joined Barnes's 12th Regiment on the left and cleared the woods of the bluecoats.[9]

Acting on Jackson's instructions, Gregg recalled his regiments to their original position. Their assignment was to draw the attention of

---

[9] Report of Lt. Col. Edward McCrady, Jr., September 1862 (otherwise undated), *OR*, ser. 1, vol. 12, pt. 2, p. 684–90.

the enemy while Longstreet got into place. No one in Gregg's Brigade knew how long that would be, and they wondered whether they could endure.

After a short interval of rest, the battle resumed. A gap of about two hundred yards opened between Gregg's Brigade and Anderson's Brigade on the right. At this point the railroad cut slanted away from the Confederate line and towards the woods. A regiment of Union solders managed to follow the cut and emerge between the Confederate brigades. Gregg sent his reserve regiment, McGowan's 14th, into the gap, and after another desperate struggle the 14th and 1st forced the attackers to retreat.

Expecting another attack, Gregg again asked Captain William Haskell to take his company, as well as skirmishers from other companies, into the woods to act as an advance line of defense. Again Berry found himself in the woods, his natural element. But how different the situation from the silence of his solitary visit to the Great Dismal Swamp! An ominous crashing of many feet announced another assault. Again, Haskell ordered one volley and retreat. As Berry turned to run to the rear, a bullet struck the sole of his uplifted shoe, a painful blow, leaving a dent in the thick leather, but no worse.[10]

Out of the trees and all along the front the blue-clad host advanced, bayonets fixed, in dreadful earnest. Outnumbered and outgunned, the Confederate line retreated from its line along the cut. The 13th, next to the 1st, began to break up, leaving the 1st to sustain the attack. In Lieutenant Colonel McCrady's words, "upon the 1st was hurled the full force of the enemy." And now even the 1st began to give way. General Branch sent in a regiment of his brigade to reinforce the 1st, but—again McCrady's words—"unused to so terrible a fire, his men gave way for a while."[11] Even Berry, as stout a fighter as any of his regiment, turned and ran, and Blackwood with

[10] Benson, "War Book," 104.
[11] McCrady's report, *OR*, ser. 1, vol. 12, pt. 2, p. 687.

him. Suddenly, Lieutenant John Munro of Company L yelled, "Benson, for God's sake stop!"[12] Munro's bravery was contagious; Berry called Blackwood and others of his company by name, and they came and stood by him, facing impossible odds. Captain Haskell and Lieutenant Pinckney Seabrook had not so much as faltered; they stood by the regimental colors. But by now the mighty force in front of them had crossed the cut, taking stands of colors and hundreds of prisoners. General Jackson, who seemed to be everywhere this day, ordered General Field's Brigade to charge through the retreating Confederates straight at the enemy. They came with a cheer, and the exhausted men of the 1st joined in the charge. The Union line broke and dissolved back into the forest. By 5:00 P.M. the entire Confederate line was back in place. The 1st had lost half of its officers, and nearly half of its men. Berry's company alone had lost eighteen.

Lieutenant Munro came over to congratulate Berry for rallying his company. In his report, Colonel McCrady singled out Captain Haskell and Lieutenant Seabrook, as well as Munro for conspicuous bravery. General Jackson asked Gregg if his brigade could withstand another assault. Gregg answered that his ammunition was about gone, but he thought he could hold the position with bayonets. Fortunately, it did not quite come to that necessity. Most of the men had discarded bayonets as burdensome impediments during their long march. Gregg pulled back the battered 1st, and placed the 13th and 14th along the cut. When the last assault came, the Confederate front held and the 1st did not become engaged.[13]

Even as the day ended, the danger continued. Enemy artillery had found the range and kept up a desultory fire. Berry and Blackwood were sitting with Haskell, talking about the day's events,

---

[12] Benson, "War Book," 104.

[13] McCrady's report, *OR*, ser. 1, vol. 12, pt. 2, p. 688; see also report of Col. D. H. Hamilton, 30 September 1862, of operations 2–20 September 1862, *OR*, ser. 1, vol. 19, pt. 1, p. 991–92.

when a stranger approached to ask Haskell a question. Suddenly the stranger screamed in pain and ran—a shrapnel fragment from a nearby exploding shell had struck him in the back. Berry inquired if anyone had been injured. Yes, he was told, the explosion killed Lieutenant Munro. Lieutenant Colonel McCrady praised Munro in his report: "When so many deserved names for gallantry, few equaled his courage and daring."[14]

That evening Longstreet closed the trap, coming up on Pope's right flank. The following day, 30 August, a massive battle raged as Longstreet routed the surprised enemy. Pope was beaten thoroughly, but he managed to save his army and retreat to Centreville. There he entrenched and waiting for reinforcements. He had lost a staggering 14,500 men. But Lee had lost 9,000 and did not dare attack Pope frontally. However, he might risk another gamble. He ordered Jackson to repeat his flanking maneuver, go around Centreville and attack Pope's flank.[15]

So on 31 August, the already exhausted men set out again on another long march, this time through rain and mud. Gregg's Brigade crossed Bull Run and reached Pleasant Valley that night. Berry's fever returned. Ordinarily the heartiest of marchers, Berry could hardly keep up. Once he had to fall out and rest. A mounted officer ordered him to get up. Berry answered that he would be grateful if the officer could make him get up, because that was something he himself could not do. The puzzled officer rode off. The muffled sound of a battle roused him. The boys were in danger and he must join them. He cut through fields, climbed over fences, and reached an outlying Confederate battery. Colonel John Pegram pointed to the location of Gregg's Brigade, in line along the slope of a ridge called Ox Hill. Berry joined them, and found the 1st lying in reserve. He ran along the line of the regiment to find Company H. The boys greeted him warmly. Captain Haskell, who knew how sick

---

[14] McCrady's report, *OR*, ser. 1, vol. 12, pt. 2, p. 688.
[15] Caldwell, *History of a Brigade*, 39.

Berry was, chided him for coming. Berry answered simply that he could not stay away while his company fought. As the rain began to fall heavily, he lay down in utter exhaustion. Quietly, William Haskell placed his own oilcloth raincoat over Berry. Berry remembered the gesture, "It was very kind, but kindness was only one good trait in many in his character. He was as cool and courageous as he was kind."[16]

---

[16] Benson, "War Book," 111.

CHAPTER 5

Sharpsburg

*"Advancing through the cornfield, there suddenly rose before us a
line of the enemy, whom we drove in disorder at the first fire."*

Berry knew that he would not be able to keep up with his regiment,
so he left early on 4 September to get a head start. He had not gone
far when the brigade came swinging down the road, buoyed by the
rumor that Lee intended to invade Maryland. Two riders clattered
along in front, one magnificently uniformed and mounted, the other
nondescript in his apparel and sitting awkwardly on his undersized
horse. Berry recognized the first as his brigade commander, Maxcy
Gregg, and the other as the legendary Stonewall Jackson. As they
passed he heard Jackson shout to Gregg, "There are but few
commanders who properly appreciate the value of celerity."[1] Jackson
had to shout because Gregg was almost deaf. Jackson got more
celerity out of his troops than any other commander.

The brigade paused for a rest at Leesburg and gave time for
Berry to catch up. Berry had not eaten anything in two days and felt
miserable. Haskell told him to go find a convenient farmhouse while
they were still in Virginia, get some milk, and stay there until he
recovered. No, Berry replied, he would stay with the boys until he

---

[1] Berry Benson, "The War Book, Reminiscences of Berry Greenwood Benson,
CSA," (Typescript prepared by Charles G. Benson, Ida Jane ["Jeanie"] Benson, and
Olive Benson), Special Collections, Reese Library, Augusta State University, Augusta
GA; hereafter cited as "War Book"), 113. A copy of the typescript is also held by the
Southern Historical Collection at the University of North Carolina, Chapel Hill, in
its Berry Benson Papers, ms. 2636. The original manuscript diary (ms. 326) is located
in the Hargrett Rare Book & Manuscript Library at the University of Georgia in
Athens. A. P. Hill still nursed a grudge against Jackson for being slow in joining the
attack at Cold Harbor, and now Jackson blamed Hill for being too slow on the march
to Manassas.

could go no farther. The brigade moved on and camped near the Potomac that night. Berry dragged himself in long after dark, and without a word, lay down next to two men who had made a mattress of straw. Sergeant Sam Wigg recognized Berry and shared his own blanket with him. It was a comradely gesture, one that Berry deeply appreciated.

Daybreak showed the Maryland hills across the Potomac, and the men buzzed with anticipation of getting into a land of plenty. Berry had to admit defeat. He told Haskell, "Captain, it ain't any use. I can't go any further. I'm played out."[2] The sympathetic Haskell scribbled a note that Berry had permission to take sick leave, and requested the help of friendly persons. It took almost all Berry's strength to creep toward a nearby farmhouse. He saw a woman sitting on the porch, smoking a pipe. He changed his course toward a larger house a mile distant. Berry had enough Southern gentility to suppose that pipe-smoking women might be generous but were not likely to be gracious. Berry preferred to die in the household of a gracious woman.

It took him most of the day to totter, fall, and crawl one mile. Once he lay in a field, put a handkerchief on the end of his rifle and waited for help. No one came, so he crawled on and collapsed on the lawn of the large house. Berry learned that the gentleman of the house was Judge Gray, and a servant carried Berry into the house and sent for a doctor. The judge's daughter, as gracious a lady as Berry could have imagined, became his nurse for a week. He grew fond of father, daughter, and young son—but particularly the daughter. Under such care, and with a wholesome diet, he recovered rapidly. Finally, on 10 September he left the house, his knapsack loaded with good things to eat, and to the hugs and tears of Miss Gray.[3]

He made his way up the Virginia side of the Potomac through the Blue Ridge Mountains, ferried across the Shenandoah, and

---

[2] Ibid., 114.
[3] Ibid., 115.

approached Winchester. He learned that Jackson had passed that way the day before and that he had besieged Harper's Ferry, only a few miles up the Potomac. He also heard that Confederate patrols rounded up stragglers and sent them to a camp to await being dispatched to any place they might be needed. Berry hated the thought of separation from "the boys." He took to the fields to avoid lurking patrols but ran right into one. "Halt! Where are you going?" a mounted rider called out. "To join Jackson," replied Berry. The soldier escorted Berry to the stragglers' camp.[4] Berry disliked being associated with stragglers even more than he disliked being guarded. He sauntered over to where a wagon hid the fence, and when the guard turned his back, he jumped over the fence and escaped through a cornfield.

On the way to Harpers Ferry, Berry heard the sound of distant thunder. Jackson's artillery ringed the Union forces in the town, and rained shot and shell on them. By the time Berry joined the army, Union General Julius White had surrendered his 11,000 men, plus an enormous hoard of supplies. In Berry's words, "the boys were 'powerful' glad to see me again, and gave me a full history of their doings."[5]

Jackson left A .P. Hill to arrange the surrender and hurried off to join Lee at Sharpsburg where McClellan, who was again in command of the Union Army, had massed a huge force against him. Actually, the capable Aleck Haskell, Gregg's adjutant, handled the business of surrender and the paroling of the enemy. During the day that Hill's Light Division lingered at Harpers Ferry, the men enjoyed an unprecedented feast. They outfitted themselves with new boots, equipment, and ammunition. The Federal prisoners marveled at the

---

[4] Ibid., 117.

[5] Ibid.; report of Maj. Gen. Ambrose P. Hill, 25 February 1862, of operations 2 September–3 November 1863, in US War Department, comp., *The War of the Rebellion: A Compilation of the Official Records of the Union and Confederate Armies*, 128 vols. (Washington DC: Government Printing Office, 1880–1901) ser. 1, vol. 19, pt. 1, p. 979–81.

ragged appearance of their captors. They seemed pleased to have been beaten by the famous Stonewall Jackson. "If we had him," one of them said, "we should whip you in short order."[6]

Captain William Haskell assigned Berry to the job of guarding the prisoners. As they milled about, guards and prisoners, they heard a sudden clattering of hooves. "Who is it?" a prisoner asked. "Jackson's coming," someone shouted. Everyone, guards and prisoners, lined the road to watch Jackson and his staff ride by. "The prisoners cheered him just as lustily and as heartily as we did ourselves," said Berry, "and we felt very kindly toward them for it."[7]

Hill could spare only a day in celebration. On 17 September he received an urgent message from Lee to come at once. The Light Division, Gregg's Brigade leading, hurried the seventeen miles from Harper's Ferry to Sharpsburg. Every Civil War aficionado knows the story of Sharpsburg or Antietam. After Lee moved into Maryland, he scattered his forces. McClellan had the incredible luck to find a copy of Lee's dispatches, indicating that he was posted at Sharpsburg with only part of his army. So McClellan moved faster than usual, pushing D. H. Hill's Division through Turner's Gap in the South Mountains. Then, puzzled by the fact that Lee stood his ground, McClellan slowed down, giving Lee just barely enough time to collect his army. Even when Jackson joined him, Lee only had 40,000 men, and McClellan had 87,000. On the face of it, it was not a good idea for Lee to tempt a fight with less than half his enemy's numbers and with his back to the Potomac. But Lee had formed a habit of doing the impossible, and his men had the utmost confidence that he would do it again.[8]

---

[6] J. F. J. Caldwell, *History of a Brigade of South Carolinians Known First as "Gregg's" and subsequently as "McGowan's Brigade"* (Philadelphia: King and Baird Printers, 1866) 43–44.

[7] Benson, "War Book," 151.

[8] Bruce Catton, *This Hallowed Ground: The Story of the Union Side of the Civil War* (New York: Doubleday and Company, Inc., 1956) 165–67.

Stonewall Jackson held the left of Lee's line, posted in a cornfield, with his artillery on a hill near the Dunker Church. D. H. Hill's Division occupied a strong position in the center, along a sunken road. Longstreet's command spread along a ridge southeast of Sharpsburg, overlooking a bridge over the Antietam River, which was really just a creek. If McClellan had sent all the troops at hand across Lee's front, he must have succeeded. However, he attacked piecemeal. The great struggle began with General Joseph Hooker's attack on Jackson's force in the cornfield. First, Hooker's artillery blasted the cornfield, making it intolerable for the Confederates, and then he sent in his infantry. The Union charge pushed the Confederates back to the Dunker Church Hill, and nearly broke through. Just in time (and this battle hinged on timing) Hood's Brigade came over from Longstreet's front and sent the Federals reeling back over the corpses in the cornfield. But there in the cornfield Hood's cheering Texans encountered a second Union corps under General Joseph Mansfield. More bodies littered the cornfield as Hood had to retreat to the ridge, but no farther.[9]

Next a fresh Union corps under General John Sedgwick attacked D. H. Hill's Division at the sunken road. The first attack failed, but the second wave gained the road. Longstreet himself worked the artillery, and D. H. Hill grabbed a musket, prepared for the worst. But again the thin Confederate line held on that sector. Now came the last big threat—General Ambrose Burnside with four divisions paraded against Longstreet's right flank in an effort to get around him. At the crucial moment, 3:40 P.M., A. P. Hill's Light Division came on the field, Gregg's Brigade leading. They could see the danger, a throng of soldiers in neat battle lines, with rows upon rows of colors flying, marched down the Antietam and around to the Confederate right. Gregg's Brigade took position on the far right,

---

[9] Ibid., 166–68; report of A. P. Hill, *OR*, ser. 1, vol. 19, pt. 1, p. 981.

the most threatened point. Colonel McGowan's 14th Regiment anchored the end of the line, facing away from the other regiments.[10]

The Federals crossed the creek and entered a cornfield. Gregg ordered Edward's 12th Regiment, Barnes's 13th, and Hamilton's 1st to form a line of battle. With their characteristic wild yell, the men charged into the cornfield just as the enemy crossed the highest ridge in the field. The Union line broke in the face of murderous fire, and the retreating soldiers tried to hide in a hollow on the far side of the field. Berry testified that this was the first time in the war that volleys were delivered as on drill. Major T. P. Alston called, "Right wing, ready, aim, fire, load—left wing, ready, aim, fire, load." Individual enemy soldiers tried to break out into the open beyond the stand of corn, but they became easy targets. Now Berry saw a stirring sight. A Union officer on a spirited black horse rode onto the field, waving his sword and exhorting his men to form their lines. Berry admired his bravery, but shot him, anyhow. The rider fell, and the horse cantered off, turned, and came back to the fallen officer, nuzzling him. The horse died, too, of multiple gunshots. Later, Berry reflected that it was his duty to prevent that officer from organizing another attack. He was glad that he never knew if his bullet killed the man; it might have been dozens of others.[11]

Suddenly, a volley from the right surprised the regiment. Their charge had separated them from the 14th, and Union troops attacked their unprotected flank. Hamilton ordered his men to fall back. Berry prided himself at being among the slowest to retreat, and this time he was even slower. His ill-fitting pants, rolled up because they were much too long, had become unraveled, and one leg had split open, almost tripping him. He stopped to rip off the pant leg while bullets whistled around him. One struck the brim of his felt hat, and two

---

[10] Report of Brig. Gen. Samuel McGowan of operations 3 September–3 December 1862, *OR*, ser. 1, vol. 19, pt. 1, p. 987–88; Caldwell, *History of a Brigade*, 45.

[11] Benson, "War Book," 118–19.

ripped through his remaining pant leg. He raced the rest of the way to join his mates in a hollow. Their situation was critical because they had used up their ammunition. Fortunately, Gregg had seen the problem and sent in Orr's Rifles under Captain James Perrin to out-flank the flankers. The 1st joined in the pursuit. With this action, the Battle of Sharpsburg or Antietam ended. The two armies occupied the same place they had at the beginning. Nothing had changed, except that 23,000 men had become casualties. Berry particularly mourned the death of his friend, Sergeant Sam Wigg, killed bearing the regimental colors into battle. A major loss to the brigade was that of Colonel Dixon Barnes, killed while leading his 13th Regiment.[12]

Even though he had lost a fourth of his army, Lee remained in place the next day, daring McClellan to attack. He and Jackson considered launching an offensive, and Jackson sent orders for his division to prepare for an advance. Lee thought better of it and countermanded the order. McClellan could have attacked. He had not used all the troops available, and reinforcements had come up—but his habitual caution held him in check. So, on the night of 18 September, the Confederates began the cumbersome operation of crossing back over the Potomac at Boteler's Ford. A. P. Hill's Light Division crossed last, with FitzJohn Porter's corps pressing on them. Hill allowed Porter's advance troops to cross, then attacked with Gregg's, Pender's, and Thomas's Brigades in the first line of battle, and followed by a second line of Lane's, Archer's, and Brockenborough's Brigades. An admiring Confederate officer reported that "Our whole front line of three brigades moved as one man, as steadily, coolly, deliberately, as if on the drill ground."[13] Union artillery opened upon the Confederate line, causing many casualties, but the ranks quickly closed and the advance continued, pushing the enemy into the river. According to A. P. Hill, FitzJohn

---

[12] Ibid., 121; report of Col. D. H. Hamilton, 30 September 1862, *OR*, ser. 1, vol. 19, pt. 1, p. 991–92; Caldwell, *History of a Brigade*, 46.

[13] Caldwell, *History of a Brigade*, 50.

Porter suffered 3000 casualties in the fighting, and many died from drowning. Berry came out of the affair unscathed, but Blackwood suffered a painful bruise from a glancing piece of shrapnel.[14]

As they went into winter quarters, Lee's troops looked more like ragged scarecrows than victorious warriors. Major Caldwell, brigade historian, painted this picture, "They now stood an emaciated, limping, ragged, filthy mess whom no stranger to their valiant exploits could have believed capable of anything the least worthy."[15] Body lice bothered the men most. Under orders, every man had to bathe in the creeks and streams, but it did little good. Lice bred in their clothing. When Berry and Blackwood built a fire in front of their lean-to, the lice in their clothing became agitated with the most uncomfortable effect on the men. The brothers had to hold their clothes over the fire to get rid of the pests. Berry felt grateful that he and Blackwood did not come down with another common ailment, the "camp-itch." Fortunately, they had had measles and mumps as children so were immune to those rampant illnesses.

Blackwood seemed the worse off, with sore and blistered feet. Like a protective older brother, Berry decided to find him a good pair of socks, a luxury most soldiers did not enjoy. He walked two miles to a farmhouse, knocked at the door, and a pretty little girl answered. She seemed unafraid despite his ragged appearance. (According to Berry's theory a man should look proud even when barefoot.) The parents proved hospitable, found socks for Berry, and invited him to a generous meal. Berry imagined what the pretty girl might look like in ten years, and resolved to make a return visit then. Walking back after nightfall, he paused on a hill to admire the scene before him. Fires gleamed in neat rows, for all the world like

---

[14] Report of A. P. Hill, *OR*, ser. 1, vol. 19, pt. 1, p. 982; Benson, "War Book," 123.

[15] Caldwell, *History of a Brigade*, 53.

lamplights in a city. Poetic impulses frequently bubbled up in Berry's psyche, and he felt a touch of fondness for the boys down there.[16]

Berry found Blackwood at Captain Haskell's campfire. They had heard news of President Lincoln's Emancipation Proclamation. Lincoln declared the slaves in the rebellious states to be free. Berry thought it made little practical difference, because the rebellious states paid no attention to Lincoln's pronouncements. Haskell treated the matter more seriously. He thought that it might divide the South, causing non-slave-holders to view the war as one for the relatively few slave owners. The proclamation would make it harder for the North and South to compromise. "He is a stronger man than I thought," mused Haskell.[17]

In early December the brigade marched to Fredericksburg in anticipation of an enemy attack at that point, and camped at Hamilton's Crossing, the same place they had been six months earlier. Blackwood had not been well, and his condition worsened; he could not eat camp fare. Berry remembered a nearby house where he and his friend Bail had gone for food. He found the house again, and the two elderly ladies welcomed him. They asked about Bail, and he had to tell them that Bail had been killed at Manassas. They supplied him with milk and provisions for his brother. In spite of the better food, Blackwood grew weaker. The brigade doctor held out little hope for his recovery. Blackwood, it seemed, would be just one of many who died that winter.

Early on the morning of 12 December, the drums' long roll roused the men. They had to fall in for a rapid march to Fredericksburg where the enemy were in motion. Berry had no choice but to leave his brother, believing that he might not see him again. He tried

---

[16] Benson, "War Book," 129–30.

[17] Blackwood K. Benson, *Who Goes There? The Story of a Spy in the Civil War* (New York: Macmillan, 1900) 379. Blackwood's novel was a thinly disguised retelling of his own experiences during the war. Like Berry, he had become very close to Capt. William Haskell and recorded their conversations in his novel.

to put the best face on it. Captain Haskell shook Blackwood's hand. He had grown fond of the younger man. Blackwood watched his friends march off to a new battle.[18]

---

[18] Benson, "War Book," 130–32.

CHAPTER 6

Fredericksburg and Chancellorsville

"Down the slope we went through the woods, firing and driving whoever they were."

On 7 November 1862, President Lincoln replaced the cautious George McClellan with Ambrose Burnside, the general A. P. Hill's Light Division had battled against at Sharpsburg. At first Burnside moved quickly. He intended to march the Army of the Potomac, now 117,000 strong, upon Richmond by way of Fredericksburg. However, at Fredericksburg on 17 November he ran into a Confederate skirmish line. Burnside waited for pontoon bridges to arrive and thereby wasted his opportunity. Finally on 11 December the massive army began crossing the Rappahannock, its screen of skirmishers chasing the last Confederate sharpshooters out of the abandoned town.[1]

The river runs north and south at Fredericksburg, and Burnside crossed from east to west. Behind the town the open ground slopes upward to a long ridge called Marye's Heights. Along the bottom of the ridge ran a sunken road. Lee posted Longstreet's Division in the road and along the ridge, supported by artillery on the heights. Lee had chosen an ideal defensive position. South of town a road followed the river and parallel to the road ran a railroad. Wooded hills overlooked the railroad, the road, and the river to Stafford Heights on the other side where Union artillery protected its army's crossing. Lee nearly waited too long to position Jackson's Division along the hills south of town. Only on the morning of 12 December, with the

---

[1] Bruce Catton, *This Hallowed Ground: The Story of the Union Side of the Civil War* (New York: Doubleday and Company, Inc., 1956) 186–88.

enemy already in possession of Fredericksburg, Jackson's men broke camp and assumed their position to the right of Longstreet.[2]

Burnside's plan might have worked if he had merely demonstrated against the unassailable Marye's Heights and thrown his considerable weight around Jackson's right where A. P. Hill was posted. Burnside commanded an army of nearly 120,000 men, divided into three Grand Divisions, against Lee's 78,000. His mistake lay in sending two of the Grand Divisions, one under Edwin Sumner, the other under Joseph Hooker, straight at the sunken road. The assaults lasted most of the day, as wave after wave of brave men marched elbow to elbow into withering artillery and musket fire, none getting closer than a hundred feet of the sunken road. Wounded and dying soldiers littered the ground, impeding the new lines, grabbing at their comrades, pleading, warning of the futility of it all. This was the scene that provoked Lee to say famously, "It is well that we know how terrible war really is else we should grow too fond of it."[3]

The frontal assault on Longstreet's lines never had a chance of success. However, the flanking movement of the third of the Grand Divisions might have worked. Confederate general A. P. Hill had to spread his troops more widely than he might have liked in order to cover his assigned front. He placed four brigades along a thickly wooded series of hills near the railroad, Brockenborough's, Archer's, Lane's, and Pender's. Hill took a chance by allowing a gap of 600 yards between each brigade. The dense forest prevented the men of one brigade from seeing their neighbors. To plug the gap if that became necessary, Hill placed Gregg's Brigade between Archer and Lane, and Thomas's Brigade between Lane and Pender. Neither Gregg's nor Thomas's men could see their front line. If General

---

[2] J. F. J. Caldwell, *History of a Brigade of South Carolinians Known First as "Gregg's" and subsequently as "McGowan's Brigade"* (Philadelphia: King and Baird Printers, 1866) 56–57.

[3] Catton, *This Hallowed Ground*, 189.

William B. Franklin, who commanded the Left Grand Division, could find those gaps, he might have succeeded. That is nearly what happened. Three brigades of 4,500 Pennsylvanians under General George Gordon Meade burst through the opening in the woods between Archer and Lane's Brigades, straight at Gregg's Brigade.[4]

If an author were writing a novel about the Civil War, he would hesitate to put his hero at the focal point of action too frequently, because it would seem contrived. Yet, the destiny that wrote Berry Benson's script put him at the siege of Fort Sumter, at the railroad cut at Manassas, at the cornfield near the Antietam, and now at the gap in the lines below Fredericksburg. Meade's men blundered into the gap, first encountering Lane's North Carolinians who diverted the attack, so that the enemy came in not directly at Gregg's Brigade, but obliquely, blindly, through the woods.

Gregg had given specific orders to his men not to fire if they saw men in front of them; they might be the first line falling back. In fact, the regimental officers made the men stack their weapons to prevent such an accident. But now Berry and his mates of the 1st Regiment could hear sounds of a battle coming at them from the right, and bullets began to whistle about. Captain Haskell set an example of coolness, sitting with his back to the danger, munching a cracker, following orders to wait. Then a mass of men came crashing through the trees, shooting at them. Men grabbed their weapons and returned the fire. General Gregg, frantic with the thought that his men were shooting at fellow Confederates, rode out in front of the 1st Regiment, waving his hat, and calling on them to hold their fire. A bullet knocked Gregg off his horse, killing him. That unleashed the fury of his men. "Down the slope we went through the woods, firing, and driving whoever they were," Berry recorded. At that point he did

---

[4] Report of Maj. Gen. Ambrose P. Hill, 1 January 1863, in US War Department, comp., *The War of the Rebellion: A Compilation of the Official Records of the Union and Confederate Armies*, 128 vols. (Washington DC: Government Printing Office, 1880–1901) ser. 1, vol. 21, p. 645–49.

not know who these people were, only that they had killed his general.[5]

The wild charge did not go far. Colonel Hamilton of the 1st assumed command of the brigade; brought the 1st in line with the 12th, 13th, and 14th regiments; and drove Meade's Brigades out of the woods back over the railroad. Hill sent Archer's Brigade to hasten the retreat. Hill recalled his brigades when they reached open ground rather than expose them to the Union artillery. As night fell, Jackson wanted to take advantage of the darkness to drive the enemy into the river, and actually gave out the order to fix bayonets. However, Lee decided that there had been enough fighting for one day and countermanded the order.[6]

Some Confederates went out scavenging after dark, taking shoes and clothing from dead men. Others, Berry, Blackwood, and William Haskell among them, ministered to the wounded, giving them water, and building fires for them. As he dragged one young Pennsylvanian to a fire, Berry asked if he would fight again. "Yes, I will!" came the defiant reply. Berry liked him the better for that. Another soldier, too badly wounded to be moved, got Berry's blanket. Berry had to share Blackwood's blanket that cold night. As they huddled around a fire they talked about the loss of Maxcy Gregg, whom they admired. They admired him, but they did not love him, as they did Lee or Jackson. William Haskell worried about his brother Aleck, Gregg's adjutant, who had been wounded in the wild charge following Gregg's death. William's other brother, John, who had lost an arm at

---

[5] Berry Benson, "The War Book, Reminiscences of Berry Greenwood Benson, CSA," (Typescript prepared by Charles G. Benson, Ida Jane ["Jeanie"] Benson, and Olive Benson), Special Collections, Reese Library, Augusta State University, Augusta GA; hereafter cited as "War Book"), 133–35. A copy of the typescript is also held by the Southern Historical Collection at the University of North Carolina, Chapel Hill, in its Berry Benson Papers, ms. 2636. The original manuscript diary (ms. 326) is located in the Hargrett Rare Book & Manuscript Library at the University of Georgia in Athens; Hill's report, *OR*, ser. 1, vol. 21, p. 645–49.646; Caldwell, *History of a Brigade*, 59–60.

[6] Hill's report, *OR*, ser. 1, vol. 21, p. 646–47.

Gaines Mill, had returned as an aide to General Lee. He stayed with Lee on Telegraph Hill during most of the battle. Toward the end of the day, Lee sent him to deliver a message to one of the generals. John rode off and a piece of shrapnel ripped through his empty sleeve. Ironically, if he had not already lost his arm, he would have lost it then. His horse bolted and he fell heavily, re-injuring the recent wound in his shoulder, and sending him back to the hospital.[7]

In all, the brigade had lost 336 casualties out of a total of 1500; 73 in the 1st Regiment. Lee's 5,000 casualties might have been considered high, except that Burnside lost 13,000. Utterly defeated, Burnside retired back across the Rappahannock. Joseph Hooker replaced him in command of the Army of the Potomac.

The Light Division went back to their winter quarters near Fredericksburg. From this camp, on 12 December, a desperately ill Blackwood Benson had to be transferred to a Richmond hospital. On 20 January 1863, the brigade was surprised by the appointment of Colonel Samuel McGowan of the 14th Regiment, as brigadier general in command of the brigade. As the senior officer, Colonel D. H. Hamilton had expected the promotion. Colonel O. E. Edwards of the 13th also ranked higher than McGowan. Hill's recommendation, with which Lee concurred, testified to McGowan's ability, and McGowan's subsequent success testified to his tact in dealing with the older colonels under him. Captain Aleck Haskell stayed on as assistant adjutant, and Lieutenant Langdon Haskell also remained as an aide on the general staff.[8]

Berry had to provide living quarters for himself, as did everyone else. He dug a square hole in the ground, pitched a tent over it, and placed poles together for a floor and broom straw for a bed. A fire at the tent opening provided some warmth. Berry did not complain; he considered it unpatriotic to complain. He summed up the experience,

---

[7] John Cheeves Haskell, *The Haskell Memoirs*, ed. Gilbert E. Govan and James W. Livingood (New York: G. P. Putnam's Sons, 1960) 113.

[8] Caldwell, *History of a Brigade*, 66, 72.

"We made out well enough." To his delight, Blackwood soon left the hospital, rejoined the company, and shared Berry's tent.[9]

A heavy snowfall provided entertainment. Most of the Carolinians had never, or seldom seen snow. Now they could make snowballs. Like small boys they began to throw at one another. Perhaps remembering his boyhood fights on the Augusta bridge, Berry led his company in a fight against another company. Then a North Carolina regiment sent a challenge to South Carolina, and the fighting spread along a broader front. Berry led the charge and got himself captured by the enemy.[10]

Each regiment in the brigade had to take turns doing picket duty on the Rappahannock to see what mischief the Federals might be brewing. Berry found picket duty particularly tedious. He and his mates livened things up by calling to the Yankee pickets on the other side. Over the weeks, the exchanges became convivial. On one side, a soldier would write a note or fold a newspaper, put it on a makeshift raft, and push it across to be answered by the other side. Once, Berry had the unexpected pleasure of listening to a Union army band. The musicians obligingly played "Dixie," and Berry's friends cheered. Then the band struck up "Yankee Doodle" and the Federals cheered. When the band played "Home, Sweet Home," everyone cheered.[11]

Foraging for food occupied much of the attention of Berry and his friends. Berry developed a taste for frog legs. Blackwood tested his theory that a roasted rat would taste pretty much like a squirrel, but Berry declined to participate in the experiment. When the ice thawed, everyone went fishing. Someone discovered that tea made from the spicewood that grew on riverbanks tasted delicious, and the tea became a staple. The constant need for firewood denuded the forests around the camp. Finally, wood had to be hauled by wagon from miles away and rationed out. The inventive Blackwood made

---

[9] Benson, "War Book," 137.
[10] Ibid., 139.
[11] Ibid., 140; Caldwell, *History of a Brigade*, 71.

trips to the railroad junction at Guinea's Station and bought candy, cakes, and cookies wholesale, and sold them at camp at retail. Everything considered, the Confederate army came out of the winter camp healthier than it went in.[12]

In April, the ponderous Union army across the Rappahannock from Fredericksburg began to stir. The new commander of the Army of the Potomac, General Joseph Hooker, massed troops and began parading about as though he intended to repeat Burnside's assault of the previous December. On 29 April, A. P. Hill's division took up its old position on the ridge below Fredericksburg. For the first time in this war, the men prepared a defensive line of fallen logs. As the Federals across the way continued their demonstration, General Jeb Stuart's scouts informed Lee that the main body of Hooker's troops had moved upriver and had begun to cross unopposed.[13]

Hooker felt confident that his strategy would work. He would duplicate Lee's tactics at Second Manassas, divide his army, and come at the Confederates from both sides. Numbers favored him. He left 47,000 troops opposite Fredericksburg under General John Sedgwick, and took 72,000 with him upriver on the flanking movement. Timing favored him also. On 30 April while Lee concentrated on the commotion at Fredericksburg most of the Union army had already crossed the Rappahannock and reached a crossroads called Chancellorsville, for the name of the family who lived in the lone house there at the crossroads. He was perfectly poised to advance down the highway, called the Orange Plank Road, upon the Confederate flank.

As in every battle, timing proved crucial. Hooker lost his advantage by delaying his advance until noon on 1 May. Lee started at 4:00 A.M., before daybreak. Leaving General Jubal Early with 10,000 men posted on the Fredericksburg heights, Lee marched with 42,000 up the Orange Plank Road, with the result that Hooker's

---

[12] Caldwell, *History of a Brigade*, 70–71.
[13] Ibid., 73.

skirmishers encountered Lee's advance forces. Hooker reacted as if
startled to find an enemy in his front when they were supposed to be
in Fredericksburg. Against the arguments of his generals, he pulled
his troops back and threw up a line of breastworks stretching across
both sides of the highway. His wagon train and reserves stretched
safely out along the road behind his front line. Secure in his defensive
position, Hooker dared Lee to attack.[14]

While Hooker's army improved its barricades during the night
of 1 May, Lee and Jackson sat around a campfire, pondering strategy.
They had learned of a country lane that cut off to the south of the
main road, passed an ironworks, and rejoined the highway west of
Chancellorsville. Lee saw the opportunity to do to Hooker what
Hooker meant to do to him, namely, circle about and attack from
both sides. Always risky, this plan to divide his forces seemed
foolhardy. Lee would retain only 14,000 men to face Hooker's army,
while Jackson attempted to get around the enemy with 28,000 men
without being seen. Usually a march of such a number of troops
would be noticed by cavalry or by one of the observation balloons
that hovered over the Union army. Hooker had sent his cavalry away
to tear up rail lines between Fredericksburg and Richmond, so he did
not have that source of intelligence, as Lee had from Stuart. Lee
learned from Stuart that Hooker was vulnerable from the rear. Even
so, the Confederate march would come perilously close to the
southernmost anchor of the Union defenses and might be seen from
there.[15]

Of course, Berry Benson would be involved in Jackson's famous
march around the enemy. It had become his habit to be part of a
campaign's most dramatic moments. Their route may be followed
today. The countryside is still wooded and sparsely settled. Jackson
began his march at 6:30 A.M., late for him. Mid-morning found the

---

[14] Hill's report, *OR*, ser. 1, vol. 19, pt. 1, p. 885–86.
[15] Caldwell, *History of a Brigade*, 75; report of Maj. Gen. James E. B. Stuart, 6
May 1863, *OR*, ser. 1, vol. 19, pt. 1, p. 886–89.

column passing the dangerous open ground. Someone saw them, either an observer in a balloon, or a soldier in an artillery battery posted two miles away on a hill. Hooker might have guessed then that the Confederates intended to get behind him, but he assumed that Lee had done the prudent thing—that he had begun his retreat to the south. Another general might have decided that this would be an opportune time to come out of the barricades and hasten the enemy retreat. Instead, Hooker stayed where he was, and merely sent a small force under General Daniel Sickles to chase after the retreating Confederates. Most of Jackson's column had passed before the artillery opened on them, and Jackson left a single brigade to engage Sickles, who immediately called for help.[16]

Jackson, with D. H. Hill's old division now under General R. E. Rodes, came out on the Plank Road at 5:00 P.M., about four miles west of the Union lines at Chancellorsville, and quietly formed a line of battle. *Quietly* is a relative term; an army cannot file out into the woods silently. So General O. O. Howard's troops of the 11th Corps, preparing their evening meals, reported some sort of suspicious activity, but the generals ignored the warning. The distant sounds of Sickle's fighting convinced them that they were out of danger. Jackson could not wait for A. P. Hill's Division to come up, and he sent Rhodes's Division of ten thousand screaming at the astonished enemy. A few brave souls snatched up their weapons and tried to resist the fierce onslaught, and their bodies marked their stand. The rest fled headlong, and Jackson pushed the pursuit for two miles as evening came on. A. P. Hill's Division followed behind the front line, passing scores of dead and wounded. An artillery battery found their range and lobbed shells that burst dangerously near the marching column. Berry Benson, who saw beauty in the strangest places, admired the long arc of fire made by the shells, reminding him of sky-rockets he had set off as a child.[17]

---

[16] Catton, *This Hallowed Ground*, 240–41.
[17] Benson, "War Book," 145–46; Stuart's report, *OR*, ser. 1, vol. 25, pt. 1, p. 887.

Around 9:00 P.M., the column halted and stacked arms, presumably for the night. Tired from the long day's march, Berry laid his head on his knapsack and dosed off. A sudden barrage of gunshots in front of the regiment caused the men to rush to their arms, prepared to fight. They did not know until later that their own comrades of Lane's Brigade of North Carolinians fired the shots, nor did they know then that those shots fatally wounded Stonewall Jackson. Jackson's front line had pushed the Federals back to their breastworks. Constructed to face an enemy from the east, the works now served against an enemy from the west. Jackson had given instructions for the front line troops of Rodes's and Trimble's divisions to fall back and for A. P. Hill's fresh troops to take their place. As he and his staff approached Hill's camp in the darkness, his own men shot him down. Before being taken from the field to a hospital, Jackson asked that General Jeb Stuart replace him in command.[18]

Following orders, A. P. Hill's Division advanced in battle line, Lane's Brigade to the left, McGowan's in the center, and Archer's on the right. The freakish necessities of war compelled the men to march blindly at midnight through tangled undergrowth at an unseen but barricaded enemy. Berry's mates of the 1st Regiment stumbled over the prostrate Confederates in their front. The brigades became separated as they went deeper into the woods. A scout revealed that the main road had been left unguarded, so the three brigades formed a column on the road, marched up within striking distance of the Union lines, assumed a battle line again, and went to sleep. Not even the prospect of facing death at daybreak could keep Berry awake.[19]

At dawn on 3 May the battle began. The huge form of General Samuel McGowan led the brigade; Colonel D. H. Hamilton walked in front of his 1st Regiment. Berry strode forward in step with

---

[18] Stuart's report, *OR*, ser. 1, vol. 25, pt. 1, p. 887; Caldwell, *History of a Brigade*, 78.

[19] Benson, "War Book," 148.

Blackwood and Captain William Haskell. As the long line came out of the woods, Union artillery and musketry opened upon them with deadly effect. Colonel Hamilton described the moment in his report, "With a shout of defiance we rushed forward, cleared the Yankee breastworks at a bound, and pushing 100 yards or so to the front, engaged the enemy." As Haskell's Company climbed over the barricade of fallen trees, the Union defenders in their immediate front fled. However, Berry looked to his right where a long line of bluecoats knelt and fired in precision at the men of Orr's Rifles, who stood shoulder to shoulder in the open, firing back and taking terrible losses. In the split second before a bullet struck him, Berry marveled at the rhythm of the Yankee guns, "Their guns came down in rapid action," he remembered, "reminding me of the play of fingers, or the revolution of the spokes in many wheels." He regretted that he did not act quickly enough to shout, "By the right flank, charge!" Battles turned on the initiative of individuals. He did not call out because a bullet smashed into his leg above the ankle, knocking him to the ground. In spite of the heat and confusion of battle, Haskell bent over to see how badly Berry was hurt, then ordered him to go to the rear. Berry used his gun as a crutch and with two wounded comrades, all three supporting one another, he hobbled to a crude field hospital out of the range of gunshot.[20]

Berry learned of the battle's progress from the day's steady influx of wounded. Stuart now commanded in the place of the wounded Jackson. By noon his lines linked with Lee's, confining Hooker to an entrenched position along the river. Then Lee took most of his troops back to Fredericksburg to deal with General John Sedgwick, who had forced his way across the river and approached along the Plank Road. Sedgwick promptly retreated across the river. When Lee

---

[20] Report of Brig. Gen. Henry Heth, 25 May 1863, *OR*, ser. 1, vol. 25, pt. 1, p. 889–92; report of Col. D. H. Hamilton, 9 May 1863, ibid., p. 902; Benson, "War Book," 153; Caldwell, *History of a Brigade*, 79–80.

returned to deliver a final blow to Hooker, that general decided to join Sedgwick on the far side of the river.

On 10 May 1863, General Thomas J. Jackson died of his wounds. Dying, he murmured that he wanted to cross over the river and rest. Did he mean that he wanted to take his army across the Rappahannock and finish the war? Most think he meant that he would cross the biblical river Jordan, and rest in heaven. Either interpretation would characterize the man. As he lay on a hospital cot near Richmond, Berry could hear the bells tolling Jackson's death. A profound somberness prevailed. Berry reflected, "Never more would we follow him to battle, never again would he be cursed by his own men for his hard marching, never again so wildly cheered by the same men as he galloped by them."[21]

The great victory at Chancellorsville proved costly in casualties. A. P. Hill suffered a wound that took him off the field. Brigade commander Samuel McGowan received a wound as he led his troops across a barricade. Adjutant Aleck Haskell, whose own injury at Fredericksburg had hardly healed, had a difficult task preserving a chain of command. After McGowan's injury, Aleck rode over to tell Colonel O. E. Edwards of the 13th that he had command of the brigade. Thirty minutes later, when an injury forced Edwards to leave the battle, D. H. Hamilton of the 1st had to assume command. At that point in the confusion, Hamilton actually controlled only the 1st and Orr's Rifles. Hamilton confused matters further by ordering the two regiments to retreat in order to replenish their ammunition. Some elements of the 1st, including Captain William Haskell and Blackwood Benson, chose not to heed the order. They remained at the front, as did the 13th and 14th Regiments. In Colonel Hamilton's sudden absence, Colonel Abner Perrin of the 14th assumed

---

[21] Benson, "War Book," 151.

command, and ordered the last successful advance on the Union lines on Chancellorsville Heights.[22]

In his report, Colonel Perrin singled out Captain William Haskell "for his accustomed coolness and daring." Perrin cast a veiled aspersion on Hamilton, "For some reason, unknown to me, the 1st (South Carolina) and Rifles had moved to their rear."[23] The busy Aleck Haskell joined his brother William in the last assault, and Aleck fell, wounded in the leg.[24] William would have to go on to Gettysburg without Aleck, and without Berry.

[22] Heth's report, *OR*, ser. 1, vol. 25, pt. 1, p. 891–92; Caldwell, *History of a Brigade*, 81–83.

[23] Report of Col. Abner Perrin, 21 May 1863, *OR*, ser. 1, vol. 25, p. 907–908.

[24] Haskell, *The Haskell Memoirs*, 114.

CHAPTER 7

Wartime Augusta

"Gettysburg!!! T'was an awful place."

After a short stay in a Richmond hospital, Berry obtained leave to report to a hospital in Augusta. He arrived at the South Carolina Railroad Depot on 4 June 1863. A wagon provided by the Georgia Relief and Hospital Association met him and conveyed him, not to the city hospital behind the medical college, but to the Eagle and Phoenix Hotel on Broad Street. Augusta had become a city of hospitals. Augusta's rail connections and the presence of the Medical College of Georgia made the city the logical place to bring the war's wounded. By 1863, the authorities had taken over the downtown hotels for the soldiers' care. When even those facilities did not suffice, churches became hospitals. St. Patrick's (the Catholic church on Telfair Street), the First Presbyterian Church down the same block, St. Paul's Episcopal Church on Reynolds Street, and the Academy of Richmond County all became infirmaries. The Reverend Joseph Wilson, pastor of First Presbyterian (and father of future president Woodrow Wilson) headed the Georgia Relief and Hospital Association.[1]

---

[1] Florence Fleming Corley, *Confederate City: Augusta, Georgia, 1860–1865* (1960; repr., Augusta GA: Richmond County Historical Society, 1995) 63–64; Berry Benson, "The War Book, Reminiscences of Berry Greenwood Benson, CSA," (Typescript prepared by Charles G. Benson, Ida Jane ["Jeanie"] Benson, and Olive Benson), Special Collections, Reese Library, Augusta State University, Augusta GA; hereafter cited as "War Book"), 159. A copy of the typescript is also held by the Southern Historical Collection at the University of North Carolina, Chapel Hill, in its Berry Benson Papers, ms. 2636. The original manuscript diary (ms. 326) is located in the Hargrett Rare Book & Manuscript Library at the University of Georgia in Athens

It seemed to Berry that overnight Augusta had become an industrialized town. Water power provided by the Augusta Canal lured factories to the city. S. S. Jones and Company produced buckles, canteens, and buckets for the Confederacy. George R. Dodge's shop dyed bolts of cloth for uniforms. Jesse Ormond moved his Savannah factory to William Hight's empty machine shop and manufactured all types of items—from wheelbarrows to railroad cars. The Georgia Railroad Machine Shop fabricated an entire train, including engine and cars for the government. Charles Rigdon, Jesse Ansley, Andrew J. Smith, and Charles R. Keen, turned out 2,359 "Confederate Colt" pistols in one year.[2]

The Confederate government established a naval supply shop in Augusta and manufactured shoes and uniforms for navy personnel. A separate Confederate Shoe Factory made shoes for the army. The Confederate Quartermaster's Office employed hundreds of seamstresses, as did the Confederate Clothing Bureau and the Georgia Clothing Bureau. The huge Augusta Factory won a contract from the government to supply cloth at favorable prices. Its 750 mostly women workers lived with their families in nearby company houses. Factory president William E. Jackson donated cloth to the many agencies serving the Confederacy.[3]

These industries, plus flour mills and lesser shops, were dwarfed by the extensive Confederate Powder Works that stretched out in its many buildings for two miles along the canal. President Jefferson Davis commissioned a brilliant engineer named George W. Rains to build a powder works in a place of his own choosing. Because of the canal's waterpower and the rail connections, Rains chose Augusta. Improvising as he went, he began construction on 13 September 1861 and turned out the first shipment of gunpowder on 13 April 1862. It became Rains's boast that no Confederate army ever lost a battle from want of gunpowder. Berry might have mentioned to

[2] Corley, *Confederate City*, 47–48.
[3] Ibid., 49.

Colonel Rains that sometimes he and his mates had to fall back on captured Yankee ammunition. The busy Rains also took over the Augusta Arsenal and used it to repair weapons and manufacture cartridges, percussion caps, fuses, and grenades. Captain I. P. Girardy, superintendent of the Augusta Foundry and Machine Works, surveyed the industrial scene and remarked that Augusta was "the heart of the Confederacy." A Columbia, South Carolina, newspaper echoed the thought, "No city in the Confederacy...are congregated more manufacturing interests, wealth and enterprise, than Augusta, Georgia."[4]

Another noticeable change that had happened during Berry's absence was the emergence of women's organizations. It seemed that women had taken charge of the war effort and formed associations for a wide variety of war-related causes. Women made up almost the entire work force in the Augusta Factory. The Ladies Volunteer Association of Richmond County made underwear, socks, and shirts for the army, while the Ladies Volunteer Sewing Society sewed uniforms. Proper ladies would not have been associated with commercial sewing before the war, (as it would have been beneath their dignity), but patriotism overcame any objection. The Ladies Lunch Association provided refreshments for transient troops at the various depots in town. The Ladies Hospital Relief and Hospital Association staffed a Wayside Home for wounded soldiers. A member of the Ladies Knitting Society sent an appeal to her sisters:

> O, women of the Sunny South
> We want you in the field;
> Not with a soldier's uniform,
> Nor sword, nor spear, nor shield,
> But with a weapon quite as keen—
> The knitting needle bright;

---

[4] Ibid., 52–59; *Augusta Chronicle*, 13 May 1864.

And willing hands to knit for those
Who for our country fight.[5]

Perhaps the most bellicose-sounding of the women's organizations was that of the Ladies Gunboat Association. The fall of Fort Pulaski at the mouth of the Savannah River caused Augustans to fear an attack upriver by Union gunboats. A group of women decided to collect money to build a gunboat in Savannah to guard against such an attack. So they conducted fairs, raffles, card parties, and auctions and donated funds for the cause, as did women in other gunboat associations across the state. They raised $115,000 to build the "Ladies' Gun-boat," the ironclad ram C.S.S. *Georgia*. Unfortunately, the vessel proved too heavy and unwieldy to move, so it remained in place at Fort Jackson below Savannah, until scuttled by its own crew at Sherman's approach. Perhaps the ladies could argue that they had succeeded in that no Yankee gunboat dared challenge their gunboat, even if it could not move sufficiently to challenge the enemy.[6]

Despite the bustle of industry, the constant train traffic and troop movement, Berry noticed signs of war weariness. Prices had skyrocketed, and on Broad Street women participated in very unladylike protests against war profiteers. The Union blockade made almost everything scarce—everything but cotton, and there was plenty of that piled in the streets. Berry might have reflected that the cotton would have been better shipped to foreign markets to secure credit for the Confederacy. Instead, the Confederate government had hoarded the cotton in an attempt to gain more diplomatic leverage with the European governments. When the men talked about burning the cotton rather than letting it fall into enemy hands, some "ladies of Augusta" addressed a sarcastic appeal in a letter to the editor of the newspaper. They suggested that even in their inferior

---

[5] Corley, *Confederate City*, 41.
[6] *Augusta Chronicle*, 23 March, 1 April, and 16 April 1862.

wisdom they could see that setting the cotton on fire would burn the city down: "All that some of us possess are our houses and homes and though we don't object to your burning your own property, we have a very serious objection to your burning ours, especially as we by our sacrifices will gain no credit, it will all be ascribed to your patriotism."[7]

A meeting of slaveholders objected to the government's proposal to impress one-fifth of their slaves. A chorus of voices protested the Conscription Act of 1862 as unconstitutional. Some of the wealthy hired substitutes to go off to war.[8]

Berry did not have to cross the river to his old homestead because his father now lived on Reynolds Street in Augusta. Mat Benson worked for Thomas S. Metcalf's Commercial Bank as an accountant. Berry, who enjoyed the work, helped his father in the evenings. Mat had rented the house from Major Stephen H. Oliver, who bore the impressive title of "Quartermaster in Charge of Transportation from Augusta, Georgia." All the war material produced in Augusta's factories had to be sent out under Major Oliver's supervision. Oliver, like so many from the North, had come to Augusta from New Jersey to seek his fortune and he found it in merchandising.[9]

Berry read all he could about the course of the war in the Augusta papers, and he looked forward to Blackwood's letters. Thanks to those letters, this narrative can follow Blackwood's progress. Berry learned from Blackwood that his regiment, the 1st South Carolina, had followed Lee into Pennsylvania. Langdon Haskell, aide to Colonel Perrin of McGowan's Brigade, told Blackwood that their destination would be Gettysburg. Rumor had it that the army would spread out after crossing into Pennsylvania and

---

[7] Benson, "War Book," 161; *Augusta Chronicle*, 7 May 1862.
[8] *Augusta Chronicle*, 6 August 1862.
[9] Benson, "War Book," 161; information about Qm. Stephen Oliver provided by Dr. Charles "Chip" Bragg.

live off the land. "The Corps will separate, and we will do splendidly, I hope," Blackwood wrote. This would certainly be the grand finale of the war, a trial of combat between the North and the South.[10]

Blackwood also described the recent reorganization of the army. General Lee created three corps under James Longstreet, Richard Ewell, and A. P. Hill. Hill commanded three divisions commanded by J. R. Anderson, Dorsey Pender, and Henry Heth. Pender's Division included the brigades of McGowan, Lane, Thomas, and Scales. Colonel Samuel McGowan remained on sick leave. When McGowan's successor, D. H. Hamilton, also fell ill, Colonel Abner Perrin took charge of the brigade, with its old regiments, the 1st, 12th, 13th, 14th, and Orr's Rifles.

The element of particular interest to Berry was the addition of a new battalion to the brigade. Captain William Haskell had been authorized to form a battalion of sharpshooters, made up of 120 men selected from each company for their courage, stamina, and prowess with a gun. Haskell would have considered character equally important. As a matter of course, Haskell selected Blackwood and promoted him to second sergeant in Lieutenant M. R. Sharp's company. This elite regiment had privileges. It marched at the head of the brigade, deployed as a first line of skirmishers, and could act independently of the brigade. The creation of the battalion of sharpshooters amounted to a recognition of Haskell's ability and judgment. The fact that more than a thousand men in the brigade applied to join the sharpshooters is the best evidence of the esteem Haskell enjoyed among the rank and file.[11]

The last of May and the first part of June passed pleasantly enough with Hooker's army still opposite Fredericksburg and Lee's

---

[10] Benson, "War Book," 164.

[11] J. F. J. Caldwell, *History of a Brigade of South Carolinians Known First as "Gregg's" and subsequently as "McGowan's Brigade"* (Philadelphia: King and Baird Printers, 1866) 90–91; Benson, "War Book," 172–73.

watching them. The historian of McGowan's Brigade summed up the action, "The two sides engaged in nothing more hostile than music and cheering."[12] If the Federals would not take the initiative, Lee would. In the boldest move of the war he decided to take his army into Pennsylvania and turn it loose in enemy country. The *Augusta Chronicle and Sentinel* worried that the South would be left undefended, and that the war resolve of the northern states would be strengthened. Blackwood and most of his mates thought the invasion a splendid idea. To Blackwood's surprise, Haskell did not share the general optimism, telling Blackwood, "Is it not absurd for a small army of a weak nation to invade a great nation in the face of powerful armies?" As the leader of his men, Haskell could not voice such sentiments publicly. The fact that he confided his misgivings to Blackwood indicates how close the two men had become.[13]

On 3 June 1863 Lee moved up the Rappahannock with Longstreet and Ewell's Corps, while A. P. Hill lingered in Fredericksburg in case Hooker caused trouble there. Indeed, when Hooker learned of Lee's movement, he thought about pushing across the river and attacking Richmond. However, President Lincoln insisted that Lee's army, not Richmond, should be the objective. Hooker reluctantly pulled out of his camp and followed Lee, allowing A. P. Hill to do the same. Hooker's grumbling about being outnumbered and needing more troops annoyed Lincoln, and Lincoln's attitude annoyed Hooker. As a result, Hooker resigned on 27 June, and Lincoln named George Gordon Meade commander of the Army of the Potomac.

By that time, Ewell's Corps had smashed a Union detachment of 7,000 at Winchester, crossed the Maryland panhandle, and entered Pennsylvania. The Augusta newspapers reported that on 25 June, Ewell's troops had reached Carlisle, that Jubal Early's division

---

[12] Caldwell, *History of a Brigade*, 91.
[13] Blackwood K. Benson, *Who Goes There? The Story of a Spy in the Civil War* (New York: Macmillan, 1900) 394. Blackwood relied upon his diaries for his novel.

occupied Gettysburg, and that Robert Rodes's division was in Chambersburg. Northern newspapers expressed indignation at the consorting of some Pennsylvanians with the invaders. People in Harrisburg were reported to be fleeing the city rather than defending it. The Augusta newspaper did not blame the Harrisburg officials for their alleged cowardice, but for impressing black men to dig fortifications: "Their entreaties to be allowed to take home their marketing were in most cases disregarded and the poor fellows, after working hard all day, were compelled to dig all night." The northern press might have thought it unusual for a newspaper that defended slavery to be concerned about the impressment of black men in Harrisburg.[14]

On 27 June, A. P. Hill's Corps marched into Pennsylvania, having crossed the Potomac near the old Antietam battlefield, and bivouacked near Hagerstown, Maryland, the night before. They found the people, if not friendly, at least cooperative. They willingly sold, and even gave, foodstuffs to the Confederates, partly from fear that it would be taken anyhow. Blackwood admitted in a letter to Berry that there was some pilfering, but that in general the troops behaved themselves.

The general feeling of good cheer reached a new level at the brigade's camp at Cashtown on 30 June. The officers allowed a rare issue of whiskey to celebrate the success of the invasion so far. Everyone knew that this larking through Pennsylvania could not last long, that a major battle loomed. Even so, they had complete confidence that with Lee at their head they would win again, and their mood was mellow. Haskell worried about it. "Lee's army will never be as strong as it is tonight," he told Blackwood as they sat at their fire.[15]

They did not know that the vanguard of Meade's army was closer than either Ewell's or Longstreet's Corps. They did not know

[14] *Augusta Chronicle*, 3 July, 4 July 1863.
[15] B. K. Benson, *Who Goes There?*, 402.

because Jeb Stuart's cavalry had gone off on a wide circle of the Union army and had not returned. On 30 June General Henry Heth at Cashtown sent a detachment to Gettysburg, as he said in his report, "to search the town for army supplies (shoes especially)."[16] They returned to report enemy troops in the town. Heth informed General Hill. Therefore, on 1 July, Hill moved eastward from Cashtown, while Longstreet followed along the same pike from Chambersburg. Ewell called his scattered forces south from Carlisle and York. All converged on Gettysburg.

On 30 June, Meade's 1st Corps under General John Reynolds camped eight miles south of Gettysburg, and the rest of Meade's army lingered about fifteen miles south of the town. Meade intended to take up a safe defensive position at Pipe Creek, just inside the Maryland border, and let Lee risk an attack.

On the night of 30 June, observers in Gettysburg could see the distant campfires of the Confederates to the west at Cashtown and the Federals to the south at Marsh Creek, each eight miles away. Among the interested spectators on a ridge west of the town were troopers of General John Buford's cavalry division. Buford dispatched a rider to inform Reynolds of the presence of the enemy. Reynolds had to decide whether he should follow Meade's directions to join him at Pipe Creek or confront the Confederates at Gettysburg. At dawn on 1 July he marched to Gettysburg.[17]

General Henry Heth's division of A. P. Hill's Corps broke camp at dawn on 1 July and headed toward Gettysburg, followed by Pender's Division. General John Buford's outriders saw the long Confederate column swinging down the road in the famous fast pace they had mastered under Jackson. Still out of range, the troopers

---

[16] Report of Maj. Gen. Henry Heth, 13 September 1863, in US War Department, comp., *The War of the Rebellion: A Compilation of the Official Records of the Union and Confederate Armies*, 128 vols. (Washington DC: Government Printing Office, 1880–1901) ser. 1, vol. 27, pt. 2, p. 637.

[17] Bruce Catton, *This Hallowed Ground: The Story of the Union Side of the Civil War* (New York: Doubleday and Company, Inc., 1956) 250.

signaled their presence by a volley of shots. Heth's column dissolved into lines of battle and advanced cautiously, not knowing who they faced. Heth's skirmishers drove back the Union pickets with little effort until they reached the line of Buford's dismounted cavalry division along McPherson's Ridge west of town. A few minutes earlier and the thin line of troopers would have broken in face of the massed Confederate infantry. However, even as Heth send all four brigades forward, the first elements of General John Reynolds's 1st Corps came running on the field in a vicious counterattack, taking hundreds of prisoners, including General Archer. The Union side suffered a major loss in the death of John Reynolds. His decision to fight at Gettysburg cost him his life, but it might have won the war.[18]

The battered Confederate brigades drew back to regroup. On the other side, General O. O. Howard, whose troops had suffered so severely at Chancellorsville, assumed command of the 1st Corps and 11th Corps. He dispatched frantic messages to Meade to inform him of the situation, and he posted artillery along McPherson Ridge. Meade had not chosen to fight here, but others had decided for him. Nor did Lee chose this place. A. P. Hill had waited for Lee at the Cashtown encampment, and the two of them came into the fight already begun.

Even before Hill came up, Heth sent Pettigrew's fresh brigade up McPherson's Ridge. They rushed up bravely, then stopped twenty yards from their enemy, the Wisconsin Iron Brigade. Standing so close to one another, they killed and were killed, both lines in the open and firing point blank. Pender then sent four of his brigades in support of Pettigrew's faltering attack. As Blackwood and the men of McGowan's Brigade passed over and through Pettigrew's exhausted fighters, they heard a cheer for South Carolina. Major J. F. J. Caldwell, who marched at the head of the 1st Regiment of McGowan's Brigade, did not mean to disparage Pettigrew's men

---

[18] Report of Lt. Gen. Ambrose P. Hill, November 1863, *OR*, ser. 1, vol. 27, pt. 2, p. 606–609.

when he wrote, "They had fought well, but like most new soldiers, had been content to stand and fire, instead of charging."[19] All Lee's victories had been achieved by charging—regardless of the cost, and the men of McGowan's Brigade, following the orders of their commander Colonel Abner Perrin charged without firing a shot. Passing through Pettigrew's troops, Pender's now became the front line and the target of terrible artillery and musketry. In spite of the great gaps created in the lines, the soldiers dressed ranks and kept going. It was grand and terrible theater, a coming attraction of Pickett's more famous charge two days later.[20]

Human beings can stand only so much carnage, and the lines wavered. Then brigade commander Colonel Abner Perrin, who had led McGowan's Brigade so well at Chancellorsville, displayed his leadership again. Ordering his men not to fire a shot, he spurred his horse to the front, raised his sword, and galloped forward. His men could not help responding to his brave call, and they rushed forward with their characteristic yell, still withholding their fire. "We were met by a furious storm of musketry and shells from the enemy's batteries," Perrin reported. Amazingly, in spite of all odds, Perrin survived the charge and broke through the stubborn defenders on McPherson's Ridge and drove them back to Seminary Ridge. Crossing the last fence about two hundred yards from the seminary, the brigade was met by "the most destructive fire of musketry I have ever been exposed to," Perrin wrote, and still his men had not fired. His brigade advanced so rapidly that they found themselves unsupported. Lane's Brigade on the right had not moved at all. Scales on the left stopped to fire volleys at the enemy. McGowan's 14th Regiment came under devastating fire from defenders behind a stone wall on Seminary Ridge. The 1st Regiment changed front and caught the Federals in the flank, flushing them out, and scattering them

---

[19] Caldwell, *History of a Brigade*, 96–97.
[20] Report of Col. Abner Perrin, commanding McGowan's Brigade, 13 August 1863, *OR*, ser. 1, vol. 27, pt. 2, p. 661.

through the streets of the town. The men of the 1st and the survivors of the 14th chased the enemy into the town, taking hundreds of prisoners and field pieces.[21]

In a manner that seemed almost miraculous to Pender's men, General Robert Rodes's division of Ewell's Corp had come down from the north and simultaneously attacked the enemy's flank. There was some controversy about which unit entered Gettysburg first, but there was no doubt in the minds of the men of the 1st Regiment that their colors flew before any others in Gettysburg that day.[22]

During the dramatic charge, Haskell's Sharpshooters ran alongside of the brigade, and then veered off to attack a troop of Union cavalry. They scattered the enemy and captured some equipment and a herd of cattle. Without an immediate objective, Haskell had to find from his superiors where best to serve. He went through channels, asking Lieutenant M. R. Sharp if he had a good man who could get through all the fighting and confusion and locate General Pender. Sharp took only a moment, "I reckon Benson will do," he said. Benson was exactly the man Haskell had in mind, "Yes, Benson will do," he replied. Blackwood relished that assignment almost as much a Berry would have.[23]

Pender had pulled his troops out of town and lined them up on Seminary Ridge opposite Cemetery Ridge. General Winfield Scott Hancock, who replaced Howard in command, rallied his troops on the two hills south of town, Cemetery Hill and Culp's Hill, and as reinforcements came up, he strung them along Cemetery Ridge. So, Blackwood had to make his way through the streets of Gettysburg, as dead and wounded soldiers lay about, and frightened townspeople

---

[21] Perrin's report, *OR*, ser. 1, vol. 27, pt. 2, p. 661–62; Caldwell, *History of a Brigade*, 97.

[22] Perrin's report, *OR*, ser. 1, vol. 27, pt. 2, p. 662; Caldwell, *History of a Brigade*, 99.

[23] B. K. Benson to Berry Benson, 7 July 1863, Berry Benson Papers, Southern Historical Collection, University of North Carolina, Chapel Hill; Benson, "War Book," 165; B. K. Benson, *Who Goes There?*, 394.

peered out of windows. Houses that had been struck by artillery and burned cast a pall over the town. Blackwood found one of Ewell's officers and asked where he might find Pender. "Over there," said the officer, pointing to Seminary Ridge southwest of town.

To find Pender, Blackwood had to pass between the armies, with shots and shells coming from both sides. "Tell the Captain to bring his men up," the general told Blackwood. Blackwood never saw Pender again. General Dorsey Pender received a fatal wound in the next day's fighting. By the time Blackwood led Haskell's Sharpshooters to Seminary Ridge, darkness had fallen, and fighting stopped. The sharpshooters took their place out in front of McGowan's Brigade as line of skirmishers.[24]

Though no longer in the 1st Regiment, Blackwood still referred to it as "our" regiment. With a degree of boasting he wrote Berry that the regiment had flushed out the Yankees from behind a stone fence, and routed them through town. "Our regiment took two flags and a battery," he wrote.[25] But there was bad news. Berry's messmate and friend Larkin lay among the dead. During the terrible day's fighting, 16,000 men on both sides had been killed or captured.

Blackwood got little sleep that night as Haskell's men did picket duty. Nearby General Lee pondered the day's events in a house near the Lutheran Seminary. By the following day he would have the reinforcement of Longstreet's Corps. He decided to send Ewell against the hills near town, at the same time Longstreet struck the southern flank. In Stuart's absence, Lee did not know where that flank might be situated. A. P. Hill would hold the center and demonstrate enough to occupy the attention of the enemy.

Meade arrived that night and took over command from Hancock. He approved the position Howard had selected, and prepared to defend it. Meade's general on his southern flank, Daniel

---

[24] B. K. Benson to Berry Benson, 7 July 1863, Benson Papers, Chapel Hill; Benson, "War Book," 166.

[25] B. K. Benson to Berry Benson, 7 July 1863, Benson Papers, Chapel Hill.

Sickles, took it upon himself to advance his troops from the ridge into a wheat field and peach orchard, ignoring two prominent features of the ridge, Big and Little Round Top.

After an exhausting march, Longstreet's Corps arrived on the field that same night. John Cheves Haskell served as an officer in Colonel Edward P. Alexander's artillery. The next morning, after only a few hours sleep, John Haskell and several others rode out to have a look at the Union position. They circled around Sickles's Division in the wheat field, and found the Round Tops guarded by only a few pickets. Haskell's party easily chased them away and took a prisoner. The hills overlooked the Union position and Haskell realized their crucial importance. He brought the news to Longstreet, and to General John B. Hood, whose division would lead the attack. Haskell did not know that his visit attracted the attention of Union General Gouverneur K. Warren, and that Warren managed to drag a battery of guns to the Round Top. When Hood's assault began at 4:00 P.M. Haskell supported it with two batteries of cannon. Hood's men drove Sickles out of the wheat field in a panic and almost gained the Round Top but Union reinforcements beat them off. Hood sat on his horse near Haskell's guns when a piece of shrapnel struck him in the arm, flinging him off his horse. That marked the effective end of the drive upon the southern flank of the Union army.[26]

Ewell's troops gained some ground at the other end of the Union line, and evening fell with Confederates clinging to Culp's Hill, and Union defenders stubbornly holding Cemetery Hill. A. P. Hill's skirmishers kept up an intermittent firing along the center. William Haskell's Sharpshooters formed the front line of Pender's Division. Haskell, always daring and unafraid, walked along the line, directing the fire of his men. Around 6:00 P.M. Colonel Perrin asked Haskell's Sharpshooters, backed by the 1st Regiment, to drive the

---

[26] John Cheves Haskell, *The Haskell Memoirs*, ed. Gilbert E. Govan and James W. Livingood (New York: G. P. Putnam's Sons, 1960) 48–51.

enemy skirmishers off the road in front of Cemetery Hill. According to Colonel Perrin, "the gallant Haskell made the most intrepid charge" upon the Federals, driving them back to the protection of their artillery.[27] To get a better view of the scene, Haskell climbed upon an outcropping of rock. A Union sniper on the roof of the Bliss Farm, five hundred yards away, took aim and fired. The bullet pierced Haskell under the shoulder, and he fell dead.[28]

Word spread quickly, and gloom fell over the regiment. When Sergeant Rhodes approached him, Blackwood knew he had bad news: "Benson, Captain Haskell is killed!" Just then, they brought the captain by on a stretcher. Blackwood thought he saw a smile on his lips. Sergeant Rhodes wept; Lieutenant Barnwell wept, and Blackwood confessed to Berry, "I broke down utterly." A man might shrug off the death of hundreds of strangers, but the death of a friend hurt deeply. Major Caldwell of the 1st South Carolina, after a long recitation of Haskell's virtues, concluded, "It was everywhere conceded that we could have sustained no heavier loss in the line, than in him."[29]

When Berry heard about Haskell's death, he grieved profoundly, "I do not hesitate to say that he was one of the best, bravest, and most promising officers in the Confederate Service, and had he lived through the war he would certainly have attained distinction."[30]

At 10:00 P.M. orders came to rest that night in line of battle. Perrin relayed word for his sharpshooters, now under Lieutenant Barnwell, to link up with Ewell's skirmish line on the left. In the reports of generals, the anonymous enlisted man who does the dangerous work of actually distinguishing friend from foe and linking up—that man is not mentioned. In this night's adventure, Blackwood

[27] Perrin's report, *OR*, ser. 1, vol. 27, pt. 2, p. 663.
[28] B. K. Benson, *Who Goes There?*, 419; Caldwell, *History of a Brigade*, 100.
[29] Caldwell, *History of a Brigade*, 104; Haskell, *Haskell Memoirs*, 114–15; B. K. Benson to Berry Benson, 7 July 1863, Benson Papers, Chapel Hill; Benson, "War Book," 166.
[30] Benson, "War Book," 170–71.

happened to be the man. When his officer, Lieutenant Sharp, appeared completely confused as what to do, Blackwood volunteered to go out alone and find fellow Confederates. He crept along a fence until he could hear voices, and still closer to see shadowy figures by the dim light of the moon. Blackwood crawled back to report to Sharp that there were people close by. In a predictable reaction, Sharp told Blackwood to go back there and see who they were.

Obediently, Blackwood made his way to the place he had left. He could hear them, so they could hear him, "Whose pickets are those?" he called out.

"Our pickets!" came the clear but unsatisfactory response.

Blackwood tried again, "Whose side are you on?"

"Whose side are you on?"

Thinking that this dialogue might go on indefinitely, Blackwood ended it by shouting, "The Rebels!"

The time the answer, "Well, we are for the Union," came to the accompaniment of a hail of bullets whistling over Blackwood's head. He scrambled out of there as quickly as he could. Lieutenant Sharp, hearing the shots and thinking Blackwood had been caught or killed, pulled his company back. There is no indication whether they ever managed to link up with Ewell's lines that night.[31]

On the next day, the fatal 3 July, the sharpshooters and 1st South Carolina held the line won by Captain William Haskell the previous day. From this point they could pick off individuals on Cemetery Ridge. Sharpshooters seldom formed regular lines of battle. They took advantage of declivities in the ground and projections above ground. Blackwood lay on his stomach and fired when he could. He counted thirty shots and saw three of them take effect. If Blackwood's rifle could reach the enemy, they could reach him. A Union bullet killed Blackwood's friend, Sergeant Rhodes, lying nearby. During the morning a line of Union infantry tried to drive the skirmishers out of

---

[31] B. K. Benson, *Who Goes There?*, 416.

rifle range, but Lieutenant Sharp led the men in a counterattack and held their original position.[32]

After noon the focus of fighting changed to the center of the field, to the right of A. P. Hill's Corps. Lee's massed artillery, 130 guns, opened upon the enemy in a furious, deafening cannonade. John Cheves Haskell commanded two batteries in the Peach Orchard from which Sickles had been driven the day before. Lee intended to silence the Union artillery on Cemetery Ridge in preparation for an assault by the Confederate infantry. Colonel Alexander, John Haskell's chief, showed him a note he received from Longstreet, telling him that when thought that the barrage had achieved its maximum effect to give orders to Pickett to march with his division. Alexander could not bring himself to take that responsibility, and the cannonade continued while the ammunition lasted. Finally, as the guns silenced, Longstreet himself sent the order, but Colonel Alexander and John Haskell heard him murmur, "It is all wrong, but he would have it."[33]

The charge is famously known as Pickett's charge. However, a portion of A. P. Hill's Corps marched out with Pickett. Heth's Division, commanded by General J. Johnston Pettigrew, and two of Pender's brigades led by General Isaac Trimble, with Pickett, formed a line a mile long numbering 15,000. John Haskell advanced five guns to support the assault. He fired into a mass of infantry that seemed poised to sweep down on Pickett's flank, and had the satisfaction of scattering them. However, he soon attracted the attention of enemy artillery. He lost two guns and a number of men. A shell struck him in the side and knocked him off his horse, but his sword hilt deflected the blow, saving his life. He had to order his men to fall back, and then he allowed them to take him to the field hospital. When he reached the barn, then being used as a hospital, he

[32] Ibid., 418.
[33] Haskell, *Haskell Memoirs*, 50–51.

was surprised to see Pickett and his staff there while his troops marched into withering artillery fire.[34]

Off to the left, Blackwood and his mates watched the drama unfold. Major J. F. J. Caldwell, then a lieutenant in the 1st South Carolina, saw it in heroic terms, "Out they marched, banners flying, arms glittering in the sun, crashing over the wheat field, breasting the storm of fire that met them, moving upon the stronghold with a bravery unsurpassed since McDonald's charge at Austerlitz." Blackwood, from the same vantage point, saw it differently, "We of the skirmishers felt our line was doomed. Men knew it would be torn apart by artillery. It was not war, neither was it magnificent. It was too absurd to be grand."[35]

Only a few made it to the stone wall with General Lewis Armistead, who died there. Trimble and Pettigrew, leading their troops, were wounded, Trimble taken prisoner. About half of the men who had set out so bravely made it back to their lines. Lee rode out to meet them. "It is all my fault," he was heard to say. There was nothing to do now but return to Virginia.[36]

Blackwood grumbled about Lee's decision in a letter to Berry, "Seriously, we don't like Lee's coming out of Pennsylvania a bit. He tried to make us take a mountain, and because we couldn't do it, he runs back into Virginia." Though no one could replace Captain William Haskell in Blackwood's estimation, he came to admire Lieutenant Barnwell, who took command of the sharpshooters. The sharpshooters acted as a rear guard as Hill's Corps crossed the Potomac at Falling Waters, and repulsed a Union cavalry charge. Barnwell rallied the men and drove off the enemy. "I tell you, he

---

[34] Ibid., 52.
[35] Caldwell, *History of a Brigade*, 101; B. K. Benson, *Who Goes There?*, 422.
[36] Catton, *This Hallowed Ground*, 191.

showed himself to be no uncommon man on that field," Blackwood wrote Berry.[37]

Berry, reading about Gettysburg in the papers, chafed at the slow healing of his wounded leg. "I so longed to be with the boys," he recalled. Gettysburg changed his life in an unexpected way. As he limped around the neighborhood on crutches, he met a twice-wounded veteran who was home to recuperate. Of course, they struck up a conversation. By a coincidence this was George L. Oliver, the son of the Bensons' landlord. George insisted that Berry come home with him and meet his sisters: Louisiana, Florida, and Alabama Jane (known as Jeanie). Berry was very happy to be introduced to the girls, and they seemed equally glad to see him. Thus encouraged, he visited the Oliver residence frequently. Florida caught his attention at first, but Jeanie finally claimed his heart. In Jeanie Oliver he found a kindred spirit. Berry has allowed us only a glimpse of the two of them sitting in the parlor, Jeanie sewing a button on his uniform, with her lips touching the button as she bit the thread, and Berry treasuring the button the more because of the imagined kiss.[38] Jeanie Oliver had all the qualities Berry admired—intelligence, sensitivity, imagination, compassion—in fact, the qualities that he also possessed. He found new delights; she played the piano beautifully, she sang enchantingly, and not only did she like poetry—she wrote it as well. If anything could have distracted him from the war, his fascination with Jeanie Oliver should have.

But the war could not be forgotten. The local newspapers printed a detailed description of the battle in Gettysburg. For a moment in September, Augusta seemed the center of military activity when two divisions of Longstreet's Corps came through town and stopped for a night. Berry visited his cousin, Henry Lindley, and heard more details about Gettysburg. Longstreet's troops then went

[37] B. K. Benson to Berry Benson, 15 August 1863, Benson Papers, Chapel Hill; Benson, "War Book," 180.

[38] Benson, "War Book," 162–63.

on to join Braxton Bragg's army and help win the battle of Chickamauga. The Augusta papers maintained a patriotic silence about Longstreet's presence, but expressed frustration when the northern newspapers printed an account of the maneuver.[39] This shifting of troops from the eastern to the western theater by rail marked an important innovation in warfare.

---

[39] Ibid., 204.

CHAPTER 8

The Wilderness and Spotsylvania

*"If a man wants to see hell on earth, let him come to this black,
bloody hole."*

Even though his leg had not completely healed, Berry decided to leave home and report to his regiment. Blackwood had written that they had taken up winter quarters, and Berry felt that he might as well continue his recuperation with "the boys." After tender goodbyes to Jeanie Oliver and a handshake to his father, he left Augusta on 2 December 1863. He was buoyed by his eagerness to be back with his company. Jeanie had only the hope of his safe return. She wrote a poem-prayer entitled "Mon Guerrier" ("My Warrior"):

> Oh, guard him, midnight stars that shine
> On many battlefields.
> Where Southern blood as free as wine
> Is spilled, but never yields!
> When bayonets leap to meet the foe
> And steel rings loud with shell
> Where death, unpitying all our woes,
> Sets his eternal seal
> Her last stanza ended with a poignant hope:
> To thee, O God of Battles, we
> Our soldier boy entrust
> We ask thy blessing, rich and free,
> With mouths laid in the dust.
> Do thou beside the cannon stand
> Directing shot and shell,

And hold his life within Thy hand,
His life—our life as well.[1]

Berry would read her poem later, but he felt her love then. He chafed at the overcrowded train's slow progress, with its many stops and its overnight stands. Finally, late in the day on 6 December he reached the depot at Orange Courthouse and limped the three miles to camp. Passing other regiments on the way to his, he heard the frequent catcall, "Hospital rat!" The men used the expression as an epithet for those who shirked duty by lying out in a hospital. Berry resisted the temptation to yell, "Go to hell!" knowing that the taunting would get worse.[2]

The greeting he received from his mates of the 1st South Carolina made up for the otherwise rude reception. Much backslapping, arm punching and joking initiated him back into Company H. He found that he ranked as sergeant as of 3 July 1863, undoubtedly a last favor to him by Captain William Haskell. Lieutenant Langdon Haskell, aide to brigade commander Colonel Perrin, did him the favor of recommending him to be acting assistant adjutant general while Captain Aleck Haskell was on furlough. That meant that Berry did much of the routine clerical copying and accounts. As a result, he could rest his leg and have leisure time for reading Hugo's *Les Miserables*, Milton's *Paradise Lost*, Meredith's *Tannhauser*, Bulwer's *A Strange Story*, and *The Life of Mahomet*. From his earliest years, Berry strove for self-improvement, partly because of the southern ideal of a

---

[1] Benson Family Papers, private collection of Arthur Dupre, Newark NJ.
[2] Berry Benson, "The War Book, Reminiscences of Berry Greenwood Benson, CSA," (Typescript prepared by Charles G. Benson, Ida Jane ["Jeanie"] Benson, and Olive Benson), Special Collections, Reese Library, Augusta State University, Augusta GA; hereafter cited as "War Book"), 215. A copy of the typescript is also held by the Southern Historical Collection at the University of North Carolina, Chapel Hill, in its Berry Benson Papers, ms. 2636. The original manuscript diary (ms. 326) is located in the Hargrett Rare Book & Manuscript Library at the University of Georgia in Athens.

cultivated gentleman, and partly because of his insatiable curiosity. He reflected later on the curious fact that he did not have a rifle until forty-seven days after reporting to camp.[3]

Berry admitted to "a slight feeling of caste" in his attitude toward conscripts. Although he and his fellow volunteers tried not to show it, they harbored a prejudice against the men who had been drafted to serve. Berry woke up one morning to see a draftee staring at him. The big stranger greeted him with a wide grin and "Howdy, Buster." Being called "Buster" by a conscript and a stranger offended Berry's sense of dignity as a sergeant and his deeper conception of himself as a gentleman. There was nothing else to do than to say "Howdy" back, as good-naturedly as possible. Major J. F. J. Caldwell of the 1st South Carolina acknowledged that a few excellent soldiers emerged from the new men, "but between discharges then or subsequently, their ill health and aversion to duty, we made very little out of the majority of them."[4]

On 19 January Berry assumed his regular duties when Aleck Haskell resumed his role as assistant adjutant general. Berry's leg had healed, and he had no excuse to get out of drills and dress parades. In fact, his first duty was to drill the recruits, overcoming his distaste in doing so. He did guard duty at night for the first time on 20 January and enjoyed the old feeling of roaming around at midnight. He finally got a gun when a wagonload of arms and ammunition arrived on 23 January. Having exhausted the available wood supply, the brigade had to move to a new camp several miles away. So Berry and his mates kept busy building new log cabins for themselves. Berry's hut measured twelve feet square, made of logs chinked with clay. It accommodated Berry, Blackwood, privates Owens and Rice. They

---

[3] Ibid., 219.
[4] Ibid., 220; J. F. J. Caldwell, *History of a Brigade of South Carolinians Known First as "Gregg's" and subsequently as "McGowan's Brigade"* (Philadelphia: King and Baird Printers, 1866) 124.

saved a space for their sixteen-year-old cousin Zack Benson, who joined them a month later.[5]

In February, President Jefferson Davis sent out an appeal for all soldiers to reenlist for the duration of the war. Most of them had thought they were doing that when they signed up for the initial three years. But with war enthusiasm flagging, the government wanted a show of determination to encourage the public. General Lee called upon his troops to renew their pledge; Generals McGowan and Wilcox echoed his appeal. Berry and his mates had no trouble repeating a commitment they had already made. The day his regiment unanimously adopted the resolution to fight to the end happened to be 9 February, Berry's twenty-first birthday, and the day he received promotion to the rank of sergeant major. By this time General McGowan had come back from sick leave to take command of the brigade, and Abner Perrin became brigadier of Wilcox's Brigade, while General Cadmus Wilcox took over Pender's Division. Captain Aleck Haskell left the brigade to become lieutenant colonel of the 7th South Carolina Cavalry, and Langdon Haskell, newly advanced to captain, stepped into his brother's position as assistant adjutant general. Aleck was much admired in the brigade and when the troops gave him a spontaneous send-off, he replied with a speech that moved some of them to tears.[6]

The most important reorganization, as far as Berry and Blackwood were concerned, was the reactivation of the sharpshooters' corps under Captain William S. Dunlop. Both Berry and Blackwood wanted to enlist, but Captain Barnwell of the 1st insisted that he could not lose two non-commissioned officers. Berry ranked as sergeant and Blackwood corporal, and the dilemma seemed insurmountable. Blackwood nobly insisted that Berry should go. Equally nobly, Berry said he would do no such thing. Blackwood had served in the sharpshooters' unit and Berry felt that his brother had

---

[5] Benson, "War Book," 226.
[6] Ibid., 228–30.

first rights to rejoin the battalion. Then Blackwood thought of a compromise; he would resign his corporal's rank and with Barnwell's consent, go in as a private. Barnwell, who liked both brothers, agreed, and the Bensons became sharpshooters. As it turned out, Blackwood soon attained the rank of sergeant, having served temporarily as sergeant at Gettysburg. Berry and Blackwood ranked as two of the four sergeants in Company A, one of three companies of about fifty men each. Lieutenant Ingraham Hasell commanded the company. Berry immediately initiated target practice for the men of the company, and wished he had done it sooner.[7]

The old wanderlust soon got the better of Berry. He obtained a pass to forage outside the picket line. Actually, he intended to spy on the enemy, but he needed a pass to show a patrol that he was not a deserter. He forded the Rapidan, walked five miles to the Robinson River, and with a spyglass spotted a Federal picket. He made up his mind to get his rifle, swim across the river, and maybe capture the soldier. If he couldn't capture him, then perhaps he could at least take a shot.

True to his intention, he set out the following night with his heavy rifle (this time without the protection of a pass), again forded the Rapidan, and reached the Robinson after dark. He had no idea how deep the river ran, so he stripped and waded into the icy water and barely made it to the other side against the swift current. He realized that he could never have crossed encumbered by his rifle and a bundle of clothes, so he reluctantly gave up his scheme. On the way back he came across a vacant schoolhouse, went in, and started a fire to warm up. Outside it began to snow, so Berry settled down for the night. The next morning, he trudged through the new snowfall to find the Rapidan now a raging river, swollen by the snow. What to do? If he walked upriver eight miles he knew he would find a bridge, but he also knew that the bridge would be guarded and he had no

[7] Ibid., 237–38.

pass. He could not face the ignominy of being arrested, and he a non-commissioned officer and a sharpshooter! There was nothing to do but strip again and carry everything across, even though he was not at all sure if he could make it. First, he crossed with one hand holding the rifle above the water. Nearly frozen, he had to swim back for his bundle of clothes. He made it across but his numbed hands would not function well enough to allow him to put on his clothes. Naked, but with his rifle and bundle, he stumbled across the field to a farmhouse. A black servant saw him coming and went out to help. He wrapped Berry in blankets, sat him down in the kitchen before a hot fire, and put a tub of hot water at his feet. The owner of the house urged Berry to stay as long as he wanted. After three hours, Berry recovered sufficiently to make his way back to the regiment. Fortunately, everyone assumed that he had gone out under permission, and he did not tell them otherwise. However his escapade became legendary among the sharpshooters because a fellow sergeant visited the same house and heard the story—with embellishments—from the gentleman of the house.[8]

In April, Blackwood went home on furlough, and as a result missed some of the heaviest fighting of the war. By now President Lincoln had found a general to his liking in Ulysses S. Grant. Grant commanded a massive force of 120,000 men north of the Rapidan and intended to use them when the weather permitted. On 4 May, the weather permitted, and he began his move, crossing the Rapidan at Germanna Ford a few miles west of the Chancellorsville battlefield and headed south. Longstreet had rejoined Lee after his adventures in the west, except for Pickett's Division doing duty in North Carolina, giving Lee a fighting force of about 65,000. Lee realized that Grant had to pass through the same dense wilderness they had fought in the year before, and the undermanned southern army would have a better chance in those thickets. On 4 May, Lee sent A.

---

[8] Ibid., 243–48.

P. Hill eastward toward the wilderness along the Orange Plank Road and Ewell's Corps on the converging Orange Turnpike. With luck they would strike the big Union columns before they moved out of the wilderness roads.

After camping at Verdiers Mill, Hill's Corps resumed its march on the next morning. Berry's sharpshooters led McGowan's Brigade along the Plank Road. Suddenly a party of Federals rode toward them. Assuming that this was one of Stuart's patrols, Captain Langdon Haskell and a few other staff officers rode out to meet them. The strangers recognized Confederates, wheeled around, and galloped off. Langdon Haskell had to take some ironic ribbing at his "victory."[9]

Around 4:00 P.M. Ewell's Corps became engaged in a line of battle along the Turnpike. McGowan's troops could hear the sound of fighting off to their left. Then Heth's Division ran into enemy skirmishers along the Plank Road and filed off into the woods. Wilcox positioned his brigades as a second line, Scales to the right of the road, McGowan to the left, and Thomas further left. Before marching into the dense woods, the brigades crossed an open field where Lee and Stuart, standing near a battery, saluted them. The noise of Heth's engagement in front of them drew them on, even though they could not see friend or foe. Crashing through underbrush, they came upon Heth's men, lying prone and firing at an invisible foe. Wilcox's Brigades passed through Heth's and became the front line, and ran the double risk of being shot from the enemy in front or from a friend in the rear.[10]

The sharpshooters out in front found the enemy line of battle and waited for the rest to come up. As sergeant major of Company A in the sharpshooter battalion, Berry's position was at the extreme

---

[9] John Cheeves Haskell, *The Haskell Memoirs*, ed. Gilbert E. Govan and James W. Livingood (New York: G. P. Putnam's Sons, 1960) 117; Caldwell, *History of a Brigade*, 127; Benson, "War Book," 250–51.

[10] Caldwell, *History of a Brigade*, 129.

right of the line. That put him at the edge of the Plank Road with a clear view up the road. About three hundred yards distant a cannon caisson stood abandoned. Berry saw a Federal step out of the woods and behind the caisson, and he took a quick shot at him. The flash of his gun disclosed his position, and the sniper fired back. The bullet painfully grazed Berry's shoulder and tore into his knapsack. For a while they carried on their own individual battle in the midst of an increasingly immense struggle. Suddenly across the road to Berry's right, the men of Scales's Brigade came pouring out of the woods and running down the road in retreat. Just then, the enemy in front of McGowan crashed through the thickets in massive numbers and the Confederate line broke, all three brigades in a panic. To Berry's dismay, even the vaunted sharpshooters joined the retreat.

Berry collected seven of the sharpshooters, all he could find, and had them put pine twigs in their hats for mutual recognition. They headed off to the west where Lane's Brigade still held. "Are you bringing in cartridges?" Lane called to them. "Only those in our boxes," Berry answered holding up his cartridge box. Then his little band pitched in with the North Carolinians. The guns on both sides fired incessantly, though neither could see the other clearly. A pall of smoke hung over the woods, and the smell of sulphur suffused the air. Two of Berry's mates fell by his side. Even after nightfall, men kept firing at the musket flashes of the enemy, and small fires burned in the underbrush.[11]

Berry had an officer sign a note saying that he and his men had fought there. Then he and the remaining five went off to find their regiment. A courier told them where their lines had reformed. In the darkness it was difficult to distinguish friend from foe. Berry heard movement, and called out "First South Carolina." A voice answered, "Here, this way." Then another, "No, that's a Yankee, come this way." Berry guessed that the second voice sounded more like a

---

[11] Ibid., 254.

Confederate and went that way, but with his gun cocked. Fortunately, he guessed right, and found Company H of the 1st Regiment. He learned that young Zack had been severely wounded in this, his first battle. He died from his wounds a month later.

Berry found the sharpshooters lying beyond the 1st Regiment and took his place along the road. The Union line was so close he could hear them talking. Soon, a bantering began between the lines. A Federal replied to a taunt by calling the Confederate a damned son of a bitch. Both sides began shooting at each other, uselessly, there in the impenetrable darkness.[12]

As the morning light filtered among the trees, Berry saw a massed line of men advancing slowly and quietly about two hundred yards in front. He alerted General McGowan, then returned to his post. There were too many of them and the sharpshooters gave way, retreating to the Confederate line of battle. To Berry's astonishment, the brigade that had fought so well so often, broke and ran without a fight. "I am ashamed to say it, but I don't think I ever saw troops behaving so badly," Berry recalled. The retreat carried them out of the woods and out to the field where Lee stood with Stuart's Artillery. Lee rode among them, and some heard him shout, "I am surprised to see such a gallant brigade running like a flock of geese." Those biting words—and the protection of the cannon—halted the retreat, and the men hastily dug breastworks with bayonets and tin cups. But the men had lost confidence in themselves, and they wondered if they could hold back the overwhelming numbers advancing toward them.[13]

Just then, after marching all night, Longstreet came riding onto the field at the head of Kershaw's and Field's Divisions, numbering 10,000 men. Major John Cheves Haskell, who commanded one of Longstreet's artillery battalions, wrote of Longstreet in admiration, "always grand in battle, he never shone as he did here." He formed a

---

[12] Ibid., 255–56.
[13] Ibid., 257–58; Caldwell, *History of a Brigade*, 133.

battle line of the two divisions, pushed through Heth's and Wilcox's demoralized divisions, and charged at the Yankee throng. After the heaviest struggle Haskell had ever seen, the enemy grudgingly gave ground and began to retreat.[14]

Longstreet's line diverged in the dense thickets. Longstreet stayed with General Micah Jenkins whose North Carolinians, jubilant at their success, gave a cheer for Longstreet. Just then, Mahone's Virginians blundered through the woods to the sound of the cheering, and fired blindly. General Jenkins fell from his horse, fatally wounded. A bullet struck Longstreet in the neck, paralyzing one arm and rendering him speechless, but he managed to ride toward Mahone's men, with one hand raised. The Virginians then saw what they had done. In the same wilderness, friendly fire had killed Jackson a year before; now it cut down Longstreet. Haskell helped him off his horse, and heard him whisper to tell Lee that the enemy verged on a rout. It took time for General Richard Anderson to come up, and by that time the initiative had been lost. Haskell tended the dying General Jenkins, his brother's classmate at military school and a family friend. He believed that the Union army would have been swept from the field if Longstreet had not been wounded.[15]

A. P. Hill advanced his corps to the left of Longstreet, meeting slight resistance, but restoring a measure of self-respect to the men. After the line halted in position, Berry prowled about through the woods deserted by the enemy, with knapsacks and equipment lying among the bodies of the slain. He came across a party of horsemen,

---

[14] Haskell, *Haskell Memoirs*, 64. In his report of 23 March 1865, of operations 14 April–6 May 1864, Lt. Gen. James Longstreet said that the charge of his troops "was made with spirit rarely surpassed." US War Department, comp., *The War of the Rebellion: A Compilation of the Official Records of the Union and Confederate Armies*, 128 vols. (Washington DC: Government Printing Office, 1880–1901) ser. 1, vol. 36, p. 1054–55.

[15] Haskell, *Haskell Memoirs*, 65.

and recognized General John B. Gordon among them. His curiosity appeased for the moment, he returned to the sharpshooters.[16]

Grant proved a different kind of general than the Confederates had faced before. He had no intention of retiring back across the Rapidan; instead he headed south along the Brock Road toward Spotsylvania, intending to get around Lee's right flank. Remarkably, Lee guessed that Grant might do just that, and moved Longstreet's Corps, now under Richard Anderson, down an old logging road parallel to the Brock Road. A. P. Hill held his position, while Ewell's Corps moved behind him from the left to follow Longstreet's troops. Hill's Corps followed, but Hill, desperately ill, had to be carried on a stretcher. Jubal Early assumed command of the corps.[17]

Anderson reached Spotsylvania before the first Union troops arrived, and hastily threw up breastworks. These works spread along a line perpendicular to the highway facing west as Ewell's Corps extended Anderson's lines. When Hill's troops under Early came in they formed a line facing east. The result was breastworks shaped like an inverted, ragged "V" blunted at the apex, or in military terms, a salient. The Confederates made use of a natural ridge to erect their works, and dug dirt from inside the works to raise the ramparts. Union General G. K. Warren must have been surprised to come across Confederates he thought to have left back in the wilderness. He attacked Anderson's position, found it too strong, and decided to wait for the rest of the Union army to come up.

McGowan's Brigade arrived on the field on 8 May and took its position facing east. Berry reflected the general feeling of relief that they would now be able to see their enemy approaching, rather than have them suddenly appear through the woods. During that day, waves of Union troops battered against Ewell's lines on the left and at the top of the salient. The Union forces opposite Early on the

---

[16] Benson, "War Book," 262; report of Brig. John B. Gordon, 5 July 1864, *OR*, ser. 1, vol. 36, p. 1076–79.

[17] Caldwell, *History of a Brigade*, 138.

right seemed curiously quiet, and remained so on 9 May. The sharpshooters took their position several hundred yards in front of the breastworks. Berry ventured out to investigate the intentions of the enemy. On the way he met Ben Powell, who held a position in the brigade Berry must have envied. Powell, by virtue of his prowess with a gun, had been given the brigade's only Whitworth rifle, made in England, having a range of 800 yards. Also, he had been given permission to act independently, to go out by himself and shoot at his pleasure. Powell met Berry outside the lines, and told him he had shot a Union officer. That night, Union pickets called across to the line of sharpshooters that Union general John Sedgwick had been killed by a sniper. Ironically, Sedgwick had just reassured a soldier that he was safe, saying, "They can't hit an elephant at this distance." Berry and Ben engaged in a bit of sniping, which provoked the enemy skirmishers to advance upon them. They retreated hastily to their lines, and Confederate artillery stopped the advance of the Federals.[18]

On 11 May, the Federal forces continued to assault the western face of the salient. Around noon, Berry asked General Wilcox for permission to go out and scout the enemy position again to see what they might be up to. Wilcox suggested that it would be helpful if Berry could manage "to get if possible in the rear of the enemy's left." The idea of getting in the rear of the enemy appealed to Berry. Ben Powell did not need permission, and he accompanied Berry. They crept between enemy pickets and came upon a farmhouse. With apologies to the owner they surveyed the situation from an upstairs window, and Berry thought he could see a way of getting around the Federal camp. After a long, circuitous hike, the two scouts

---

[18] Benson, "War Book," 270, 273–74. In his history of the sharpshooters, Maj. W. S. Dunlop accepts as a fact that Powell was the sniper who killed Sedgwick (W. S. Dunlop, *Lee's Sharpshooters; or the Forefront of Battle* [Little Rock AR: Tunnah and Pittard, Printers, 1899] 49).

heard voices ahead in a wooded area. Creeping forward through the trees, they saw soldiers at campfires, cooking their evening meal. Someone came toward them; they heard his cough. In whispers, they decided to take him prisoner. However, he stopped short, picked up some firewood, and returned to the camp. As it grew darker, Berry cautioned Powell to wait for him. He moved to the edge of the camp clearing, near an outlying tent. Just then a courier rode up, and an officer came out of the tent to speak to him. Berry heard the courier give orders about the disposition of troops and address the officer as "colonel." He tried to remember the names of the units he heard mentioned in order to relay the information to General Wilcox.[19]

Although General Wilcox might have been satisfied with the information gathered so far, Berry was not. He had been asked to locate any possible breastworks, and so far had not seen any. He decided to put a bold face on it and walked out into the camp, being careful to remain on the fringes and out of the firelight. He called over to a group sitting around a fire, and asked where a certain regiment might be. They cheerfully shouted out the answer. He thanked them, looked about, and decided that he had all the information he wanted. His route back took him by the colonel's tent. The colonel worked inside by the light of a lantern. Twenty feet in front of the tent stood the colonel's horse, a magnificent animal. Berry weighed the chances for a moment, then decided to steal the horse. He circled around so that the horse would be between him and the colonel. Calming the horse, he cut the tether with his knife and quietly led him away. He found Powell, frantic with anxiety, and suggested that they might find a horse for him, also. After reconnoitering, they could find no likely prospect, so decided to let well enough alone. Their appearance at camp, leading a horse with a colonel's blanket and sidearms, caused quite a stir and added to Berry's reputation. As a sharpshooter and a scout, Berry had no need

---

[19] Benson, "War Book," 275–80.

of horse, so he sold it to brigade quartermaster Harry Hammond, who lived at Redcliffe plantation near Hamburg. Berry saw the horse from time to time after the war. The Hammond family displayed the colonel's pistols as souvenirs of the war.[20]

Thus far, Hill's Corps had escaped serious fighting, while Anderson's and Ewell's had withstood the worst of the Union attacks on the salient. That changed suddenly on the early morning of 12 May. Lee anticipated another attempt by Grant to get around his right flank and withdrew his artillery on the evening of 11 May in preparation to counter Grant's movement. He sent the guns back into position early on 12 May, but too late. General Winfield Hancock's corps launched an overwhelming attack on the angle of the salient; his troops poured over the breastworks and captured General Edward Johnson, and 2,800 men of his division. Lee himself rode among the retreating Confederates to check their panic. General George Steuart's brigade of Johnson's Division held firm on the left, and Lane's Brigade of Wilcox's Division held on the right. Lee attempted to lead John B. Gordon's division into the gap, but the men cried out "Lee to the rear!" Gordon's fierce charge checked Hancock's advance and pushed him back to the breastworks.[21] McGowan's Brigade came at a run to support Gordon. McGowan fell wounded. The senior colonel Brockman fell. Colonel J. N. Brown assumed command and pushed his men into the masses of the enemy. McGowan's troops became intermixed with General Nathaniel Harris's Mississippians. Berry lost contact with the sharpshooters, but found his old H Company and took a position alongside Major T. P. Alston. The Federal troops retreated to the

---

[20] Ibid., 288, 549.
[21] Report of Brig. Gen. John B. Gordon, 5 July 1864, OR, ser. 1, vol. 36, pt. 1, p. 1078–79.

outer line and then over the works to the outside, where they clung tenaciously.[22]

Now occurred the most bizarre struggle of the entire war as men fired down on each other from opposite sides of the works. It had rained all day, and it kept raining. Water red with blood and dead bodies filled the dug-out hollows on either side of the works. Great masses of Union infantry waited outside the lines for their forces to break through the salient, and the Confederate artillery played upon them with terrible effect.

The din of musketry was deafening. Minie balls cut limbs from trees. Incredibly, an oak tree measuring fifty-five inches in circumference crashed, cut through by bullets.[23] Berry's friends died around him: Sergeant Mackay, regimental commander Colonel W. P. Shooter and his brother Lieutenant E. C. Shooter. Colonel McCreary (who replaced Colonel Shooter), and Captain Barnwell were wounded. When Federals pointed gun barrels down on them, Berry's mates would seize the muzzles and divert their aim, or try to wrestle the gun away. Only the foolhardy raised their heads above the works to get a shot; there were many of those, and their bodies covered the parapets. The lines held all day and into the night. While firing continued all around him, Berry—always unpredictable—fell asleep. He had not slept in two nights, and though he did not intend to, he succumbed to sleep. No one paid attention to one more inert body among so many.[24]

---

[22] Caldwell, *History of a Brigade*, 140–41; Dunlop, *Lee's Sharpshooters*, 63–68; Benson, "War Book," 283–85; report of Brig. Gen. Samuel McGowan, *OR*, ser. 1, vol. 36, pt. 1, p. 1093–94.

[23] Maj. Dunlop of the sharpshooters stated that after the battle he measured the circumference and the diameter of the tree. The diameter was slightly more than eighteen inches (Dunlop, *Lee's Sharpshooters*, 73). Gen. McGowan stated that the tree fell on men of the 1st South Carolina Regiment (*OR*, ser. 1, vol. 36, pt. 1, p. 1094). McGowan singled out his assistant adjutant general, Capt. Langdon Haskell, for gallantry.

[24] Benson, "War Book," 285.

Late at night a whispered command passed along the ranks to fall back to an interior line of new works. Berry woke to find himself abandoned and hurried to join his companions. With daylight, companies and regiments sorted themselves out, and awaited a renewal of the struggle. But none came that day, 13 May. The next day, McGowan's Brigade moved back to the east wall of the salient. Berry walked alone over the abandoned ground within the works that from then on would be known as the Bloody Angle. Dead bodies, some blackened and swollen, still littered the ground. Berry could not bring himself to look into the staring eyes of the dead Federals. Confederates had taken away their dead and wounded. Berry saw where they had buried Colonel Shooter and his brother, near the works where they fell. He looked out over the works. Discarded rifles and equipment lay strewn about. He mused that if a man wanted to see hell on earth, he should come and look into this black bloody hole with its wet, muddy graves. As he walked along the breastworks, the sight of a soldier sitting atop the parapet startled him. He opened his mouth to speak to the young man, when with a shock he realized the man was dead. The burial detail had passed him by, assuming he was resting.[25]

Back among the sharpshooters, Captain Dunlop asked for volunteers to go on a dangerous mission. Berry volunteered. Dunlop told him to report to the adjutant, Captain Langdon Haskell. Haskell knew Berry and liked him, but nevertheless gave him the most difficult assignment in Berry's wartime career. General Lee wanted to know the motions of the enemy out in front. Berry suggested that he could get around the enemy flank and into their rear as he had done before and be back the next day. Haskell said no—Berry must be back in two hours! "This was a stunner," Berry later wrote in his journal. He took it as a compliment that Haskell thought that he, or anyone, could penetrate the enemy lines, look around inside their

---

[25] Ibid., 287–88; Caldwell, *History of a Brigade*, 147.

camp, and return in two hours. Nevertheless, he would try. It was the least he could do for General Lee.[26]

[26] Benson, "War Book," 296–97.

CHAPTER 9

From Point Lookout to Elmira Prison Camp

"I kept on, at work in the dark, as long as I could stand it."

After dark on 16 May, Berry with two volunteers climbed over the earthworks and set out on his mission. Moving silently, he came upon his own pickets and found them sound asleep. Berry welled up with righteous indignation. Only four days earlier, the enemy had surprised Johnson's Division at the Bloody Angle because of inattentive pickets. Berry woke the men and demanded to speak to their officer. When the man came Berry berated him for allowing his men to sleep on duty. "It won't happen again, Colonel," replied the officer, assuming that no one with a lesser rank would speak with such authority.[1]

Berry and companions advanced into no-man's land. He took for granted that anyone who walked into enemy lines would be arrested; he did not see how he could avoid it. But he figured that he could look around the camp and then try to escape. He told his two men to wait to see what would happen and then walked up to the Union picket line. "Who goes there?" called a sentry. "A friend," answered Berry as innocently as he could manage. He was allowed in. Berry strolled in among the enemy soldiers and explained that he was a

---

[1] Berry Benson, "The War Book, Reminiscences of Berry Greenwood Benson, CSA," (Typescript prepared by Charles G. Benson, Ida Jane ["Jeanie"] Benson, and Olive Benson), Special Collections, Reese Library, Augusta State University, Augusta GA; hereafter cited as "War Book"), 297. A copy of the typescript is also held by the Southern Historical Collection at the University of North Carolina, Chapel Hill, in its Berry Benson Papers, ms. 2636. The original manuscript diary (ms. 326) is located in the Hargrett Rare Book & Manuscript Library at the University of Georgia in Athens.

Union man who had gotten lost. He thought his explanation sounded plausible, but they took him to their brigadier anyway. "What regiment are you with?" asked the colonel. Berry named a New York regiment. "You are a southern soldier," said the officer. Berry earnestly assured him that he was indeed a New Yorker and suggested that he be sent under guard to General Hancock who could prove his identity. The colonel lit the lamp in his tent and saw Berry's grey uniform. To Berry's surprise, his captor laughed.

Berry knew the game was up. The officer introduced himself as Colonel Jacob B. Schweitzer; Berry told who he was, and the two shared "light, cheerful talk" in Berry's words.[2] Clearly Schweitzer admired Berry's nerve. The corporal to whom Berry was consigned showed less appreciation for Berry's nerve or attitude, especially when—out of sight of the colonel—Berry made a dash for the woods. The burly corporal chased after the spry Confederate with a slim chance of catching him, but his cries alerted the sentries who closed in and cornered the prisoner. The panting corporal directed a string of oaths at Berry. Berry took offense and reprimanded the corporal for using unsoldierly language. The exasperated man prodded Berry with his bayonet and used more choice epithets. Berry appealed to the men who stood around, was it not his soldierly duty to try to escape? Then what crime had he committed? Some of them nodded in agreement, but the corporal denounced him as a damned spy. Until then, Berry had not thought of the consequences of spying, and visions of Major John Andre flashed through his mind. They tied his hands and took him to General Meade's headquarters.[3]

One of Meade's adjutants questioned Berry, accusing him of spying. Worried now, Berry asked how he could have been spying.

[2] Benson, "War Book," 299. Berry thought Schweitzer was a general, and later he was brevetted to that rank. Ironically, Schweitzer had been a prisoner of war in Richmond for more than a year (*Biographical Encyclopedia of Pennsylvania* [Philadelphia: Galaxy Publishing Co., 1874] 646–47).

[3] Benson, "War Book," 304.

Wasn't he caught outside the Federal lines wearing a Confederate uniform? Berry thought that he had never been as eloquent as he was in his defense of himself at General Meade's headquarters. The officer remained unconvinced and told Berry that he would be tried as a spy by a court martial. As he was taken to an enclosure where there were several other Confederate prisoners, Berry planned another attempt at escape rather than face death by a firing squad. Presently, the guards brought in another prisoner. "Are you Benson?" the man asked. When Berry answered that he was, the newcomer said that as he waited to be interrogated by the same officer who had questioned Berry, he heard the officer say that Benson would be treated as a prisoner of war. Berry took the news as an enormous relief. While in the Union camp, Berry listened in amazement to the routine cursing he heard from the guards. He heard expressions he had never heard before. Men called each other by names that would have provoked a fight in a Confederate camp. The guards came for the prisoners the next morning and marched them off to Fredericksburg.[4]

From Fredericksburg the prisoners, now twenty-five, walked under guard to Belle Plain where they lodged in a stable. A sentry heard a soldier named Ellison, one of Ewell's scouts, talk about escape. The guards took him out and told the rest of the prisoners that the man had been hanged. That information cast a pall on the others. The prisoners boarded a steamer that carried them down the Potomac to Point Lookout, a camp on a spit of land where the Potomac joins Chesapeake Bay. The camp had been established to house the prisoners taken at Gettysburg in July 1863. Planned to accommodate 10,000 prisoners, the camp held up to 20,000 at one time during its two years of existence. The drainage was poor and

---

[4] Ibid., 312–14.

because of that and other causes, more than 3,000 prisoners died there over twenty-two months.[5]

Berry sized up the place the first day. He noticed that the privies were positioned several yards out into the bay, reached by narrow planks. During the day men could go through the guarded gates and use the privies. He did not see why he could not take advantage of the opportunity the privies afforded. So, on the second day of camp, he waited until near dark, walked out to the privy and slipped into the water. He could not believe how easy it was. A good swimmer (thanks to his boyhood adventures) he had no trouble going two miles up the coast, but then cut his feet on the oyster-studded bottom. He climbed out of the water and slept in the woods. The next morning, limping because of his injured feet, he trudged through Leonardstown. He made a strange spectacle, a barefoot man wearing a Confederate uniform. Several people looked at him with suspicion, so he took the precaution of hiding in the woods outside the town. Sure enough, a patrol of Union Calvary came galloping by, probably looking for him. He resolved to avoid the roads and the towns and go through the countryside. That he did, eating when he could, once with an hospitable black woman, again with a suspicious white man who thought he was a deserter from Lee's army. Berry encouraged the notion, though it pained him to be thought a deserter.[6]

For six harrowing days, Berry walked across fields and through woods, avoiding people. On 30 May 1864, he reached the Potomac and could see Virginia, the promised land, on the far side. Steamers and small craft plied the mile-wide river. He could make out the church towers of Alexandria, and beyond loomed the unfinished Washington Monument. But how to swim the wide river without detection? Resourcefulness was Berry's strong point. He found two

---

[5] Ibid., 315–17. There is now a state park on the site. See also Edwin Warfield Beitzell, *Point Lookout Prison Camp for Confederates* (Washington DC: Kirby Lithograph Co., 1972).

[6] Benson, "War Book," 340.

fence rails, tied them together with twine he had found, waited until dark, and then waded out into the river. He hoped anyone on a passing boat would not pay attention to floating logs. A huge paddle-wheel steamer narrowly missed him, but he made it across safely, though exhausted from the exertion. With matches he carried in his hat brim, he started a fire and spread his two possessions to dry, a diary and a New Testament given him by his mother. Then he slept.[7]

Next morning, happy to be in his own country, he headed south. Although Federal troops occupied northern Virginia, Berry hoped the people he met would be friendly. So, he did not try to avoid two young men who approached him. They asked what he wanted. To find a job he said. They told him to go with them to a nearby miller who needed help. Berry went along, hoping the miller would be a decrepit old man he could deal with. Unfortunately the miller stood a strapping six-feet something, and he wore a pistol at his belt. Doubly unfortunate, the man happened to be head of a contingent of home guard on the lookout for Confederate raiders. He interrogated Berry who dodged and improvised as best he could, but to no avail. The miller turned him over to a patrol of the 8th Illinois Cavalry, and Berry found himself a prisoner again.[8]

On the morning of 1 June 1864, the patrol and their prisoner entered the town of Alexandria with its handsome cluster of eighteenth-century brick houses. The guards delivered Berry to the town jail that housed Confederate prisoners, Union deserters, and common criminals. Berry failed to convince the provost marshal that he was a deserter from Lee's army. Almost immediately, he began to devise plans for an escape. He thought of trying to scale the fourteen-foot walls of the exercise yard.[9] Before he could try an attempt, he

---

[7] Ibid., 360–63.
[8] Ibid., 370–72.
[9] As of this writing, the walls still stand, though the prison has been demolished.

and a group of Confederates were taken by steamer to Washington, DC, and locked in the Old Capitol Prison.[10]

The prison, erected around 1800 as a tavern and boarding house, had an interesting history. After the British burned Washington in the War of 1812, the United States Congress occupied the building. By 1825 Congress moved into the new Capitol, and the vacated building became known as the "Old Capitol" even while it was used as a school, hotel, and boarding house. Vacant in 1861, the government converted the building into a prison. During the war it acquired notoriety because of its prisoners, among them Confederate women "spies" Belle Boyd and Rose O'Neal Greenhow, and because Captain Henry Wirz, commander of the Confederate prison at Andersonville, Georgia, met death by hanging in the prison yard. The same fate befell the conspirators implicated in the assassination of Abraham Lincoln, including Mary Surratt.[11]

Berry found congenial companions in the prison, notably a group of Mosby's men, troopers who had ridden with the legendary "Gray Ghost" of the Confederacy, John Singleton Mosby. Berry admired these robust young men as made "of better material than the average of soldiers." Berry met a schoolmate from Augusta, Captain William B. Young, who later became mayor of Augusta and remained one of Berry's good friends. He was surprised to meet Ellison, who had been taken from Belle Plain and supposedly hanged. Berry decided that the story of his death had been concocted to prevent others from trying to escape.[12]

---

[10] Ibid., 373–74. I am indebted to T. Michael Miller, research historian of the Office of Historic Alexandria, for a copy of his article, "Prison Life in Civil War Alexandria," *Northern Virginia Heritage* 9/3 (October 1987): 9–13. I visited the site of the prison in December 2003.

[11] Background information on the prison may be found in Richard M. Lee, *Mr. Lincoln's City* (McLean VA: EPM Publications, 1981) 42–43. The United States Supreme Court Building now occupies the site of the prison.

[12] Benson, "War Book," 388–91.

Berry refused to complain about his prison treatment. It would not do to grouse about meager food rations when he had less when free and in the field. He later doubted the stories about the abusive treatment of prisoners in northern camps. Of course, some guards were overbearing. One struck Berry without reason, just hurrying him along. Berry barely resisted retaliation, knowing that it would bring recrimination. He concluded that some people were naturally mean, but he retained his general faith in people.

New prisoners brought rumors of an improbable attack on Washington, DC, by an army under Jubal Early, who had commanded Hill's Corps at Spotsylvania. Lee had fallen back to Petersburg, continuing to shield Richmond from Grant, and had sent Early on a Stonewall-like raid into the Valley. Early took advantage of the opportunity to sweep aside a Union detachment at Lynchburg, cross the Potomac and approach Washington from the west. With little opposition, he reached Silver Springs, only six miles away from the Capitol. The prisoners grew frantic with excitement. They could hear Early's guns and see the shells bursting. They cheered at every explosion. Outside, townspeople hurried about in a panic. Berry saw a motley crowd of militia marching toward the sound of fighting in a disorderly manner. Early should easily deal with the likes of these. But Early did not come! "Oh! If it had been Jackson!" lamented Berry, "If it had been Gordon!" Berry did not know that General Horatio Wright's 6th Corps had stopped Early, not the rag-tag army he had seen. Early's raid represented a political blow to the Lincoln administration. How could the war be going well when Lee still had room to maneuver? The grim fact that Grant in Virginia and Sherman in Georgia had lost 90,000 men added to the frustration of many in the North. President Lincoln doubted his reelection chances that July.[13]

---

[13] Benson, "War Book," 401–403; Bruce Catton, *This Hallowed Ground: The Story of the Union Side of the Civil War* (New York: Doubleday and Company, Inc., 1956) 332–33.

Berry devised several escape plans and considered it his soldierly duty to do so. To wait for an exchange amounted to a failure of nerve. He and Baxter, his bunkmate, actually began to whittle a hole in the wooden floor under their bunk. This tedious work was interrupted by guards who conducted Berry and six hundred other prisoners to a train and sent them off to Elmira, New York, to a new prison camp there. A former Union army camp had been converted into a prison in June 1864. Its thirty-five barracks could accommodate five thousand prisoners. By late July when Berry's contingent arrived, that number had been reached. A month later ten thousand crowded the camp. The enclosure became a city of tents, with many sleeping in the open. Pneumonia and smallpox took their toll. By the end of 1864, 1,264 prisoners had died. When the camp closed in July 1865, 2,933 men had died in the single year of the prison's existence. The camp came to be known as "Hellmira." During the year only seventeen men would manage to escape, ten of them at one time. One of the ten would be Berry Benson.[14]

The six-hundred-man contingent of Old Capitol prisoners marched through the streets of Elmira on 24 July through crowds of staring townspeople to the camp on the edge of town. Berry started plotting escape even before the entered the gates. He saw a large tree overhanging one corner of the prison and thought he might try to get into that tree. Through the gate, the prisoners stood for the roll call, and then went to their assigned quarters. Berry and Baxter shared a bunk in one of the pine barracks. Neither had a sheet or blanket, so they slept on the bare boards. Next morning Berry scouted out the prison. It occupied roughly one square mile between the town and the Chemung River in mountainous country. An old

[14] Benson, "War Book," 410; Clay W. Holmes, *The Elmira Prison Camp: A History of the Military Prison at Elmira, N.Y., July 6, 1864 to July 10, 1865* (New York, G. P. Putnam's Sons, 1912). The copy of Holmes book in the Special Collections of Reese Library (Augusta State University, Augusta GA) is richly annotated in Berry Benson's handwriting.

bed of the Chemung channeled a sluggish pond that flowed through the camp. Berry thought that the pond offered possibilities of escape. He wondered if he could make a breathing tube and walk under water, following the pond out under the fence. But a guard was stationed just there where the pond went under the fence. Guards patrolled the interior of the fence, and other guards marched up and down on a raised platform outside the circumference of the fence. Escape would not be easy.[15]

Berry found old friends including some from Augusta. John Perrin, James W. Bohler, and Billy Kernaghan had been his schoolmates in Augusta. He met Benjamin G. Bogan from his old Company H in the South Carolina 1st. Bogan and Berry had the same initials, the Union guard who called the roll, kept referring to Berry as Benjamin. Berry liked the mild-mannered Bogan, called him "Judge," and knew that he would never be a partner in escape. Sergeant J. M. Hood, also of the 1st South Carolina, brought a surprise to Berry. Berry had carried his cousin Zack Benson's knife, but he had dropped it when he tried to get away from the burly corporal at Meade's headquarters. The corporal had found the knife. When he learned that Sergeant Hood was in Berry's regiment and that they would likely be together in prison, he gave him Zack's knife to return to Berry with his compliments. Berry told Hood that he therefore forgave the corporal for sticking his bayonet into him. He met acquaintances from Point Lookout—Ferneyhaugh, Russell, and Johnson. He had left his vest, shoes, and other belongings with Johnson when he swam out of Point Lookout, and remarkably, Johnson now returned the items to him.[16]

Berry's first impulse was to involve his Augusta friends in an escape plot. He persuaded Perrin to cut a window in the barracks next to his bunk, admitting access into the narrow space between that

---

[15] A photostat of Benson's map of the camp, taken from the original manuscript diary, appears between pages 410 and 411 of the "War Book" typescript.

[16] Benson, "War Book," 291, 415.

building and the next. Fences covered the front and back of the space, so a man could get under the barracks without being seen. Perrin cut the window and they went to work immediately on a tunnel under the barracks. The distance to the fence was a daunting eighty feet, but they worked with a will. They had barely begun when one of the Augusta party discovered that another tunnel was farther along. Those tunnelers wanted to talk to Berry about joining forces.

Thus, Berry met Joe Womack, a sergeant major in Wade Hampton's legion. Womack and his friends had started a tunnel under a hospital building closer to the fence. Womack argued that it was futile to dig competing tunnels, because when the first one was used there would be a general search for other possible tunnels. Berry readily agreed to join forces. Joe Womack and Berry became good friends. Womack later reflected upon his stay in prison, "Prisoners of war quickly seek to find companionship and friends. At the Elmira Prison camp in 1864, I found both in the person of Berry Benson, a sergeant of the 1st South Carolina Volunteers." Womack described Berry as "gay, fearless, imperturbable."[17]

They had not worked on their tunnel long, when they learned that two other tunnels had been started under two adjacent hospital buildings! The situation called for a summit meeting of tunnelers. They disagreed with Womack's argument that they should concentrate on one outlet, and decided to continue to dig two, and hope they could finish both at the same time. Neither Berry nor his new friends realized that one of their fellow prisoners was a Union soldier posing as a prisoner. Sergeant Melvin Mott Conklin mingled among the conspirators and kept Major Henry Colt, the superintendent, aware of their plans. Colt decided to let the prisoners dig. It would be good exercise and keep them out of other trouble. Conklin would tell him when the tunnel neared completion; then it would be closed down. Tunneling seemed to be a prison industry at

---

[17] Womack's story is in Holmes, *The Elmira Prison Camp*, 151–52.

Elmira. After the war Conklin boasted that he had foiled seven tunnel attempts, admitting that he missed "the big one."[18]

After several days of work, Berry's crew discovered that their tunnel had been blocked up with dirt. Unaware of Conklin's real identity and purpose, Berry assumed that the rival diggers had done it for some reason. One night he went over to the other hospital. To his surprise, a number of men loitered about, sure to attract the attention of guards. Suddenly the men began to scatter. One of them told Berry that the guards had discovered the tunnel and blocked it with stakes driven into the ground. Berry didn't believe it. How would the guards know where the tunnel was located in order to drive stakes down into it from above ground? Berry guessed that the tunnel leaders had started the rumor themselves to clear out the crowd. He handed his coat and shoes to Billy Kernaghan and crawled under the hospital. None of the three men at the mouth of the tunnel objected as he crawled into the opening and inched along in the intense darkness. He reached the end, sure enough, no stakes! Pushing back with elbows and toes, he returned to the opening and asked for a knife. Someone, he could not see who in the dark, gave him one and he wiggled back to the head and began to dig. When he accumulated a pile of dirt, he had to back up, raking the dirt with his arms, a most tedious task.[19]

The men at the mouth seemed glad to have Berry do their work. He asked for a candle and matches and they gave him one. However, the candle soon went out for lack of oxygen in the tunnel. Matches would not light. Berry worked as long as he could stand it, nearly suffocating. He and the remaining unknown few alternated all night. Finally Berry, at the mouth of the tunnel, heard one say to the other worker that he had reached a fence post and they should be ready to go out the next night, but if the tunnel were discovered the speaker

---

[18] Ibid., 71, 161.
[19] Ibid., 153; Benson, "War Book," 423.

had another tunnel in progress that no one knew about. "I'll see you tomorrow," the same man said. "You will know me by this."[20]

Berry got back to his barracks just at daybreak, avoiding the night patrol, and told Baxter to be ready to go out that night. During the day, the guards demolished the tunnel with pickaxes and shovels. Several of the diggers were rounded up and locked in the guardhouse. Berry did not know their names and wondered if his co-laborers of the night before were among them. The word got out that Major Colt respected the diggers, and the prisoners in general felt kindly toward him for that. Even the guards gave them preferential treatment, referring to them as "the engineer corps" rather than criminals, and exempting them from the most menial jobs.

The discovery of the tunnel on the verge of success discouraged many from trying again. Berry pondered the words he remembered. Another tunnel had been started by the man who said "You will know me by this." By what? A written message? Suddenly it came to Berry. He had seen a man with an usually long fingernail and wearing a long Confederate coat loitering about the tunnel hospital. He guessed that the man scraped his nail across the arm of his companion, and said those words. Now he had to find the man, if he were not already in prison.

While looking for the man with the fingernail (he called him "my Chinese friend"), Berry concocted other schemes for escaping. He and a prisoner, Jack Kibler, made pieces of a ladder that could be assembled when needed. They planned to wait for a dark night, place the ladder on the fence, and escape. Berry told Baxter about it, but Baxter had lost his yen for excitement, and preferred to wait for an exchange. At the same time, Berry and two other sergeants named Johnson and Wilder, concocted an Armageddon-like plot. Wilder had achieved the heights of military bravery by standing waist-high

---

[20] Benson, "War Book," 425; Traweek's story can be found in Holmes, *The Elmira Prison Camp*, 193.

on the breastworks at Spotsylvania, firing down on the Yankees, while lesser men handed up loaded rifles. The plan called for each of the three sergeants to recruit as many trustworthy men as possible. On the agreed-upon time, one would rush the prison arsenal and seize the guns while the others stormed the prison fence. After the successful breakout, the prisoners would confiscate all the guns in Elmira and march south. Several thousand armed prisoners would make a formidable force. They would face armed opposition, but that they had faced—and expected to face again.[21]

One day Joe Womack of the failed hospital tunnel approached Berry. He had obtained a book from the prison library, a library contributed by the townspeople and some of the prison authorities. He showed Berry a blank form for a pass to and from the prison that he had found in the book. "You can get out with this, Joe," said Berry. All he had to do was forge Major Colt's name to the blank form. Berry knew a good forger. But Womack worried that the form might have been planted to test him, and could not bring himself to try using it. He returned the book with the form still enclosed.[22]

Prison life worsened as the crowding became excessive. Rows of white tents lined both sides of the pond. The pond became fouled and dead fish floated on the surface. On 18 August 1864, the food ration was cut, allegedly in retaliation for the poor treatment of the Union prisoners at Andersonville, Georgia. Wagons conveyed corpses out of the camp on a daily basis. Berry thought of getting into one of those coffins somehow, and being smuggled out of the camp. He couldn't quite figure out the details. Men turned to religion for solace, and prayer meetings multiplied. Preachers from town came in; one named T. K. Beecher happened to be the brother of Henry Ward Beecher.[23]

---

[21] Benson, "War Book," 461–64, 471.
[22] Holmes, *The Elmira Prison Camp*, 153; Benson, "War Book," 467–69.
[23] Benson, "War Book," 444.

Berry haunted the prayer meetings and other places where men gathered, looking for his "Chinese friend." He watched men marching in and out of the mess hall, almost despairing of finding the man among the ten thousand prisoners. Then one day he saw the man in the long coat saunter toward the pool, sit down with his coat falling about him, and begin emptying his pockets. Berry approached him and said, "You'd better be careful of what you are doing."

The man responded, "I am not doing anything."

"You are putting stones in the water," observed Berry.

"Well, there's no harm in that."

"No, if you are not digging a tunnel," Berry said. Berry offered to sit beside the man, and help conceal what he was doing. The man finished in silence, then said to Berry, "Follow me." They walked to a less-crowded place and the man introduced himself as Washington Traweek of the 9th Alabama Artillery. Berry identified himself and explained to Traweek that he had been with him in the hospital tunnel. Traweek admitted that he and his friends were at work on another tunnel and if Berry would swear an oath of secrecy, he would be admitted to their company. Nothing could have pleased Berry more. Traweek told him to come to the third tent in the second row from the fence at a certain hour to meet the "gang."[24]

Berry could hardly wait for the appointed time. He could imagine the anxiety of Traweek's companions when they were told that a sergeant from the 1st South Carolina had found them out. As he entered the tent, he saw three men with Traweek and learned their names—J. Fox Maull, J. P. Pretegnat, and Frank Saurine, all from Alabama. Traweek produced a Bible and swore Berry to secrecy under pain of death if he revealed the work in progress. Berry did so, even though it meant dissembling before his other friends. Traweek told how they, like Berry, had been taken at Spotsylvania and sent to Point Lookout where Traweek attempted Berry's exploit of

---

[24] Holmes, *The Elmira Prison Camp*, 193–94; John Fox Maull's story can be found in Holmes, *The Elmira Prison Camp*, 174; Benson, "War Book," 445.

swimming to safety. A patrol boat turned him back. At Elmira, Fox Maull conceived the idea of digging under his tent, and he recruited the others. On 24 August they began digging, first a shaft straight down, waist deep, then a tunnel from the bottom of the shaft. They worked by day as one of them guarded the flap of the tent. By night and during inspections, they concealed the shaft with sod-covered boards. Needing more workers, they had admitted three others of the 9th Alabama Artillery: Cecrops Malone, known as "Cyclops;" George "Hickory" Jackson; and William H. Templin. Glenn Shelton, a Mississippi preacher in civilian life, came in after Berry. Shelton, a good worker otherwise, had a habit of interrupting the work to hold prayer meetings.[25]

Fox Maull, in his memoir about his prison experience, said that he welcomed Berry, who "proved to be one of the best men we had, ready to work at all times, his head full of excellent ideas, which immediately began to crop out." Cyclops Malone echoed the sentiment, "We took Benson in and found him to be one of our best workers." After administering the oath to Berry, they opened the pit and he went down to take a look. They had progressed ten feet or so, and estimated that they had at least fifty feet farther to go.[26]

The first of Berry's good ideas concerned the removal of dirt. The diggers had been using Pretegnat's spare shirt, the only one in the tent, as a bag to remove dirt. The digger would fill the bag, and then inch backward, dragging the bag to the mouth where Maull or Shelton was waiting to dispose of it. Maull found it impossible to enter the tunnel without gagging and vomiting, so he volunteered for the disposal work. Shelton suffered from claustrophobia and worked outside with Maull. They had to be clever about disposing dirt and stones. New dirt spread on the ground would show suspiciously. The men took the dirt to the pond, and threw stones under buildings. Sometimes several members of the disposal team would throw the

---

[25] Holmes, *The Elmira Prison Camp*, 171–72; Benson, "War Book," 446–49.
[26] Holmes, *The Elmira Prison Camp*, 174, 201.

stones at imaginary rats at the edge of the pool. There were plenty of rats, so the ruse did not arouse suspicion. Berry's innovation concerned the removal of dirt. He suggested tying ropes to both ends of a shallow box. The digger filled it, knocked on the box as a signal, the man at the mouth pulled it back, emptied it, and the digger pulled it back to refill it. The system saved the digger the tedious task of dragging the debris out of the tunnel. Maull pronounced the box system "a great success."[27]

Berry thought it might be a good idea to see how far they were away from the fence. He suggested that two men go out where they thought the tunnel ran, and bang on tin, pretending to make spoons, not an unusual occupation in the camp. The man in the tunnel would call back directions that would be relayed to the pounders: "He says move to the right." More pounding, then, "More to the right." Finally they located the place above the tunnel, far to the right of a straight line. If they had continued the way they were going, their tunnel never would have reached the fence. How could they have gone so wrong? Berry thought about it and concluded that the reason must be that all the diggers were right-handed, and naturally favored that side. Obviously, however, the "mistake" had been a fortunate one, and, after discovery of the tunnel, the bend in its direction, an observer thought to be "artful engineering."[28]

Another of Berry's contributions was the "ventilator." As the tunnel grew longer, digging became an excruciating exercise for lack of air. Berry suggested punching a hole in the roof, and widening it so that it would not only admit air, but allow a back-up digger to rest huddled up in the space. Maull recalled that he asked Berry how they were going to locate the proper spot above ground for the air hole. "In ten minutes," Maull wrote, Berry was back with a ramrod. He crawled under and punched the rod to the surface where some of the team stood around. They marked the spot with a stone. Open a few

27 Ibid., 174–75; Benson, "War Book," 450–53.
28 Holmes, *The Elmira Prison Camp*, 176.

inches at the top, the aperture widened toward the bottom. During the day, someone had to sit near the opening playing cards or mumbly-peg to keep it hidden. At night the hole would be covered with a stone.[29]

Berry considered Traweek the best worker, with himself a close second. The two of them could stand the dreadful lack of air better than the others, and they had greater stamina. Traweek had an advantage that Berry did not. One of the Confederate sergeants who had been appointed a "sick sergeant" by the authorities, would bring to Traweek's tent extra rations. The sergeant, "Parson" Scruggs, had authority to bring food to the sick, and Traweek let him in on the secret. Berry did not know that his fellow diggers kept their strength up by this extra food supply.

One day the guards came to arrest Traweek. His friends thought that they had been discovered and expected to be taken in also. Someone, probably Conklin the informer, had given Traweek's name to Major Colt. The superintendent demanded to know the names of the tunnel-diggers. Traweek, not nearly as diplomatic as Berry would have been in that situation, said, "I will see you in hell as far as a blue bird could fly in a year before I would tell." Colt commented, "He is a sassy son of a bitch and should be shot," and locked Traweek in with an earlier digger, James W. Crawford of the 6th Virginia Cavalry.[30]

Traweek managed to get word back to his friends by the "sick sergeant" Scruggs that their secret was safe and that they should keep at it. Maull used Scruggs to smuggle a file, concealed in a chunk of bread, to Traweek. Crawford, the cellmate, guessed what they were doing, and Traweek asked the guards for a Bible, which they gladly gave the supposedly repentant sinner. Traweek used it to swear Crawford to secrecy. As it happened, he did not have to use the file. After three weeks he decided to apologize to Colt for his improper

---

[29] Ibid., 176; Benson, "War Book," 474–76.
[30] Holmes, *The Elmira Prison Camp*, 195.

language. Colt assumed that Traweek had learned his lesson, and let him out. The superintendent had been told by his informer that no tunnels were underway.[31]

In Traweek's absence, Berry assumed the leadership of the diggers. In spite of splitting headaches, he kept working every day, and the tunnel inched closer to the fence. Berry could hear the inside-fence guard pacing up and down over his head as he lay prone, scraping with his knife, filling the box. By the time of Traweek's return, they were almost to the fence. On 5 October 1864, Traweek called back to Berry (who waited by the ventilator) that he had hit the fence post. Berry relieved him and dug around the post. Desperate for air, he turned on his back, and with eyes shut, he reached up, pushing his fingers through the soil. When he broke the surface, a draft of sweet air rewarded him. Berry savored the moment, breathing deeply the air of freedom. Then, he gave way to Traweek who hollowed out the escape shaft, leaving only a thin layer of topsoil. The two diggers came out to tell the good news to the others. They could go out the next night, 6 October.[32]

Berry hated to keep the secret from Baxter, Kibler, Womack, and his other friends, but he had sworn an oath. Without attracting attention, he gathered some essentials—a tin saucer made from a canteen, a compass, a hand-made map, some matches, and a few other items. As darkness approached, the team gathered in Maull's tent, and drew straws for the exit. Traweek would go first, followed by his cellmate Crawford. The two decided to stay together on the outside. Traweek and Crawford would be followed in order by Maull; "Parson" Scruggs, the sick sergeant; "Cyclops" Malone; Pretegnat; Shelton; Benson; "Hickory" Jackson; and William Templin. Berry was desperately afraid that the first ones would be caught before his turn came. One after another disappeared into the hole. Then it was Berry's turn—but Shelton came back out! "They are still

---

[31] Ibid., 196.
[32] Benson, "War Book," 480–86.

in there," he said. Something must have gone wrong. Berry crawled in as far as the ventilator, finding no one. He took precious minutes to go back and tell Shelton that the way was clear; then he went on without waiting. Emerging from the outlet, he found himself under the platform that ran around the camp. Over his head he could hear the heavy tread of the sentinels. Across the street other soldiers huddled around a fire. He marveled that six of his friends had escaped detection. The darkness hid him from the guards across the street, and he crept along under the platform until he reached the corner. This was the moment of greatest danger. He had to step out in plain view of the guards on the platform, and risk being shot in the back. He waited under the platform until the soldier above reached the corner, then turned to retrace his steps. Then he stepped out across the street into a front yard, through the backyard, over the fence, and up the mountain he had seen so often from camp. He looked back, expecting a stir, but the camp lay quiet in the moonlight, and the unsuspecting sentinels continued to patrol their beat.[33]

He was free! As daylight began to tinge the camp, he turned toward the forested mountain.

The historian of Elmira Prison called the morning of 7 October, "the most momentous and exciting witnessed in the history of the prison." Morning roll call revealed men missing, and the guards would not say how many. The exit hole was soon discovered and the prisoners flocked to the fence to gawk. Joe Womack hurried to Berry's barracks to tell him about it. Baxter informed him that Berry had gone out that night and had not come back. "It was not pleasant to be left behind," wrote Womack. He decided that if Berry could take such chances, so could he. He went back to the library, found the blank pass in the same book where he had left it, forged Major Colt's name, underwent some tense moments as the guards examined his papers, then walked across the street. "The farther I got away, the

---

[33] Holmes, *The Elmira Prison Camp*, 177–78; Benson, "War Book," 487.

faster I walked," he recalled. Womack was the eleventh man to escape Elmira.[34]

---

[34] Holmes, *The Elmira Prison Camp*, 168, 154–55.

CHAPTER 10

Through Enemy Country

*"I lay at my ease, drifting, for the moment without
a thought or care."*

Few escaped prisoners have enjoyed their flight through enemy
territory as much as Berry Benson did his. The air of freedom, the
thrill of living by his wits, the challenge of new adventures, all added
a zest to life, especially to one whose obsession for four months had
been to put himself exactly in that situation. Here he was, in real life,
emulating those escape artists he had read about as a child.

He searched about on the mountain outside Elmira the night of
his escape, calling out occasionally for Traweek and Maull, but he did
not waste much time doing so. He climbed up the mountain and
collected ears of corn from a field and apples from an orchard on the
way. At daybreak he rested on top of the mountain, with a beautiful
view of the Chemung River winding through rolling hills. Berry
laughed to think of the sergeant's face at roll call that morning when
he called out "Benjamin Benson" (he always made that mistake) and
no one answered. Down the mountain, avoiding roads, he followed
the river heading west, knowing that the roads leading south would
be guarded. After dark, he risked using the river road, passing
through the village of Big Flats at midnight. By daybreak he reached
Corning, and crossed the Chemung River on a bridge, and now his
course lay to the south.[1]

The coincidence of hunger pangs and a nearby flock of chickens
tempted him. He chased a rooster all over the yard, over a fence, and
across fields. Berry gave up, but saw the humor: "I think he ought to

---

[1] This chapter is based on Berry Benson's "War Book," 489–561.

have let me catch him, for the honor of being eaten at such a critical time in the history of the Civil War." An observer might have noted that it takes a certain amount of bravado to chase chickens about the neighborhood when one is an escaped prisoner only twenty miles from Elmira. About ten miles south of Corning he slept for the first time in two nights and days.

On 10 October, he crossed the Pennsylvania line. He celebrated by catching a chicken from a coop, finding potatoes from a barrel, and roasting both—a better meal than he had in four months in prison. He walked all night along a railroad track, and in the morning came to a coal-mining village. He passed miners on their way to work, heads down, lunch pails in hand. He had no idea where he was, but knew that he had passed through Canton on the train to Elmira, so he had to find the way to Canton. He approached a house that lay near the woods so that he could make a run for it if the occupant took him for an escaped prisoner. His luck held. The man of the house, a genial Scot, invited him in for tea. Berry accepted. Instead of tea, he sat down to an ample supper. "I destroyed everything but the crockery," Berry recalled. During the meal the man asked questions and Berry made up as many lies. He learned what he needed to know. The village was called Falls Brook, and Canton lay only nine miles to the east.

He set out briskly for Canton that night. The weather had turned cold, so as he left the village, he helped himself to a pair of trousers and socks hanging on the back porch of a miner's cottage. He put them on, and with daylight discovered that his legs were covered with coal dust.

Walking steadily, he reached Canton early on the morning of 11 October. He went through the deserted town, following the railroad in a southerly direction. A few miles south of town he came to a shack next to the tracks, probably housing a railroad employee. He took a few potatoes from an outside barrel. An open window aroused his curiosity. He peeped in and heard a man snoring. A thick coat hung just next to the window. Berry leaned in head and shoulders, lifted the coat from its hanger, and pulled it out the window. The owner continued to snore. Though somewhat worn, the coat was warm and quite respectable. Berry thought it made him look more like a Broadway dandy than an escaped prisoner. Best of all, he now had enough pockets to carry provisions.

He continued walking at night on 11 October. He caught a chicken for breakfast, priding himself on his skill in this new form of foraging. During the pleasant morning of the next day, he walked along the Lycoming River near Ralston, alive to the beauty of the scenery. (The area is now part of a state park.) Suddenly a train roared through the valley, loaded with Federal soldiers heading south. Some of them yelled at Berry, and he waved his hat at them, as if to say. "On to Richmond!" the very picture of a patriotic Yankee.

He napped for a while and at dusk continued his long walk, reaching Williamsport at dawn. He spotted a henhouse, of recent days his favorite target, crawled in, and grabbed two chickens. He walked through Williamsport with a chicken under each arm. He camped on Bald Eagle Mountain outside town, roasted the chickens, and ate them both. Late on 13 October he started out again. Now the road wound between the mountains on his right and the Susquehanna River on his left as he headed south. He decided to take the advantage offered by the river. He found a boat tied to a tree, unfastened the rope, and rowed out into the current. He tried rowing for a while, but found it easier to let the boat drift in the swift current, while he ate chestnuts stowed in his many pockets. He felt poetic, musing, "The clear Susquehanna shut in by the dark, wooded mountains that showed a hundred shapes and shadows, and the full moon overhead in a clear sky. I lay at my ease, drifting, for the moment without a thought or care."

His serene river passage lasted until he heard the rushing of the shoal waters, and decided not to risk the rapids. He walked all day on 14 October, passing the town of Milton and reaching

Northumberland that night. He figured that he had come 115 miles from Elmira. He stopped at a respectable house, told a plausibly pitiful story, and received a good meal. At the Northumberland depot he saw a train that seemed ready to start. He hid in one of the freight cars, and congratulated himself on his good luck. He had just settled down, when the train stopped at Sunbury, only three miles from Northumberland. He waited for it to start. It did not start. He got out, only to find that his car had been left behind by the rest of the train.

However, on a nearby track a passenger train got up steam. Berry waited until it started then stepped up between two cars. This was more like it. Soon, he saw the conductor coming down the aisle. He stepped down on the bottom step, and with one hand on the rail, swung around on the outside of the car. He came up when he heard both car doors bang shut. He could not believe his good luck and rode fifty-three miles to Harrisburg without a ticket. He changed trains at Harrisburg, boarding the one to Baltimore. When the conductor came along he tried his trick of swinging outside the train, but felt a tap on his arm. The conductor wanted to know just what Berry thought he was doing out there. Berry quickly improvised a sad tale about a dying sister in York who had sent for him, but he had no money, etc. The conductor scolded Berry for not coming in and asking him for a seat instead of hanging outside like that where he could get hurt. He led Berry to a vacant seat and told him to stay there until the train reached York. Berry regretted that his fictitious sister was dying in York instead of Baltimore, but he enjoyed the ride and slept most of the way. At 2:00 A.M. he got off at York in deference to the conductor's instructions. He had covered eighty-four miles that night!

Having rested, he walked all that night and all day on 15 October, and crossed the Mason Dixon line singing "Dixie." The next day he reached Cockeysville, just fifteen miles from Baltimore. He calculated that he had walked forty-two miles from York. At the depot he met an elderly gentleman who told him stories of Early's troops passing through and the damage they had done. A train puffed to a stop. The man told him that the cattle on the train were for Grant's army at Petersburg. Federal soldiers rode atop the cars as guards against Confederate raiders. Since Berry could not get inside with the cattle, he climbed atop the car and sat down next to a soldier, admitting that "it took a great deal of cheek." Berry assumed that the soldier would not suppose that an escaped prisoner would do such a thing. The soldier asked Berry if he lived in the neighborhood. Berry answered that he did. The soldier asked if Berry had been here when the Confederates came through and what the damage had been. Thanks to the elderly gentleman's information, Berry was able to say they burned that barn, destroyed that bridge, and did such and such other mischief. That is how it was that Berry Benson, escaped prisoner, rode into Baltimore, chatting companionably with a Union soldier.

The train pulled into the station at mid-morning on Sunday, 17 October. People passed through the streets on their way to church. Some pesky boys followed Berry, saying that he looked like a rebel. Berry hurried out of town, trying to avoid further attention. He slept that night at Ellicot Mills, ten miles outside Baltimore. The next day, he almost walked into a Federal bivouac. Fortunately, a stranger alerted him to the fact that the camp was just ahead. Berry's first instinct was to circle around it. His innate perversity got the better of him again. He decided to reconnoiter the camp. Just as in his scouting days, he crept up on the camp, approaching from the woods, getting close enough that he could hit one of the soldiers with a stone. Except for the satisfaction at honing his scouting skills, there was not much point to this particular adventure. He resumed his journey.

Passing through Clarksburg, he helped himself to a change of clothes from a convenient clothesline. He would return to the Confederate States better outfitted than he had left it. He reached the Potomac on 19 October. He felt a thrill as he gazed across to his own country. First he had to cross the Chesapeake and Ohio Canal that ran along the Maryland side of the river. As he looked, a Federal patrol came clattering along the towpath between the canal and river. Berry decided to wait until night to try the crossing. As he lay secluded, he heard the distant thud of cannon, indicating a battle in progress. He later learned that on that day Jubal Early's army staged a surprise attack on the Union encampment at Cedar Creek, gaining an almost complete victory. Early's hungry men fell to plundering the Yankee stores while a rear guard of the enemy still fought. At Winchester, twenty miles away, General Phil Sheridan heard the same sound of battle that Berry heard. Thomas Buchanan Read immortalized Sheridan's ride in a poem that caught the fancy of the public in the North. Sheridan charged into the ranks of his retreating army, damning the men in his fiercest oaths. The men responded to his terrible wrath, stopped running, and followed him back into battle, overwhelming the disorganized Confederates. It was a bitter defeat for Early that tarnished his reputation. Whether he had permitted the men to plunder, or whether he had lost control, he had to take the blame for the defeat. Sheridan's success boosted Lincoln's reelection chances.

In the evening, Berry prepared for his second crossing of the Potomac. He thought that he would like to enter Virginia mounted upon a horse, so he visited a nearby farmyard and caught a horse. He fashioned a bridle out of cord, climbed onto the horse's back, and led him to the canal. The horse absolutely refused to enter the water. Berry kicked and coaxed in vain, but the horse had made up his mind. Berry had to give up his hope of traveling through Virginia like a cavalier. He crossed the canal on one of the locks, found a heavy plank, tied his clothes into a bundle, and keeping one end of the plank out of the water, swam across. His clothes, tied on the upper end of the plank, stayed dry.

Berry knew this part of Virginia. He had recuperated at Judge Gray's house near Leesburg before the Battle of Antietam. He stopped at a mansion and asked where Judge Gray lived. In the course of conversation, Berry revealed that he was an escaped southern soldier and a friend of the Grays. He was told that the family had moved into Leesburg, but Federal patrols were out that day and he should lodge there for the night. The next day, 21 October, Berry went into Leesburg and had no trouble finding Judge Gray and his family. They greeted him like a lost son and insisted that he stay two days. Miss Gray was as solicitous as before, but now Berry had a sweetheart in Augusta and could not be equally solicitous in return. She insisted that he take a respectable grey coat, and he reluctantly did so, though he would have preferred the coat with many pockets that he had stolen.

He left Leesburg on 23 October, trudged on all day, and enjoyed an evening meal at the house of a hospitable stranger. Berry asked where he could stay for the night, and learned that all available houses in the neighborhood had been taken by Mosby's men. Berry had blundered into "Mosby's Confederacy" as four northern counties were called. In that region Colonel John Singleton Mosby conducted a two-year guerilla war against Union forces guarding Washington, thereby immobilizing those troops. In addition, he destroyed the Manassas Gap Railroad, for a time preventing Grant from getting reinforcements from Washington. Mosby had become a legend in his own time as the "Gray Ghost," as daring and dashing a figure as Berry could imagine. He rode with only a few men at a time, as few as thirty and as many as two hundred fifty. He would select a target, send riders out to summon his men to a rendezvous, then strike quickly and scatter to homes and hiding places. Berry had happened upon one such rendezvous.

Berry asked the same hospitable stranger if he could sleep in his barn. The man said he would have to ask his houseguests. Two men entered the room and began to question Berry. They listened suspiciously to Berry as he recited his adventures, but when he told of meeting two of Mosby's men in the Old Capitol Prison, they relaxed, and called to their friends in the other room, "Boys, here's a man who knows Ben Crowley and Underwood." Now Berry found himself a hero, surrounded by Mosby's men, who listened avidly to his story of escape. They pulled out their wallets and forced money on him. They had a meal in mellow fellowship, and one of the raiders insisted that Berry take his bed that night; he would sleep in the barn. As Berry retired he made up his mind to join these gallant fellows on their raid the next day. He admired the raiders and commented, "Not only were these men much better dressed than soldiers ordinarily, but I am quite sure this band was of better calibre in all respects, physically and mentally."

The next morning the rest of the band rode up, including Mosby himself. Mosby would like to accommodate Berry, but he had no spare horse. He advised Berry on the best way to Early's camp. Then Berry's new friends saluted, wheeled their horses, and dashed away. Berry watched them go, a little envious. Mosby's report of the action that day understates the risks he ran and indicates the success he achieved: "I have returned from a successful trip to the valley, captured a brigadier general (Duffie), capturing ambulance horses, etc. Sent them out, then returning by another route captured seven wagons, fifty-five prisoners, and forty-one horses."[2] It seems that Berry missed getting his horse by one day.

Berry proceeded to follow the route suggested by Mosby, westward toward the Shenandoah Valley rather than southerly toward Petersburg where his unit lay encamped. He managed to get supper in a stately mansion occupied by three lovely ladies named Gibson. They apologized for not being able to afford him a decent meal. Berry discounted their apology, assuming that a poor meal for them would be an excellent repast for himself. However, he felt

---

[2] James A. Ramage, *Gray Ghost: The Life of John Singleton Mosby* (Lexington: University of Kentucky Press, 1999) 330–31.

sympathy for them when he sat down to a supper of chestnuts and milk, the same meal they had earlier. Their "servants" had left them. (People of society used this term instead of "slaves.") Their brother, a Confederate officer, had come home to get in the crop and was even then working late in the fields. Berry wondered if their fate presaged things to come.

On Sunday, 25 October, Berry walked through the village of Paris and reached the beautiful Shenandoah River, winding, he thought, "like a silver thread" among the hills. He slept that night by the side of the road in Ashby's Gap. Next day, he followed the turnpike from Fort Royal to Culpepper Courthouse, though he had to dodge Union patrols along the way. He found himself in a no-man's land between Sheridan's and Early's forces. Locals seemed terrified of "Jessie's Scouts," Union guerillas dressed like Confederates. Originally they had acted as scouts for General John C. Fremont's Mountain Department and used the name of Fremont's attractive and assertive wife, Jessie Benton Fremont. Though Fremont resigned his commission in June 1864 to run for the presidency and had not been in command since 1862, Jessie's Scouts still roamed the region. People he met regarded Berry suspiciously, suspecting him of being one of the scouts. One man told him he did not know whether Berry was a scout or was not, but he could have supper anyhow.

On 27 October, Berry encountered a patrol of gray-clad troopers. Fortunately, they were authentic Confederates belonging to Early's command. The patrol conducted him to the headquarters tent of General Bradley T. Johnson. Johnson began asking Berry questions, becoming more interested with each answer. Finally, he said, "Sergeant, begin at the beginning, and tell us the whole story." Berry protested, "General, I'm quite willing, but I tell you, you've got to give me my supper first." The general's servant brought food, and set it on the general's traveling chest. Berry ate his fill while curious officers and the general waited for his story. They gathered around when he finally put down his fork and listened intently to the entire saga. By the time he finished it was approaching midnight. General Johnson paid him a compliment, saying "The sergeant talks mighty well, don't he?" Johnson insisted that Berry sleep in the general's tent, as befit a hero. So, in spite of his mild protests, Berry slept on the floor with the general's blanket over him and his head resting on the general's saddle. Before leaving Johnson's company the next morning, Berry enquired why Early had not attacked Washington when his army was so close. Johnson explained that it had been Early's intention to free the prisoners at the Old Capitol and at Point Lookout, but the "untimely arrival" of the Federal 6th Corps thwarted them. Johnson gave Berry a pass to Newmarket, the headquarters of General Early.

Berry rode in comfort atop a wagon to New Market. As he entered camp, he heard jeers from soldiers who thought he was another one of those who had fled to the mountains in the rout at Cedar Creek. He located the 12th Georgia Regiment and his Augusta friend "Hoody" Hitt. Hitt looked up startled, "Is this not Berry Benson?" Berry assured him that it was indeed. Hitt explained that all Berry's friends had heard that he had been killed in an attempt to escape from Point Lookout. After chatting with Hitt and other acquaintances, Berry reported to General Jubal Early, and found him sulking in his tent, brooding over his recent defeat. Unlike General Johnson, Early showed no interest in Berry's adventures. He merely authorized an order for the quartermaster to provide Berry transportation to his unit at Petersburg.

Berry rode atop a stagecoach with the driver as far as Staunton. There he called upon an Augusta friend, Dr. Bob Eve, then working as a surgeon at an army hospital. On 1 November he boarded a train for Richmond, enjoying the luxury of being a legitimate passenger by virtue of his pass. At Richmond he telegraphed his father that he had escaped and was well. He spent the night with a cousin. The next day he happened to see an officer in McGowan's Brigade on the street.

After a warm greeting, the officer offered to conduct Berry to his unit at camp about three miles south of Petersburg. Petersburg seemed like a ghost town as they passed through. Outside the town the Confederate tents lined up in orderly rows behind deep entrenchments that ran for forty miles. A mile of no-man's land separated them from the Federal works.

As Berry walked among the tents, he heard repeated exclamations, "Isn't that Sergeant Benson?" Soldiers stopped what they were doing and stared as if seeing a ghost. Some came out to shake his hand and slap him on the back; he told them he had to find his brother first. He saw the men of Company H grouped around a fire, Blackwood among them. A man called out, "Blackwood, there's your brother!" Without a word Blackwood rushed up to Berry, hugged him, and began pounding him on the back. The others crowded around, "When were you exchanged?" Berry savored the moment, "I wasn't exchanged, I escaped." Blackwood started pounding on him again.

The day after his triumphant return, General McGowan sent him out on a scout.

CHAPTER 11

Campaign for Savannah

It was a musical sound, in the dead of the night, to hear the "clink-clank, clink-clank" of the horses' iron feet as the troopers rode down the brick pavements.

As the war in Virginia settled down to a nine-month-long siege of Richmond and Petersburg, the attention of the nation turned to Georgia, and William Tecumseh Sherman's famous march. At this point a writer of fiction would bring his hero down from Virginia and put him in Georgia where the spotlight of history would focus on him. A writer of fact would not dare do so, except in the case of Berry Benson. Berry Benson came home on furlough in early December 1864 to a city terrorized by the near passing of Sherman.

By 21 November Sherman's army of "bummers" had reached Milledgeville, the state capital. Augusta braced itself for attack. Sherman's target, as everyone assumed, must be Colonel Rains's magnificent Powder Works, upon which the Confederate armies depended for powder and ammunition. Fortifications in the form of cotton bales surrounded the city. General Birkett Fry dispatched dozens of telegrams naming generals who brought reinforcements to Augusta: Braxton Bragg; William Hardee; Ambrose B. Wright; James Chesnut; Albert G. Blanchard; Pierce W. B. Young; even Berry Benson's friend of a fleeting moment, Colonel John S. Mosby. The local newspaper reported, "Our streets were enlivened with the sound of martial music and the tramp of soldiery."[1]

The telegrams told a partial truth. The generals came, but they brought few soldiers. There were probably 15,000 men in Augusta to

---

[1] *Augusta Chronicle*, 24 November 1864.

oppose Sherman's 60,000. But the telegrams worked as well as General Fry might have liked. Sherman believed that a considerable force defended Augusta, and he could not afford a lengthy siege. His men had to live off the land, and he needed to get to a sea-base as soon as possible. General Joe Wheeler's cavalry skirmished with the Union's General Judson Kilpatrick at Waynesboro on 3 December, and that was as close as Sherman came to Augusta. Sherman himself verified the effectiveness of the Confederate deception: "When I reached Waynesboro," he wrote, " I learned that General Bragg with Longstreet's Corps and other troops was in Augusta prepared to defend the place, which forced me to abandon its destruction and rapidly move to my new base of supplies, Savannah."[2]

When Berry reached Augusta, Sherman had already passed and begun his siege of Savannah. After warm welcomes and hasty goodbyes, he set off to join the Augusta battalion of volunteers then on the lines outside Savannah. Sherman's men had torn up all the rails leading to Savannah on the Georgia side, but the railroad through South Carolina was still open, and operated as Savannah's last lifeline. So Berry took the train to Charleston. It was risky business going from Charleston to Savannah, because the Union lines reached the Savannah River, and the railroad passed within cannon range of Union artillery. The locomotive engineers had learned to keep a head of steam and go full throttle through the gauntlet of Union artillery. Berry blessed the inaccuracy of the enemy guns as the train rumbled across the Savannah River and the shells dropped harmlessly round about.[3]

[2] Florence Fleming Corley, *Confederate City: Augusta, Georgia, 1860–1865* (1960; repr., Augusta GA: Richmond County Historical Society, 1995) 91.

[3] Berry Benson, "The War Book, Reminiscences of Berry Greenwood Benson, CSA," (Typescript prepared by Charles G. Benson, Ida Jane ["Jeanie"] Benson, and Olive Benson), Special Collections, Reese Library, Augusta State University, Augusta GA; hereafter cited as "War Book"), 564. A copy of the typescript is also held by the Southern Historical Collection at the University of North Carolina, Chapel Hill, in its Berry Benson Papers, ms. 2636. The original manuscript diary (ms. 326) is located

Sherman had tried to cut this last link by ordering by ordering an idle army of 5,000 at Hilton Head on the Carolina coast to come up and break the line. The Georgia militia under General Gustavus W. Smith defended the road at Honey Hill near Grahamville, South Carolina, and against all odds, beat back the more numerous Federals. Smith's troops returned to defend Savannah, surprised at their victory and better armed from the spoils of the battlefield. Berry located the Augusta battalion and found them all equipped with new Enfield rifles discarded by the enemy.[4]

General William Hardee commanded the Confederates, and he had relied upon Augusta native General Lafayette McLaws to plan the defenses of Savannah. The town sits on a peninsula between the Savannah and Ogeechee Rivers. The Union line stretched from one river to the other. Fort Jackson and the gunboats in the Savannah River prevented Union gunboats from that river access to Savannah. Earthen Fort McAllister on the Ogeechee blocked approach by that river. Thus the seaside seemed well guarded. McLaws's defense line stretched for ten miles between the two rivers, taking advantage of the flooded rice fields behind Savannah. Even so, he had only 10,000 to Sherman's 60,000. The rice fields were so shallow that the Federals could have waded across, but they did not.[5]

Berry joined the Augusta Battalion commanded by Major George T. Jackson. Berry knew several of them, including John U. Meyer, future mayor of Augusta as well as Berry's future brother-in-law. A veteran like Berry might have felt superior to these newcomers to warfare, but he admired them for their good fight at Honey Hill and now for their willingness to stand against a more numerous enemy. A flooded rice field lay in front of them. Confederate pickets

---

in the Hargrett Rare Book & Manuscript Library at the University of Georgia in Athens.

   [4] Ibid.; Alexander A. Lawrence, *A Present for Mr. Lincoln: The Story of Savannah from Secession to Sherman* (Macon GA: Ardiwan Press, 1961) 170.

   [5] Charles C. Jones, Jr., *The Siege of Savannah in December, 1894* (Albany NY: Joel Munsell, 1874) 112–15; Lawrence, *A Present for Mr. Lincoln,* 171–74.

guarded the dams that crossed the fields. On the other side stretched a field of straw, and beyond that a wooded area that concealed the Federal troops.[6]

On 13 December, Fort McAllister fell, giving Sherman access to his supply ships.[7] For a week afterwards, the Federals on the lines did nothing except strengthen their position. Colonel Charles C. Jones, Jr., one of the Confederate defenders, wrote, "It seems marvelous that General Sherman should have contented himself with setting down before our lines, erecting counter batteries, engaging in artillery duels and sharp-shooting, feeling for weak points day after day." Jones knew very well that Sherman could have marched into Savannah if he chose to do so.[8]

Berry had been in camp only a few days when he felt the old yen to go out scouting, "to see whether I couldn't run across some of Sherman's men," as he put it. With Major Jackson's approval, he selected two men and used a dam to cross the rice field. They crawled through the high grass in the open field, getting closer to the woods. Suddenly a rain of bullets pelted around them. Berry took a quick shot and fled. He had disturbed a hornet's nest. Now a line of Union skirmishers came out of the trees, as though annoyed by Berry's trespassing. The Confederates across the rice field waited until the Yankees were within range, then opened with muskets and artillery. The Federals began to throw up earthworks on their side of the flooded field. That evening Berry wrote his father about the day's excitement, "Tell Blackwood I wish the battalion of Sharpshooters was here; we could drive these Yankees out of field opposite."[9]

While Sherman prepared a major offensive, General Hardee constructed a pontoon bridge across the Savannah River to

---

[6] Benson, "War Book," 565.
[7] Richard Wheeler, *Sherman's March* (New York: Thomas Y. Crowell, Publishers, 1978) 127–29.
[8] Jones, *The Siege of Savannah*, 115–16.
[9] Benson, "War Book," 568–69.

Hutchinson Island, from that island to Pennyworth Island and then to the South Carolina marshes on the far side. The crossing would be hazardous because Union troops occupied the upper portion of Hutchinson's Island. Sherman might easily have prevented the Confederate escape by throwing a brigade or two across the Savannah River at any point, but he did not. On 20 December, the evacuation of Savannah began. The Confederates used up their shot and shells by an intense firing upon the Union position and then, at dusk, spiked the cannon.[10]

Major Jackson stationed Berry with the pickets guarding the dams across the rice fields and instructed him to keep up a sporadic firing to deceive the enemy. He quietly asked Berry to manage the last withdrawal that night, even though a lieutenant had nominal command. Giving orders to the rear guard to wait until 11:00 P.M., Jackson's battalion withdrew at 8:00 P.M. The young lieutenant soon began to fidget with anxiety about being left behind with no protection from the horde of enemy troops so close. He began to repeat aloud, "I don't know what to do; I don't know what to do." Berry spoke up, "Lieutenant, there is only one thing to do; obey orders, stay here till 11:00 o'clock, and then go." And that is what they did.[11]

Berry's was the last infantry unit to march through the sleeping city of Savannah. With them rode the rear guard of cavalry, the "clink clank" of the horses' hooves echoing on the cobbled streets.[12] If the streets were quiet, the scene at the river was chaotic. Men, horses, and wagons crowded across the unsteady bridge, some falling into the water. Berry's squad crossed last on the bridge about 3:00 A.M. Then the engineers scuttled the rice barges used as pontoons.

---

[10] Bruce Catton, *This Hallowed Ground: The Story of the Union Side of the Civil War* (New York: Doubleday and Company, Inc., 1956) 360–361; Jones, *The Siege of Savannah*, 133–34.

[11] Benson, "War Book," 572–73.

[12] Alexander Lawrence quoted this passage from Benson's unpublished journal in *A Present for Mr. Lincoln*, 199–200.

The flotilla of Confederate gunboats was destroyed by their own crews, except for the *C.S.S. Macon* and *C.S.S. Sampson* that escaped upriver to Augusta.[13] It will be remembered that the ladies of Georgia had gone to a great deal of trouble to subsidize a gunboat remarkable for its immobility. Colonel Jones described her fate in this laconic passage, "The Ladies Gun-boat, or iron-clad *Georgia*, was sunk at her moorings, abreast of Fort Jackson, on the night of the 20th."[14]

Most of the retreating Confederates had a miserable time of it, trekking through swamps on a cold morning, and marching all day. They must have been amazed at Berry Benson's attitude. He later wrote, "It was a real treat to me to march through this country, so different from Virginia with its innumerable hills; here all was flat with great pine forests, here and there a clearing with the beautiful spreading live oaks to see one of which was worth a summer's campaign."[15] When they reached the railroad, the Augusta battalion returned home, and Berry with them. They thought they might need to defend their own town as Sherman moved up through South Carolina.

While the Confederate army tramped through swamps, the Union army entered Savannah. Major General John W. Geary's division probed the Confederate works at dawn, found them empty, and marched to Savannah on the river road. The mayor of Savannah and a delegation of citizens came out to surrender their city. General Geary savored the moment: "My entire division entered the city of Savannah at early dawn and before the sun first gilded the morning clouds our National colors, side by side with those of my own division, were unfurled from the dome of the Exchange and over the U.S. Customs House."[16] To his credit Geary promptly put a stop to

---

[13] Wheeler, *Sherman's March*, 134–36.

[14] Jones, *The Siege of Savannah*, 154. My great-grandfather served on the crew of the *Georgia*.

[15] Benson, "War Book," 574.

[16] Wheeler, *Sherman's March*, 137–38.

the looting that had already begun and imposed strict order. He sent two regiments to occupy Fort Jackson below Savannah on the river. The only remaining gunboat, the *C.S.S. Savannah*, lobbed a few shots at the Union soldiers as they marched along the river. Then its crew disembarked on the Carolina side and set the ship afire. The vessel exploded with an immense volume of flame and a thunderous roar.[17]

All day long on the 21 November, Union troops paraded into Savannah. General Sherman joined them the next day. He reported, "I was disappointed that Hardee had escaped with his army, but on the whole we had reason to be content with the substantial fruits of victory." Then he sat down to write his famous message to President Lincoln, "I beg to present to you as a Christmas gift the City of Savannah, with one hundred and fifty heavy guns and plenty of ammunition, also about twenty-five thousand bales of cotton." He notified General Grant that he intended "to punish South Carolina as she deserves."[18]

As he lingered in Savannah, Sherman let it be known that his next target would be Augusta or Charleston.[19] Having no intention of attacking either, he hoped to keep garrisons in those cities and out of his way. His ploy had the desired effect. General Hardee remained with his troops in Charleston to defend that place, and Generals Daniel H. Hill and Pierre Beauregard hastened to Augusta to direct the defenses of that city. Berry returned to an Augusta demoralized and paralyzed. No one accepted Confederate currency. Farmers declined to bring produce into the town because they knew that Confederate money would soon be worthless. Local militia remained on the alert for an attack. General Daniel H. Hill ordered the cotton piled in bales along the downtown streets to be burned to prevent its falling into the hands of the enemy. Burning of the cotton would likely destroy the city—a matter of no great moment to the general,

---

[17] Jones, *The Siege of Savannah*, 154.
[18] Ibid., 139.
[19] Ibid., 152.

but of great concern to the women of the town. Mayor Robert May compromised by agreeing to burn the cotton when the enemy reached Hamburg across the river.[20]

As the people worried about Sherman, a flood swept over Augusta on 12 January 1865, causing more damage than Sherman could have done. The canal overflowed and the mills had to stop production. Streets remained full of water for two days. Berry could not get back to his house and had to stay the night with a friend. The next day he waded through the flooded streets to his home. An attractive young lady stood on a corner, afraid to cross. Berry picked her up, waded thigh-deep across the street, and set her down—all without a word. He always regretted not having asked the lady her name.[21]

The train to Charleston still ran; Sherman's troops would not destroy it until 8 February. If Berry wanted to rejoin "the boys" in Virginia he had to leave Augusta while he could. The remnants of General John B. Hood's Army of the Tennessee made use of the train through Augusta, on their way to join General Joseph E. Johnston and form a new force to stop Sherman. Instead of remaining in Georgia to oppose Sherman, as President Jefferson Davis wanted him to do in the first place, Hood had gone off into Tennessee in the vague hope of cutting through to join Lee in Virginia. Instead, he had dashed his army against a strong Union position at Franklin and suffered a complete defeat at Nashville. Many of the survivors went home; the more resolute traveled to South Carolina to fight again.[22]

On 17 January Berry said goodbye to his father, Mat; his brother Brad; his sister, Callie; and to lovely Jeanie Oliver and her sisters. Sixteen-year-old Brad wanted to go with him, but Mat decided that the boy should wait. For a week Berry rode the train to Charleston

---

[20] Corley, *Confederate City*, 89–90.
[21] "Berry Benson's Girl Problem," *Augusta Chronicle*, 15 October 1911.
[22] Catton, *This Hallowed Ground*, 362–63.

and on to Richmond. He took advantage of the Wayside Homes for food and shelter along the way. At Richmond he called upon Judge Baxter to tell him that the judge's son Will had been his prison mate at Elmira and that he was well when he last saw him. The train to Petersburg stopped short of the town because of the proximity of the Union lines. Berry walked the last three miles to his camp. Blackwood and the boys greeted him warmly. Nothing seemed to have changed since he left in December, except that on 15 January, the Federals had captured Fort Fisher and closed the last Confederate port at Wilmington, North Carolina.[23]

Major Caldwell, historian of McGowan's Brigade, wrote about the mood of the times: "The people not only did not reinforce us with soldiers, not only did not supply us with decent food and clothing, but they refused us the small comforts which our deeds wrung even from our enemies—admiring and sympathetic words."[24] The war had become unpopular. Families urged their men to desert, and too many did. The women of the Confederacy who had cheered sons and brothers off to battle now summoned them home.

---

[23] Benson, "War Book," 590–91.

[24] J. F. J. Caldwell, *History of a Brigade of South Carolinians Known First as "Gregg's" and subsequently as "McGowan's Brigade"* (Philadelphia: King and Baird Printers, 1866) 192–93.

CHAPTER 12

The Lines at Petersburg

*"For myself, I cried; I could not help it. And all about were men
crying—plenty of them."*

By 1 February 1865, the Union and Confederate armies had faced
each other for eight months in a grim trench warfare with no
perceptible gain on either side. General Grant had pivoted around
Richmond, unable to break through, and now his lines faced almost
north, below Petersburg, the back door to Richmond. Lee's troops
defended the South Side Railroad, the line that came in from the
West and supplied Petersburg and Richmond. The works extended
nearly forty miles, from east of Petersburg to a stream called
Hatcher's Run. The trenches on both sides measured at least six feet
deep and eight feet wide. The excavated dirt piled to a height of six
feet above the trench allowed the men to move through the works
without being seen. In front of the trenches stretched lines of felled
trees, their sharpened ends pointing toward the enemy.

Lee had 50,000 men in his works; Grant had 120,000.
Longstreet's Corps held the left of the Confederate line nearest
Petersburg, Gordon the center, and A. P. Hill the right. Heth's
Division of Hill's Corps occupied the extreme right near Hatcher's
Run, with Wilcox's Division next. McGowan's Brigade of Wilcox's
Division adjoined Heth's Division.[1] The most conspicuous landmark
in McGowan's front was a large brick house belonging to a family
named Jones. Blackwood and the sharpshooters had become familiar
with the Jones House over the previous months, as they skirmished

---

[1] Douglas Southall Freeman, *R. E. Lee: A Biography*, 4 vols. (New York: Charles
Scribner's Sons, 1934–35) 4:8.

around it, using the house as protection. Now Berry came to know the neighborhood.

When Sherman set out across South Carolina on 1 February, he faced no serious opposition until 22 February when Lee asked General Joseph E. Johnston to pull together whatever troops he could find and oppose Sherman. To his credit, Johnston managed to recruit 17,000 infantry, including the veterans of Hood's army, and 6,000 cavalry. But Sherman had 60,000 with more coming in from Wilmington. Johnston accepted the responsibility like a good soldier, but told Lee, "I can only annoy him."[2]

The Confederate Congress debated an issue with profound implications—whether or not to recruit slaves into the army. The Confederacy was based on the premise, as Alexander Stephens had explained it, that there was an inherent inequality between the races. Jefferson Davis, in his response to the Emancipation Proclamation, had threatened to enslave all the blacks in areas conquered by Confederate armies because "helotism" was the natural and proper condition of black people. Now President Davis proposed a way to free the slaves. Georgia's Howell Cobb remarked, "If slaves will make good soldiers our whole theory of slavery is wrong...." But Lee thought that they would make good soldiers, and his prestige carried the measure through the legislature. Lee put dependable Richard Ewell, then defending Richmond, in charge of recruiting black troops with the promise of freedom at the end of service. Gertrude Clanton Thomas of Augusta wondered to her journal, "I take a woman's view of the subject, but it does seem strangely inconsistent, the idea of our offering to a Negro the rich boon—the priceless reward of freedom to aid us in keeping in bondage a large proportion of his brethren, when by joining the Yankees he will instantly gain

---

[2] Ibid., 4:13.

the reward which Mr. Davis promised after a certain amount of labor and danger incurred."[3]

Out of courtesy, General Lee asked the men their opinion regarding the enlisting of black soldiers. Major Caldwell recorded that the men of McGowan's Brigade raised no objection. However, the request was disheartening because it indicated the desperate straits of the Confederacy. The men regarded the Hampton Roads Conference of 3 February, as another sign that the end was near. Confederate vice president Alexander H. Stephens, Judge John A. Campbell, and Senator R. M. T. Hunter, acting as representatives of Jefferson Davis, walked across the lines under a flag of truce to see General Grant. Grant informed President Lincoln that the visiting gentlemen wanted to speak to him. So, Lincoln and Secretary of State William Seward came down to Hampton Roads to have a chat aboard the steamer *River Queen*. Lincoln greeted his old congressional colleague Stephens warmly, but made it clear that he did not intend to negotiate. The commissioners proposed the strange idea that the Union and Confederacy should pause in their fight and go down to Mexico and expel the French. Lincoln thought that might be a good idea, but only after the Union had been restored. The soldiers in the trenches who had cheered the commissioners on their way, now silently witnessed their return, knowing that the mission had failed.[4]

---

[3] Virginia Ingraham Burr, ed., *The Secret Eye: The Journal of Gertrude Clanton Thomas, 1848–1889* (Chapel Hill: University of North Carolina Press, 1990) 243.

[4] J. F. J. Caldwell, *History of a Brigade of South Carolinians Known First as "Gregg's" and subsequently as "McGowan's Brigade"* (Philadelphia: King and Baird Printers, 1866) 201; Berry Benson, "The War Book, Reminiscences of Berry Greenwood Benson, CSA," (Typescript prepared by Charles G. Benson, Ida Jane ["Jeanie"] Benson, and Olive Benson), Special Collections, Reese Library, Augusta State University, Augusta GA; hereafter cited as "War Book"), 596. A copy of the typescript is also held by the Southern Historical Collection at the University of North Carolina, Chapel Hill, in its Berry Benson Papers, ms. 2636. The original manuscript diary (ms. 326) is located in the Hargrett Rare Book & Manuscript Library at the University of Georgia in Athens.

Men who had fought valiantly began to desert. McGowan's Brigade, one of the finest in the army, lost nine men from Orr's Rifles, four from the 14th Regiment, twenty-six from the 13th, and eleven from the 1st. Five of these latter were arrested, including several who had fought bravely in many battles. One of the deserters was pardoned because of his youth. The other four were shot by a firing squad made up of their comrades of the regiment. The executions dampened the spirit of the regiment. When the regiment was ordered out to watch the executions on 9 March, Berry disobeyed orders. He stayed by himself in one of the huts, noting later that "I could not bring myself to witness the cool, deliberate killing of men, however necessary and justifiable."[5]

The sharpshooters did most of the fighting during the lull in major operations. When General McGowan wanted information, he would have Dunlop's Sharpshooters sweep along the Union picket line and bring in prisoners. Major Caldwell described their tactics: "They would move out of the picket line a little before day, creep close to the enemy, form, rush in (generally by the flank) and sweep up and down the works. They always captured some prisoners and a good deal of plunder, and sometimes killed a few of the enemy, but I never heard of a single casualty among them."[6] Berry relished this kind of fighting and excelled at it. On 27 February Berry wrote Mat Benson that the sharpshooters had adopted an emblem worn on the left arm, a green stripe for each campaign, and for every gallant act a red star.[7]

On 25 March Lee launched a major offensive—his last as it turned out. He wanted to stop Grant from continually extending his left and threatening the railroad supplying the Confederates. If Grant could be made to contract his lines, perhaps Lee could make a junction with Johnston's army retreating before Sherman in North

---

[5] Benson, "War Book," 608.
[6] Caldwell, *History of a Brigade*, 195–96.
[7] Benson, "War Book," 599.

Carolina. He stripped men from the right of his lines to give Gordon nearly half of his army in the center. Gordon's immediate objective was Fort Stedman, east of Petersburg, the anchor of Grant's right flank. A more important objective was the railroad guarded by Fort Stedman that supplied the Union army from Petersburg down. If he could break that line, Grant would have to pull back his entire left flank.

At 4:00 on the morning of 25 March, Gordon began his attack. His men quickly overran the Union picket line, and his axemen cut through the abatis and other obstructions in front of the works. He took Fort Stedman and trenches on both sides for several hundred yards. But the Federals threw up another line defending the railroad and Gordon could not break that. The men retreated in the face of withering artillery fire; the Federals closed in from both sides, and there was nothing left to do but to go back to the Confederate works, with the loss of 4,000 men.[8]

The attack seemed to arouse a sleeping giant. On the evening of 25 March the Union army demonstrated all along the front. Berry saw them coming out of their works a mile away across a treeless plain. A long line of infantry wound down the distant ravines and gullies and formed a skirmish line. They advanced upon the brigade's pickets who lay in their shallow rifle pits. The Confederates held their fire just long enough, then blasted the attackers, driving them back. A reinforced skirmish line came forward again, with the same results. It would take more than a skirmish line to break through. They realized that on the other side, and now advanced a line of battle, in perfect step, shoulder to shoulder, their colors waving grandly, and their mounted officers encouraging them on.[9]

The thin picket line could contain such an offensive but for a moment. They caused the line to pause, but a courageous color bearer broke into a run, and then the whole Yankee line cheered and

---

[8] Freeman, *R. E. Lee*, 4:14–19.
[9] Caldwell, *History of a Brigade*, 203–204.

charged, clearing the rifle pits for half a mile, and taking most of the defenders prisoners. Now the Confederate artillery opened upon the Federals, and musket fire erupted along the breastworks. The Federals got no farther than the rifle pits. They occupied the pits and took cover in and behind the Jones House.

At night the sharpshooters crept out on their usual duty of harassing the enemy, but now the enemy lay in the Confederate rifle pits and Berry's mates had to dig new ones. Berry crawled out ahead of the others, taking advantage of slight depressions in the ground and took shots at Federals passing in front of the Jones House, which they had set afire. During the next day, he remained out in front of his own rifle pits, shooting at enemy skirmishers. Making himself a nuisance, he soon attracted so much return fire that he dared not raise his head. He stayed there all day, and under cover of night he and the other sharpshooters retired to their works.[10]

Berry was surprised that General Lee himself had taken an interest in their fight. Lee suggested that it would be desirable if the Federals were pushed back beyond the Jones House to where they had come from. Sharpshooters from Mahone's and Heth's Divisions joined the four hundred of Wilcox's Division. "What a trim little band of say 400 this was!" Berry wrote. All of them picked men from their battalions, and each man determined to prove his battalion the best. They lined up at dawn on the chilly morning of 27 March. Officers rode along the lines giving orders to move quietly and hold fire. The line marched out in perfect formation, moving swiftly. A Yankee skirmisher fired a shot. In response, the sharpshooters gave their wild rebel yell and charged at the half-awake enemy. It was over quickly. The Federals fled in a panic, out of the rifle pits, back behind the smoking ruins of the Jones House, all the way to their works. It was a small victory, but Lee noticed it and complimented the men. Major Caldwell, who watched the action, wrote, "It was admitted to

---

[10] Benson, "War Book," 614–16.

be a very handsome affair." They could not have known then that they would not again have occasion to give vent to the rebel yell.[11]

Tuesday, 28 March, passed quietly enough for the Confederates in their works. From the other side came sounds of massive movement, bugles blowing, drums beating, creaking of wagons. Grant was moving 50,000 men to smash the right of the Confederate line at Hatcher's Run and cut the South Side Railroad. On 29 March, General Bushrod Johnson took a position on McGowan's right to bolster that end of the line. All day long Pickett's Division marched farther to the right to anchor the Confederate line at a place called Five Forks, beyond Hatcher's Run. Lee had scraped up 11,000 men for Pickett and ordered him to hold Five Forks at all costs. The general who opposed Pickett was the formidable Philip H. Sheridan. Earlier in March, Sheridan had routed the remnants of Jubal Early's Shenandoah army and come east to join Grant. Now, with 10,000 cavalry, he intended to deal with Pickett at Five Forks.[12]

It rained all night that day and all the next day, delaying action. McGowan's Brigade slogged through the mud to connect with Bushrod Johnson's division at the extreme right of the Confederate position at Hatcher's Run. Men feared the worst. Berry noted their demeanor: "They hung their heads despairingly and said the time was not long when it would be all over, and we would be a conquered people."[13]

At daybreak on 30 March, General McGowan rode up to the sharpshooters' camp and called for Benson. Generals did not often pay social calls on sergeants, and Berry approached with some degree of anticipation. McGowan asked if Berry would be willing to pick his

---

[11] Caldwell, *History of a Brigade*, 206; Benson, "War Book," 620.

[12] Freeman, *R. E. Lee*, 4:27; Benson, "War Book," 622.

[13] Benson, "War Book," 207. Gen. Bushrod Johnson described the events of 28 March–1 April in his report of 10 April 1865, in US War Department, comp., *The War of the Rebellion: A Compilation of the Official Records of the Union and Confederate Armies*, 128 vols. (Washington DC: Government Printing Office, 1880–1901) ser. 1, vol. 46, pt. 1, p. 1286–87.

own squad and act independently of the brigade. He told Berry that General Lee himself had suggested Berry for such a command. Berry replied, "Of all things, it was what I most desired." McGowan gave Berry a hand-drawn map of their situation. Berry immediately began thinking of men he wanted—Blackwood, of course, and Ben Powell. But such adventuring would have to wait for the outcome of the big battle shaping up.[14]

McGowan ordered Dunlop's Sharpshooters to form a front line four hundred yards in front of the works. As usual, Company A occupied the right of the line and Berry the right of Company A. There should have been a detachment from Johnson's Division to link up with and complete the line, but Berry could see no one on his right. He walked back to report to his acting lieutenant (Ingraham Hasell had not returned from furlough) that the sharpshooters were unsupported and could easily be flanked. He noticed the men laughing and pointing. He saw why. The young lieutenant skulked behind one of the few trees on the field; the man had clearly lost his nerve. Berry called his fellow sergeants together and told them to ignore the lieutenant; he was assuming command. Berry later reported the officer for cowardice.[15] Berry then went out alone to find the Confederates on the right. When he found them several hundred yards away, he persuaded them to extend their position to meet McGowan's Sharpshooters. Even so, a gap of about fifty yards remained between Berry and Bushrod Johnson's men. He knew that the gap would not be tested by the enemy during daylight, but worried that they might try to exploit it at night. After dark, he put a

---

[14] Benson, "War Book," 622. Other than Berry's statement and his lifelong belief that Lee had recommended him for independent command, there is no proof that Lee did so. However, Lee was with McGowan at the time, and might have done so. See Freeman, *R. E. Lee*, 4:34.

[15] According to Maj. Dunlop, a Lt. Ballinger had replaced Hasell on 28 January 1865, and Ballinger gave way to Lt. N. G. Dicen on 25 March 1865 (W. S. Dunlop, *Lee's Sharpshooters; or the Forefront of Battle* [Little Rock AR: Tunnah and Pittard, Printers, 1899] 238).

few men in the gap, and they soon caught a Federal scout probing the weakness.[16]

The weather cleared on 31 March. Before the expected federal offensive could begin, Lee beat them to it, launching an attack of his own in hopes of disrupting the enemy operation. He ordered McGowan's Brigade and Gracie's Brigade of Johnson's Division to move out of the Confederate works, follow a road that took them to the end of the Federal line, and attack in the flank. Grant intended to do exactly the same thing on the same day on a larger scale, using Sheridan to enfilade the Confederate line while Gouverneur K. Warren attacked frontally at Hatcher's Run.

Berry remained in the rifle pits, with his mates keeping up a sporadic firing to mask the movement of the brigade. Therefore, he was in position to see the Confederates emerge in line of battle across the field, close-ordered as in a drill, rolling back the enemy line. "It was our brigade," wrote Berry, "driving them before them. It was a beautiful sight." The retreating Federals backed into the sharpshooters' range of fire. "And all the time we had a flank fire from our pits which galled them severely," Berry wrote. The retreating Federals and advancing Confederates soon disappeared from view. The roar of musketry grew fainter, then louder as Federal reinforcements pushed the Confederates back. Again the two lines moved across the sharpshooters' front, now in reverse. Though outnumbered, the Confederates maintained perfect order, and reached the safety of their own works. Colonel C. W. McCreary of the 1st Regiment was killed in the engagement.[17]

The victorious Federals now turned on their tormentors, the sharpshooters. They marched across the field in double line-of-battle, flags flying, men cheering. The sharpshooters put up a fierce fight, checking the advance momentarily. A courageous Yankee flag-bearer broke into a run, and the whole line followed. Berry stood on

[16] Benson, "War Book," 624–25.
[17] Ibid., 627; Caldwell, *History of a Brigade*, 210–11.

a stump for a better view, even though he made a better target, and discharged all the bullets in his Spencer rifle. Then he retreated, the last in his company to do so, and regained the breastworks. Curiously, the Federals did not attempt to penetrate the works. Lee, who had witnessed the battle, congratulated McGowan on the gallant conduct of his brigade.[18]

Lee had gained a day, but on 1 April, Warren followed orders to link up with Sheridan. His scouts did not know the terrain, and his infantry blundered about most of the day, to Sheridan's intense annoyance. Sheridan, as the superior officer, removed Warren from command, a harsh treatment for one of the heroes of Gettysburg. When Sheridan finally launched his attack, late in the afternoon of 1 April, Pickett was away at a fish fry with congenial companions. By the time he returned to the front, his line had been broken, with Sheridan taking 5,000 prisoners. Lee was as furious with Pickett as Sheridan had been with Warren, and with better reason.[19]

All this action took place to the far right of the position of McGowan's Brigade. General McGowan wondered where the enemy had gone. He approached Berry early on the morning of 1 April, and told him that he must go out and find them. Berry promptly set out, taking with him Shade Thomas, who had Native-American ancestry. They crept cautiously through the woods that concealed the enemy works and saw a long line of infantry on the march. Berry ran back to report to McGowan. The general told Berry to lead the way; the sharpshooters would follow, and the brigade would come along behind. Berry selected Thomas again, as well as his old friend Ben Powell, and the three of them moved through the forest, fifty yards apart. The sharpshooters followed at a distance. As they came out into the open they saw the Federal works three hundred yards in front of them. Were they occupied? Any number of troops could be hidden behind the high breastworks. Berry figured that the only way

---

[18] Caldwell, *History of a Brigade*, 212–213; Benson, "War Book," 628–29.
[19] Freeman, *R. E. Lee*, 4:29–40.

to find out was to climb the breastworks and look inside. With a heightened sense of anxiety, he approached the works, mounted it, looked inside, and saw a confusion of equipment lying about, but no enemy. He stood on the works and waved to the brigade to come up. They quickly occupied the trenches and helped themselves to the equipment.

Meanwhile, Berry, Thomas, and Powell crossed the open space behind the works and entered another wooded area. Suddenly, three Federal soldiers stepped out from behind trees and called upon Berry to surrender. Thomas and Powell were too far on either side to know what was going on. Thoughts of Elmira flashed through Berry's mind, and as quickly he decided on a bluff. He raised his gun (unloaded because he had used all his bullets) and called on the enemy to surrender. "You are cut off and surrounded," he yelled. Incredibly, the ruse worked and the three Federals threw down their weapons and marched out of the woods with Berry following. He delivered them to the sharpshooters and noticed several of his mates looking at the good boots of the prisoners. Berry knew they would take them, so he decided to take the best pair for himself. He had never taken anything from a prisoner, but he reasoned that the boots would help him do his job better. Therefore he owed it to his country to take the boots! McGowan's Brigade remained in the abandoned Federal works the rest of the day, listening to the distant sound of battle around Five Forks where Sheridan broke Pickett's line.[20]

Lee had withdrawn men from A. P. Hill's Corps farther up the line to supply Pickett. Grant did what Lee tried to do at Gettysburg, and attacked the weakened middle. General George G. Meade had defended the center at Gettysburg; now he led the 6th Corps in an offensive against Lee's center early in the morning of 2 April. The

---

[20] Benson, "War Book," 634–35.

out-manned Confederates made him pay dearly, accounting for 2,000 Federals, but inevitably the force of numbers overwhelmed the defenders and broke through the lines. A. P. Hill came riding furiously to the point of attack, rallying his men. A Pennsylvania soldier took aim and put a bullet through Hill's heart. When Lee heard about the break-through, his thought was for his trusted lieutenant. "He is at rest now," he said, "and we who are left are those who must suffer."[21]

On the same morning, McGowan received orders to pull out of the lines and follow Bushrod Johnson's troops to defend the South Side Railroad, now vulnerable to Sheridan. The sharpshooters were the last to leave. Berry had received no official orders to begin acting in an independent capacity, but he decided to begin unofficially. He had no trouble picking his team—Blackwood, Thomas, Powell, Hensen, and a few others. Nothing of value to the enemy should be left behind; therefore, they began breaking discarded weapons, smashing them against trees. Whether the well-equipped Yankees would have wanted used Confederate rifles was beside the point. Having finished that business, his squad lagged behind the brigade, acting as a rear guard. As they passed through a cluster of winter huts used by their brigade, they searched for malingerers and found one hiding in a hut, hoarding an enormous amount of plunder. He had quit the war and decided to sell the stuff to the highest bidder. Berry disliked "skulkers" even more than the enemy, and this was a champion skulker. He prodded the man with his gun and made him march. The man grumbled, whined, and dragged along. "I declare that two or three times I was on the point of ordering the men to shoot him," Berry remembered. Instead he told Blackwood to take the good shoes hanging around the man's neck, and bid him good riddance. They could not afford to dally, because enemy sharpshooters came into sight and took shots at them.[22]

---

[21] Freeman, *R. E. Lee*, 4:47.
[22] Benson, "War Book," 638–29.

Twice, Berry's little band took shelter behind trees and fired at their pursuers, hoping to slow them down. But there were too many. Berry would have liked to burn a bridge he crossed but there was no time. Federals trotted across the bridge right behind them. The four brigades in retreat had stopped and already thrown up a low embankment, Berry's men tumbled over the works on the right of the line among Bushrod Johnson's men. He learned that McGowan's Brigade held the left of the position, but there was no time to join them because the Federal sharpshooters immediately formed an attack line and ran toward the Confederates. The overconfident Yankees were surprised by the fierce fusillade that met them, and they quickly fell back. Berry and some of his men jumped out of the works to chase after the enemy, but none of the other defenders were inclined to follow. The Battle of Sutherland's Station had begun.[23]

Their first attack on the right of the Confederate line having failed, the Federals tested McGowan's Brigade on the left. Major Caldwell described how they were met, "Lee's veterans were not to be frightened by sounds or appearances. They rolled a perfect sheet of lead across the open interval, striking down scores of the enemy, opening great gaps in their line, and destroying all concert and all order." The Federals fell back and took advantage of a sunken road about 400 yards distant, and continued firing. Berry threw away his Spencer and picked up an Enfield when he first reached the works; "We had some right lively sharpshooting," he wrote. He swore that he saw a bullet coming at him a fraction of a second before it whizzed past his ear.[24]

After a pause, the Federals massed on their right, the Confederate left, intending to outflank McGowan's Brigade. McGowan swung Orr's Regiment of rifles out to protect his flank. Now the enemy came on silently with dreadful earnestness. The rifles had to give way, exposing McGowan's position. Then, certain

---

[23] Ibid., 641; Caldwell, *History of a Brigade*, 220.
[24] Caldwell, *History of a Brigade*, 220; Benson, "War Book," 642.

of victory, the Federals in front and the ones on the side started cheering and advancing rapidly. They came, wrote Caldwell, "Like the converging currents of a storm." The brigade crumpled from left to right. Berry and his band on the extreme right were the last to go. One after another fled, but Berry, Blackwood, and Hensen kept shooting. Berry called to Hensen to fire and run, then the same to Blackwood, then he fired—as far as he could tell—the last Confederate shot in the Battle of Sutherland's Station. He described "a veritable shower of bullets" that followed him, but his incredible luck held and the three of them caught up with their mates.[25]

The four Confederate brigades that had been engaged now lost all semblance of order. A number of officers had been captured, including Captain Dunlop of the sharpshooters. They had lost six hundred men, and they had lost the railroad. Sullen, dispirited, and angry men kept moving until they reached the Appomattox River. Heavy rains of the previous days had swollen the river, and there was no way to cross, except for a small boat that could ferry four at a time. Many threw down their guns and tried to swim; some drowned. Most simply plodded along the riverbank, heading west, away from the enemy. At dusk, the exhausted men halted in a clearing by the river. The second of April had been a terrible day.[26]

Berry sought out General McGowan and found him lying on the leaves with a few other officers, as demoralized as the rest. He frankly admitted that he did not know where they were or how they might cross the river. If McGowan did not want to take the initiative, Berry decided that he would. After all, McGowan had said that he intended that Berry lead an independent command. He rounded up as many sharpshooters as he could find and gave them a speech worthy of a general, but devoid of the typical rant. He told them that if they stayed where they were, all would be taken prisoners. For himself, he believed it a duty to get away and fight again. If any felt the same way

---

[25] Caldwell, *History of a Brigade*, 223; Benson, "War Book," 643.
[26] Freeman, *R. E. Lee*, 4:64–66.

they should come with him. He warned them that they would have to march all night: "It is mighty little rest I shall give you." Some who wanted to join him could not because of sheer exhaustion. Blackwood, Bell, Clark, Hensen, Ruff, and a few others—fifteen in all, including a barefoot teenager—stood up to follow Berry.[27]

He gave them mighty little rest indeed. They followed the river until blocked by a swift-flowing tributary. They had to detour up the creek to find a crude bridge of logs partly afloat. They managed to cross safely. Berry's band returned to the river path to continue on. They came upon three Union soldiers, unarmed and calmly sitting by the path. They explained that they had been captured, but that their captors went off in a hurry. Berry did the proper thing; he told them to get up and march. He let his barefoot soldier take shoes from one of the prisoners, but he refused to allow anything else to be taken. One of the three, a sergeant major, expressed his appreciation by offering Berry a silver coin. Berry declined the offer, saying that the sergeant would need the money in prison. He thought to himself that he had a better chance of imprisonment than his captives.

At about 3:00 A.M. they came up an encampment of a Texas regiment, and they turned their prisoners over to the Texans and kept going. At 4:00 A.M. Blackwood told his brother that he could not move another step. It had been nearly twenty-four hours of marching and fighting. Berry gave them two hours rest, then they moved off again. They reached Kidd's Ferry, twenty-one miles from Petersburg, and crossed the Appomattox. Three hours later the Federals reached the ferry.

Later in the day, Berry permitted another rest. He sent Blackwood and another soldier to a farmhouse to get food. Blackwood dutifully approached the house, and to his surprise the door was opened by General Henry Heth. Heth was a distant cousin of General Lee, and one of the very few Lee called by his first name.

---

[27] Benson, "War Book," 646.

Lee meant for Heth to take over command of A. P. Hill's Corps, but in the confusion could not find Heth and turned the corps—the remnants of it—over to General Longstreet. Heth greeted Blackwood warmly and appealed to the owner of the house to provide enough flour for all of Berry's men. Blackwood returned to his camp, flushed with success, only to be told by Berry to go out and get some meat. So, the younger brother took his gun and a companion and went foraging. Berry heard one shot. Blackwood and the other soldier came back with two pigs. Berry scolded Blackwood for killing an extra pig, but Blackwood explained that his one shot killed both of them. They found a big wash pot, kindled a fire, put both pigs in it, and fell asleep. When they woke, the pigs had boiled to the consistency of jelly. They ate them anyhow.[28]

On 4 April, Berry's troop overtook Longstreet's Corps, marching from Richmond along the north side of the Appomattox. Everyone seemed to be on his own, dispirited and straggling. Berry had his men form a column of twos, arms at right shoulder, and go swinging off as they had done when following Stonewall. Many a veteran looked up in surprise and cheered them on. Berry could not have been prouder, and his attitude spread to his men. Reuben Ruff started singing a marching song, in a loud, clear voice, a slave song they had learned from the Yankees: "Ole Massa run away / De darky stay at home / I believe in my soul / Dat the kingdom am acomin' / And the year of jubilo!"[29] And all sixteen took up the chant verse after verse; Berry remembered all the verses years later. So they marched, singing and in formation, an echo of the days when hundreds chanted and marched with a swagger. Now they were only sixteen, but the troops they passed remembered, and for a moment forgot their misery.

They came to Goode's Bridge and crossed to the south side of the river. To Berry's surprise, there he found General McGowan and

---

[28] Ibid., 650.
[29] Ibid., 651.

the rest of the brigade, perhaps three hundred now. McGowan had marched along the south bank of the river and got there before Berry. Lieutenant Ingraham Hasell had returned from furlough to resume command of Company A of the sharpshooters, and that was the end of Berry's adventure in independent command. Other than Berry's gallant fifteen, there were only twenty-five sharpshooters left in the battalion.

The weary Confederates expected to find supplies at Amelia Courthouse on the Richmond and Danville Railroad, but they had not arrived. Nor had Ewell's Division come in from Richmond. Almost automatically, the men began to dig entrenchments. Lee wasted a day waiting for supplies that never came. They could not continue on the rail line because Sheridan blocked the way at Jetersville. On the evening of 5 April the hungry army left the railroad heading west, heading back toward the curving Appomattox. Even so, Lee's rear guard came under constant harassment from Sheridan's Cavalry. On 6 April, Ewell's Corps, lagging behind, was cut off by Sheridan's Cavalry and Wright's 6th Corps at Sayler's Creek with a loss of 7,500 men and much of the wagon train. The rest of the army kept moving toward Farmville, a station on the South Side Railroad where it crossed the Appomattox. They expected to find food there.[30]

As McGowan's Brigade entered Farmville, Confederate cavalry under Fitz Lee pushed in among them, running from Sheridan. There followed a mad crush of horses and men trying to cross the narrow bridge over the river. Union artillery unlimbered on the hill behind them and sent shots and shells crashing down among the demoralized Confederates. Major Caldwell, as intelligent and brave as any, confessed that he was never so bewildered as then. Berry shouldered through the crowd and raced up the opposite hill with the rest of them, helter-skelter. Berry had the capability of keeping his

---

[30] Freeman, *R. E. Lee*, 4:66–73.

head while others lost theirs. So when he saw a large pot of beans cooking over a fire, he yelled at Lieutenant Hasell to come over. They used Berry's gun to hoist the pot, and they ran with it through the gauntlet of artillery fire.[31]

When the men stopped running and the brigade reorganized, Berry and Hasell had to go out on picket duty with the other sharpshooters. So they left their pot of beans to finish cooking. When they returned from duty every last bean was gone. Fortunately, Berry found an abandoned haversack with some food in it.

On the evening of 7 April, the sharpshooters again assumed picket duty. The pursuing Federals came up before nightfall and set up a skirmish line in full view on a ridge crowned by a farmhouse. Berry suggested to Hasell that he could take a few men and go capture that house. Not to be outdone, Hasell decided to come along. After dark the two Bensons, Hasell and three others crawled along on hands and knees until within two hundred yards of the house. There were men inside the house. Clearly, capturing and holding the house would be impossible. However, Berry suggested that if they rushed the house they might at least take a few prisoners and get away. Hasell thought the idea too risky, and they crawled back to their lines.[32]

Berry hated to give up. He had developed a grudge against the house and the men in it. So he passed the word to his men that they should be careful not to shoot him when he returned. He had no trouble reaching a ridge about four hundred yards from the house; he could see it outlined against the clear night sky. He aimed and fired. He could hear the bullet strike the house. He fired again, and saw a flash in a window and heard a shot hit near him. He exchanged a few rounds with the man in the window. He knew he could hit the house

---

[31] Caldwell, *History of a Brigade*, 233; Benson, "War Book," 654–57; Freeman, *R. E. Lee*, 4:100–101.

[32] Benson, "War Book," 659.

at that distance, but he had to get closer to hit an enemy soldier. He circled around the house, taking advantage of an outlying shed. He thought he saw a sentinel in front of the house and took a shot at him. Instantly someone shot at him. His little duel had put them all on alert. He fired one last shot for good measure, then ran back to his lines. He was nearly killed by one of his own men who forgot that they should not shoot at Sergeant Benson.

They were relatively undisturbed as they resumed the march on 8 April. Someone had started the rumor that they would be safe once they reached Lynchburg. The reassurance of safety made the men feel better, but there was no basis for the rumor. In fact, Sheridan was even then racing to Appomattox Courthouse along the south side of the river from Farmville with the intention of cutting off the Confederate retreat. The pleasant April weather lifted drooping spirits, and when they bivouacked four miles east of Appomattox Courthouse that night, they enjoyed their first good sleep since leaving the lines at Petersburg.

Early the next morning they set out again, McGowan's Brigade pushing through wagons, artillery, and straggling infantry. But after going only two miles, they received orders to file out into a field and rest. Two hundred or so gaunt soldiers straggled in after them. Someone asked what regiment they were, to which they replied that they were the remainder of Kershaw's Division. Up ahead, near the courthouse, sounds of battle could be heard. Gordon's Corps gallantly struggled against Sheridan's Cavalry in a vain effort to open the road, but Federal infantry arriving in increasing numbers checked them and forced them back And now, as they waited in the field, a black line of Union infantry appeared on the encircling ridges.[33]

Berry believed that most of the Confederates camped in the field expected a last fight to the finish. General McGowan ordered Berry to form a skirmish line with the sharpshooters. Then, to his surprise,

---

[33] Caldwell, *History of a Brigade*, 234.

the General sent word for him to return to the brigade and line up on the road. Presently a mounted federal officer came dashing along the road, waving a white handkerchief. What could this mean? Had this officer surrendered? But there was nothing of surrender in the man's demeanor and everything of bravado.

One-armed colonel John Cheves Haskell has not been part of this narrative since Gettysburg because he served with Longstreet's artillery on a different sector. At Appomattox, Longstreet had sent artillery under Haskell to support Gordon. When Gordon ordered him to cease firing, he rode back to Longstreet. He told Longstreet that in the event of surrender he intended to join Joe Johnston in North Carolina. Longstreet said that he might go, too, and take as many as would come. He was prepared to fight his way out of the trap, and he would need Haskell's artillery to do that. However, first he wanted to see if Lee could get honorable terms from Grant.

As they were talking, the rider who had passed Berry came up waving a white handkerchief. "He was a most striking picture," wrote Haskell; "A rather young man dressed in a blue sack with the largest shoulder straps of a major general that I ever saw, with long red hair hanging in oily curls down near to his shoulders, a gorgeous red scarf in which there was a gold pin nearly two inches in length...with big letters 'George A. Custer, Major General.'"

Custer dismounted and swaggered up to Longstreet demanding his "instant surrender." Longstreet asked what authority Custer had to make such a demand. Was he sent by Grant? Custer boasted that he and Sheridan were independent of Grant, "and we will destroy you if you do not surrender at once."

Longstreet answered calmly but sternly, "I suppose you know no better and have violated the decencies of military procedure because you know no better. But your ignorance will not save you if you do so again. Now go, and do as you and Sheridan choose, and we will teach you a lesson you won't forget. Now go!" Haskell noted that Custer went away "with his tail between his legs."[34]

Then Haskell accompanied Longstreet to the McLean house where they met Grant and his senior officers. Lee had already been there and worked out satisfactory terms of surrender. Grant and Longstreet had been at West Point together, and they chatted about old times. Grant asked Haskell to work with his officers in handling the details of disbanding Lee's army.[35]

Even now, in the ominous quiet, Berry refused to believe that Lee would surrender. He asked Captain Barnwell of Company H what was going on. Barnwell did not know. Berry approached General McGowan. He had no information either. Berry said bluntly that he had been in prison once and did not intend to go there again. He would not surrender; he would go off to join Johnston. McGowan told him to wait until they heard definite news of surrender; then Berry could go with his blessing.

Berry found Blackwood and told him his plan. They talked to Ben Powell and a few others. Then Berry went back to see McGowan. The general was changing into a clean uniform, preparing to surrender the brigade, and tears ran down his face. Berry then cried openly, and men all about were crying. McGowan's Brigade surrendered its arms on a rainy morning of 12 April. They marched to Appomattox Courthouse through a line of Federal soldiers on each side of the road. McGowan ordered his men to stack arms and colors, then return to camp. That afternoon those who remained of Wilcox's Division, the brigades of McGowan, Lane, Scales, and Thomas, marched back through Federal lines, on their way south. McGowan's Brigade remained together for a day.

[34] John Cheeves Haskell, *The Haskell Memoirs*, ed. Gilbert E. Govan and James W. Livingood (New York: G. P. Putnam's Sons, 1960) 93–95.
[35] Ibid., 97–98.

McGowan gave his men a brief farewell address, and they broke up into smaller parties.[36]

Only Blackwood of their regiment went with Berry to fight again. Before they left on the afternoon of 9 April, Berry tried to buy Ben Powell's telescopic rifle, but Ben wouldn't sell. Berry gave Captain Barnwell two greenback dollars he had received from his father, thinking that Confederate officers would probably go to prison. "So B. K. and I left the little, tattered, weary, sad and weeping army there on the hill with their arms stacked in the field, all in rows, never to see it anymore." That night as he attempted to sleep in the woods with Blackwood beside him Berry cried as he had not since his mother died.[37]

The war left an indelible impression upon Berry Benson, upon Blackwood, and, indeed, on all the men who had taken part in the epochal four years. For both brothers, the war coincided with the formative period in young adult life when identity is fixed. The early stories Berry had read of knighthood and adventure merged with the mature reality of daring deeds unimagined in his childhood. He had been measured by his own standards of courage, honor, sacrifice, and patriotism, and he had passed the test. His life would go on, but the war experience would never leave him. The friends he made in war would always be his best friends. The memories of his first shot at Sumter, of the clear moon on the night Jackson was killed at Chancellorsville, of the Gray family who had nursed him to health outside Fredericksburg, those images and dozens like them remained etched in his mind and came flooding back at the sight of and even the thought of the battle-scarred Confederate flag.

Berry carried two books with him when he and Blackwood walked away from Appomattox. One was his mother's Bible, which represented a pledge he had made to honor his mother's memory and to do right by God. The other was Walter Scott's poem *Marmion*,

---

[36] Benson, "War Book," 664–66.
[37] Ibid., 666.

which included the stirring tale of the battle of gallant Scots' battle against overwhelming numbers of English, and their inevitable defeat. Gallantry demanded that he act bravely, and religion prepared him to die with resignation. Berry later regretted that he had never carried the colors in any of his battles; he had tried to snatch the flag once, charging at Spotsylvania, but the bearer would not give it up. To carry the colors and live would have been the most supreme test of all.[38]

[38] Ibid., 689; *Augusta Chronicle*, 7 May 1914.

CHAPTER 13

The Emergence of the Lost Cause

"I am certainly proud, naturally and properly proud—of having
been chosen to represent the private Confederate soldier whose
figure was to crown the monument."

Many years after the war, Berry Benson wrote,

> Northward poured the victor's legion,
> Organized, armed, firing well,
> Their returned heralded with music and with salvos of
> cannon.
> But for us:
> Never a drum beat anywhere,
> Never a bugle blew,
> When we came home from the war.[1]

When the Benson brothers came home to Augusta on 15 May 1865, no crowds greeted them; no bands played, no one made a speech. They had been sent off to war as heroes; they had fought as gallantly as men could, and now no one paid attention to their homecoming. They wasted no time in feeling sorry for themselves. They knew that they looked like hundreds of other dirty, ragged veterans who crowded the town in the wash of war. They dared not sleep in a bed until they had rid themselves of lice, their constant companions for years. In his quiet way Mat Benson was glad to see his sons. Callie, now fourteen, and ten-year-old Elizabeth, greeted them shyly, for they had hardly seen their brothers in four years. Brad grumbled that

---

[1] Collected poems of Berry and Jeanie Benson, Benson Family Papers, in private collection of Arthur Dupre, Newark NJ.

the war had ended before he got into it. Ironically, Brad had been spared the danger of battle, only to die of natural causes a decade later.[2]

In the streets deserters and criminals mingled with once-proud veterans, recently "discharged," but "paid off in worthless Confederate notes." Earlier in the month these men had gone on a rampage, looting and vandalizing, disgracing themselves and their uniforms. The Confederate military authorities lost control, and Mayor Robert May had no police to call upon. When Augustans thought about the post-war period during later years, they remembered it as a time of terror. They forgot that the worst period of anarchy were the weeks before the Federal occupation. A semblance of order had been restored by the Federals who marched into Augusta the week before Berry and Blackwood returned.[3]

The Bensons had left their comrades at Appomattox on 9 April and started on their long trek to find General Joseph Johnston's army in North Carolina. On the 10 April they crossed to the north side of the James near Amherst Courthouse, heading west. Two days later they reached Lynchburg. Continuing west towards Leesville, they began to meet paroled Confederate prisoners who stared at them curiously because the brothers still carried their Enfield rifles. Through Pittsylvania to Danville, they mingled with parolees and jostled with them for food from Confederate commissaries.

They rode the train to Greensboro that night and walked six miles to Johnston's camp. They reported to the 2nd South Carolina Regiment only to learn that an armistice had been declared. Berry found General Bradley Johnson who remembered him as the man who had escaped from Elmira. The general told him that Johnston and Sherman were negotiating terms of surrender. Berry and Blackwood had not surrendered at Appomattox, and they would not

---

[2] Brad died on 30 March 1875.
[3] Florence Fleming Corley, *Confederate City: Augusta, Georgia, 1860–1865* (1960; repr., Augusta GA: Richmond County Historical Society, 1995) 93–94.

surrender at Greensboro. They left again, heading south. If partisan
bands were active on the Carolina coast they meant to join them.[4]
They found only discouragement and defeat. At home they
encountered a disorienting new social reality.

Religious-minded Augustans had been sure that God blessed
their cause. Gertrude Clanton Thomas wrote in her journal that
Lee's defeat made her doubt the Bible.[5] White Augustans—brought
up to believe that black people should occupy the lowest position in
society—now saw the 33rd Colored Regiment, United States
Infantry, march proudly up Greene Street, dressed in red pants and
blue jackets, chanting and followed by hundreds of excited black
Augustans who escorted them all the way to the Arsenal on the Hill.[6]
For this writer's grandmother, who witnessed the parade as a child,
the event had a traumatic influence. In the dementia of declining
years she would take me aside and whisper, "Edward, they came
marching up Greene Street!" I kept waiting to hear what terrible
things they had done. In time, I realized that they had done nothing
but march, sing, carry weapons, and in general act like white soldiers.
In my grandmother's world, they were not supposed to act like that.
It seemed that almost overnight the subservient had assumed
authority.

If Berry read the local newspaper the day after he returned, he
would have been surprised that the editorial denounced the doctrine
of secession as "never more than a mere doubtful political
abstraction." The editor praised the Federal military commander,
Brevet Major General Edward Molineux as "the gentlemanly and
obliging commander of the post."[7] Molineux, the commanding

---

[4] Ibid., 681–82.

[5] Edward J. Cashin, *The Story of Augusta* (Augusta GA: Richmond County Board
of Education, 1980) 128, quoting the unpublished journal of Ella Gertrude Clanton
Thomas.

[6] Edward J. Cashin, *Old Springfield: Race and Religion in Augusta, Georgia* (Augusta:
Springfield Village Park Foundation, Inc., 1995) 44.

[7] *Augusta Chronicle*, 16 May 1865.

officer of the 159th New York Regiment, made it his business to repair the damage done to streets and houses by the January freshet. Berry might have thought it strange that a Yankee officer accomplished what Confederate and civilian authorities could not or did not. When Molineux left Augusta, the town's leading citizens vied to pay him compliments. Ironically, as time went on, Augustans remembered the occupiers as oppressors.[8]

The post-war decade was filled with other ironies. People expected terrible things to happen—rape, pillage, insults of all kinds—but the actual violence was minimal. During the last months of 1865, the period the editor of the *Augusta Chronicle* called a "reign of terror," Augustans exhibited a remarkable resilience. They displayed an almost Yankee fondness for making money. As if embarrassed by their success, Augustans exalted the theme of the "Lost Cause," thereby demonstrating their fidelity to the southern way of life. Berry Benson found himself caught up in these currents; he worked for the factories of the New South, and he posed for the most conspicuous image of the Lost Cause, the soldier atop the magnificent Confederate monument in the center of town.[9]

Most of the violence during the 1865 "reign of terror" consisted of petty crimes, vagrancy, and random shooting of firearms. General Molineux declared martial law and imposed a 9:00 P.M. curfew. Black Augustans complained that the military took away their guns, but not those of the whites. Curiously, the only confrontation between groups of whites and blacks was a street fight between white Union soldiers of the 159th Regiment and black soldiers of the 33rd Regiment. Three ex-Confederates murdered white Captain Alex Heasley of the 33rd Regiment on a public street, apparently without provocation. The subsequent trial of the three men attracted enormous attention, but no demonstrations of any kind. Two of the

---

[8] Corley, *Confederate City*, 98; *Augusta Chronicle*, 25 June 1865.
[9] The "reign of terror" expression is from the *Augusta Chronicle*, 3 January 1866.

three were acquitted, and the third was sentenced to a fifteen-year prison term.[10]

In another racial incident, white policeman Tom Olive shot and killed Private Isam Simmons, a black soldier of the 136th Colored Regiment. The 136th Regiment replaced the 33rd at the Augusta Arsenal. The men of the 33rd had two years of military training and conducted themselves well; the newcomers of the 136th had been mustered in Atlanta in July. They had trouble adjusting to military discipline. Olive turned himself in to the military authorities. Colonel Richard Root, a veteran of distinguished service in the western theater and commanding officer of the 136th Regiment, presided over the trial. Though Root might have had reason to blame Olive for killing one of his own men, he acquitted him.[11]

The final (and by far the worst) racial incident happened on 28 December and again involved the unfortunate 136th. Four soldiers went out for a walk on that afternoon. They stopped at the farmhouse of Mrs. Elizabeth T. Freeman and asked for water from the well. Mrs. Freeman told them to drink from a gourd. Instead, the soldiers used the bucket. The lady of the house remonstrated with them, and angry words were exchanged. One of the soldiers approached the widow, brandishing a musket. Matthew Freeman, her sixteen-year-old son appeared on the porch, armed with a pistol. The soldiers left, warning that they would be back.

Those in the house included other sons, Willie, a twenty-year-old former Confederate soldier; Henry, age eighteen; a twenty-year-old cousin, Milton Parks; two daughters; and two of the daughters' friends. Later in the same afternoon, eight soldiers returned. One of them shot the dog in the yard, and several fired shots through the

---

[10] The trial was closely followed in the *Chronicle* during the first thirteen days in September 1865, and again on 10 November 1865.

[11] For more information about this incident, see Russell K. Brown, "Post-Civil-War Violence in Augusta, Georgia," *Georgia Historical Quarterly* 90 (Summer 2006): 196–213.

windows. The family took refuge upstairs. From a window, Willie Freeman shot one of the men with a shotgun, wounding him. That caused a lull, as the soldiers carried off the wounded man.

Frightened, Mrs. Freeman called a neighbor, an ex-Confederate named Charles Martin, to stay the night. His sister was one of the girls visiting the Freemans. Martin posted Henry Freeman and Milton Parks outside as lookouts. A larger number of soldiers returned clearly bent on trouble. They fired at the two young lookouts and chased them away. They made angry threats about the people inside, then broke down the door with an axe. While the family huddled in fear on the second floor, the men smashed furniture downstairs, then turned their attention to the stairway. Four of them climbed the stairs, the leader holding a lantern. As the first soldier reached the top of the stairs, Willie Freeman shot him dead, then shot the second man. Martin and the boys fired at the others in the stairwell, and two more fell. The others retreated momentarily.

Astonishingly, they stormed the stairway again and were again driven back. Some climbed on the roof, looking for a way to enter. Others prowled about, firing at windows. Near dawn, they began dismantling the front porch to make a bonfire, hoping to burn down the house. Just in time, a company of soldiers headed by Colonel Root appeared on the scene. The soldiers had been reported missing, and Root had gone looking for them. He arrived in time to avert an even bigger tragedy. Four soldiers had been killed and three wounded. A week later, the 136th Regiment was disbanded.[12]

Military occupation of Georgia ended in 1870; not so for neighboring South Carolina. Federal troops lingered there to protect a Republican administration. Prince Rivers, a black man, represented

---

[12] The initial report in the *Augusta Chronicle*, 30 December 1865, was graphic but not racially inflammatory. The retelling of the incident by Charles B. Martin and W. F. Freeman in the *Augusta Chronicle*, 12 January and 2 February 1908, reflected a wave of racial animosity that afflicted Georgia.

the government in Hamburg where he served as justice of the peace and major general of the militia. He later testified that he did not call out the local militia on 4 July 1876, and that he had nothing to do with the militia that assembled under the leadership of a man named Dock Adams.

That day marked the centennial of the signing of the Declaration of Independence, and Dock Adams called the militia together to parade in the town streets. The men bore arms supplied to them by a white Hamburg native named Louis Schiller. It happened that two young residents of Hamburg, Thomas Butler and Henry Getzen, returned from selling produce at the Augusta market to find their way blocked by the parading militia. For whatever reason, the militia refused to let them pass; angry words were exchanged. Finally, after the show of force, the militiamen allowed the two white youths to drive their buggy through.[13]

That might have been the end of it, except that "black rule" and military occupation had caused simmering resentment among whites of Edgefield County in which Hamburg was located. Senator Benjamin Tillman, speaking about the affair in 1909, stated frankly that "It had been the settled purpose of the leading white men of Edgefield to seize the first opportunity that the negroes might offer them to provoke a riot and teach the negroes a lesson."[14] Thomas Butler's father, Robert, hired General Matthew C. Butler, to prosecute Dock Adams for impeding passage on a public thoroughfare.[15]

---

[13] Though Berry Benson did not mention his part in the Hamburg riots in his journal, his son Charles Benson provided a handwritten account in the "War Book," opposite page 693.

[14] Sen. B. R. Tillman, *The Struggles of 1876: How South Carolina Was Delivered from Carpet-Bag and Negro Rule. Speech at the Red-Shirt Reunion at Anderson* (N.p., 1909).

[15] Butler enjoyed hero status in South Carolina. His uncles on his mother's side were national heroes, Commodore Oliver H. Perry for the Battle of Lake Erie, and Commodore Matthew Cailbraith Perry for opening Japan to American trade. A volunteer captain in Wade Hampton's legion at the beginning of the Civil War,

General Butler presented the complaint to Judge Prince Rivers, who subpoenaed Dock Adams. At the hearing on 8 July, Adams replied insolently to the judge's questions, and Rivers charged him with contempt of court. Expecting arrest, Adams called his company together and occupied the Sibley Building, a two-story brick structure near the railroad trestle in Hamburg.

Judge Rivers went to the Sibley Building and made a personal appeal to the men to surrender their weapons. Adams replied that he would be defenseless against the angry whites if he did so. Rivers asked General Butler to guarantee the safety of the militiamen if they gave up their guns. Butler agreed to ship off the weapons to Governor Chamberlain and let the men go. Adams declined the offer.[16]

Butler then rode over the bridge to Augusta and asked for help, and at least a hundred men responded. By 7:00 P.M. a large crowd gathered on the river in Hamburg and under the trestle near the Sibley Building. Suddenly, with a defiant yell, the militiamen began firing. Some of the balls crossed the river to Augusta. The besiegers returned fire. Twenty-three-year-old T. Mackey Meriwether, standing on the riverbank, fell dead of a shot to the head. His friends carried his body to Augusta. Exaggerated rumors of a general armed uprising of blacks caused intense excitement in the town. Some men took a cannon belonging to the Washington Artillery to the Hamburg side and fired four rounds into the Sibley Building, instantly silencing the opposition inside. The defenders sought refuge in the basement, but refused to surrender. One of them, James

---

Butler lost a foot at the battle of Brandy Station, rose in rank to major general and commanded the rear guard opposing Sherman's march through South Carolina. Though Berry Benson did not mention the fact in his journal, Butler thought so well of Berry that he may have arranged Berry's first job after returning home, that of teacher at Sweetwater Church School near Cherokee Ponds, some eight miles from Augusta. In fact, Butler invited Berry to lodge at his house during the time he taught at Sweetwater. Berry Benson did not mention his teaching at the Sweetwater school. Charles added that information in the "War Book."

[16] *Augusta Chronicle,* 9 July 1876.

Cook, the town marshal, crawled out of a window and made a run for it. He fell, his body riddled with bullets.

During the lull, Berry Benson persuaded General Butler to allow him to try negotiation. He had known several of the men inside since childhood. It required an unusual degree of independent thinking on Benson's part to make the suggestion. With Meriwether's death, a vindictive frenzy had seized the white crowd. At the risk of being shot by blacks and being despised by whites, Berry entered the building and talked to the leaders. Again, they refused, whether from fear or from misguided courage. The whites outside resumed sporadic firing.

Later that evening twenty-nine militiamen surrendered. A reporter wrote that two Augusta gentlemen interceded for three of the prisoners, vouching for their character. The Augustans brought the men to the Georgia side and let them go. We do not know whether Berry, and perhaps his brother Blackwood, might have done the humanitarian deed, but it would be typical of both men. Berry had tried to save them all; perhaps he saved three.

Nine of the militiamen who had remained in the Sibley Building were shot: five of them killed, four wounded. An editorial in the *Augusta Chronicle and Sentinel* condemned "the cruel and unnecessary murders." If such a thing had happened in wartime, it "would have received the execration of all civilized nations." The newspaper praised the calm conduct of Augusta's black population. On the other hand, Republicans in Congress characterized the riot as a "massacre" and used it as a reason for continuing military occupation of South Carolina for another year. In spite of military control of the state, the legislature elected Butler to the United States Senate in 1876. His appearance in Washington touched off more acrimony.[17]

The attack by black soldiers on the Freeman home in 1865 and the white attack on the black militia in July 1876 marked the most violent local episodes of the Reconstruction era. As time went on,

[17] Charles Benson, "The Hamburg Riots," insert in the "War Book," back of p. 692; *Augusta Chronicle*, 11, 22 July and 12 August 1876.

many began to think of the period as one of "Negro Rule" and grinding oppression of whites. Generally forgotten was the fact that all but one of the casualties during the decade were members of the occupying army or militia.

The nightly curfew imposed by the military in 1865 bothered Berry Benson hardly at all. "Many a night when I have been out visiting some of the girls," he wrote, "I have had to sneak back home, with both eyes open, dodging now to the right and now to the left, and making roundabout circuits to keep from being caught by the patrols." The girls in question were undoubtedly the Oliver girls with states for names, Alabama Jane (Jeanie), Louisiana, and Florida. Dodging patrols must have been a lark compared to scouting through enemy lines, but Berry probably enjoyed the consternation expressed by the girls at his daring. Blackwood tried nocturnal social calls, and, in Berry's words, "came home missing." He spent a night in jail.[18]

Berry occupied the first months of his civilian life as teacher in Sweetwater Church School, boarding with the Butler family. Other of Berry's friends and fellow Confederates became teachers. Martin Calvin, principal of Houghton School, helped write legislation establishing Georgia's public school system, and acted as the first superintendent of Richmond County's public schools. Joseph Derry opened his own school and taught future president Woodrow Wilson, and future Supreme Court justice, Joseph R. Lamar.

Already by the end of the year 1865 Augusta's economy had begun to rebound from the depression of the war years. Martin Calvin published a city directory in which he referred to "the chaos of uncertainty" at the close of the war as contrasted with the bright prospects at year's end. "We witness stores undergoing repairs, business houses and dwellings, phoenix-like, rising out of the ashes...The stores are stocked with goods; the streets thronged with men, hurrying to and fro, all speaking silently, yet loudly, our city's

---

[18] Benson, "War Book," 690.

praise—all proclaiming her rapidly increasing prosperity."[19] So far, in this post-war era, no one lamented the "Lost Cause."

When in October 1865 acting Governor James Johnson called a state convention to draft a constitution according to President Andrew Johnson's stipulations, he had to borrow money from wealthy Augustans: Thomas Metcalf loaned the state $20,000 in specie; William Jackson's Augusta Factory loaned $5,000; E. M. Bruce $10,000; C. F. McKay $5,000; and J. M. Newby $2,500. The Augusta Factory returned a remarkable twenty percent return to its stockholders for the year 1865 and for seven years in succession. Clearly, not everyone in Augusta was destitute.[20]

Black Augustans were poised to take advantage of their freedom. Augusta's five hundred or so pre-war free black population provided leadership for the newly freed slaves. Springfield Baptist Church acted as a school for freedom. The church has legitimate claims to being the oldest in the country, having been established at Silver Bluff on the Savannah River below Augusta before the Revolution and removed to Augusta after the Revolution. It operated under black pastors all during the antebellum period, and its members found ways to integrate into the urban economy. The Freedman's Bureau provided emergency assistance for the hundreds of former slaves who flocked into Augusta and settled on the south side of town in Verdery's Territory, or simply "the Terri." Captain John Emory Bryant remained in Augusta after he left the Freedman's Bureau and acted as an advocate for black rights.

Springfield Church hosted the first Emancipation Day celebration on 1 January 1866. Henry McNeal Turner of the 1st Regiment, United States Colored Infantry, gave thanks that blacks could now meet without supervision (though Springfield churchgoers had met without supervision since its beginning): "We were watched, feared, and suspicioned. Three colored men could make a threat and

---

[19] Introduction to *Calvin's Augusta and Business Directory, 1866.*
[20] Cashin, *Story of Augusta*, 130.

five hundred white men would rush to arms." On 10 January, thirty-eight delegates from eleven counties met at Springfield to form the Georgia Equal Rights Association, the forerunner of the Republican Party in Georgia.[21]

Also in January, John Shuften, a black Augustan, issued the first black newspaper, the *Colored American*. It carried an account of the Emancipation Day activities, and provided a partial directory of black churches and businesses. All five of the black churches had started schools by that time. The newspaper listed black-owned grocery stores, restaurants, and barbershops. The Union Hotel advertised itself as catering to "traveling people of color." Harper and Ladeveze sold art supplies and musical instruments at their store. Zeke Williams offered his services as a dentist. Within ten years Augusta could count a black professional class of teachers and lawyers. In 1867, William J. White founded Augusta Baptist Institute, a school that moved to Atlanta ten years later and in time became Morehouse College.[22]

The facts that white and black Augustans were positioned for economic success within only a few months of Appomattox and that acts of violence were isolated indicate that the "reign of terror" was mainly psychological.

The political future also seemed promising. As early as June 1865 wartime mayor Robert May called a meeting of leading citizens. One after another rose to propose resolutions of loyalty to the Federal government under President Andrew Johnson, horror at the assassination of President Lincoln, and thanks to General Edward Molineux for maintaining good order. In October a statewide convention repudiated slavery and secession and adopted a constitution, as required by the guidelines of the Andrew Johnson administration. Augusta's moderate Charles J. Jenkins was elected

---

[21] Cashin, *Old Springfield*, 47.
[22] Ibid., 49; *The Colored American*, 2 January 1866, Special Collections, Reese Library, Augusta State University, Augusta GA.

governor, and senators and representatives were sent to take their seats in Congress. Politics continued without rancor on the municipal front as James Gardiner defeated former mayor Foster Blodgett in a close mayoral election. Berry Benson gave up his teaching career to go to work as a clerk for Mayor Gardiner. Gardiner attempted to win black Augustans away from their reliance upon the Freedman's Bureau by promising public schools for black children.[23]

During 1866 many Augustans, particularly the former Whigs, seemed inclined to support the Republican Party. Mayor Gardiner and a number of other leading citizens, included Generals Ambrose Wright and Lafayette McLaws, signed a statement in July supporting President Johnson's policies. General Wright and Linton Stephens were elected to the House of Representatives, and Alexander Stephens and Herschel Johnson to the United States Senate.

Unfortunately for the political stance of the moderates, radical Republicans won control of the United States Congress in the elections of 1866. They nullified the president's authority by initiating impeachment proceedings, and enacted their own reconstruction plan in 1867. The legislation declared that the former Confederate states were reduced to the status of territories, thereby giving Congress control over them. By Congress's order, federal troops returned to occupy the cities and towns to maintain order, to register voters, and to supervise election of delegates to a constitutional convention. Congress required the convention thus elected to draft a constitution that would grant black men the right to vote. Elections were then held for a state legislature that ratified the 14th Amendment to the United States Constitution, conferring citizenship upon all persons born and naturalized in the country.

Berry Benson's opinion reflected that of many moderates, "The radical Republicans, were, in legislation, very bitter upon the South, and treated us harshly, so that very rancourous feelings were

---

[23] *Augusta Chronicle*, 24 July 1966.

naturally entertained toward them in return."[24] Augustans faced a difficult political choice. They had cooperated with the federal government; should they continue to do so? Governor Jenkins set an example by leaving the state in protest, taking the great seal with him. Union general George G. Meade, the victor at Gettysburg, then acted as governor. Most Georgians opposed the new order; however, a significant minority, led by war governor Joseph E. Brown, decided to cooperate with the military authorities. That meant an alliance with the "carpetbagger" John Emory Bryant, the former Freedman's Bureau agent and proponent of civil rights for black Georgians. Several prominent ex-Confederates joined Brown, among them former mayors Foster Blodgett and Benjamin Conley.

At a rally for freedmen at Augusta's city hall, Bryant welcomed Brown and Blodgett to the Republican Party. The *Augusta Constitutionalist* took a cynical view of the event in a ditty: "How doth the busy bee improve each shining hour, See Bryant, Blodgett, and Brown unite for place and power." Place and power came quickly. Blodgett became military mayor of Augusta, and chairman of the statewide Republican Party. He ran the convention that drafted a new constitution conveying the vote to the freedmen. In the new state legislature, Blodgett used his influence to elect Governor Rufus Bullock and Lieutenant Governor Benjamin Conley. For a time, the "Augusta Ring" of Blodgett, Bullock, and Bryant dominated politics. However, most of the legislators were Democrats, and they returned Joshua Hill and D. V. M. Miller to the United States Senate over the candidacy of Foster Blodgett and Joseph E. Brown.[25]

After the ratification of the 14th Amendment, the Federal troops withdrew from the state. The General Assembly then expelled the black members of the legislature on the grounds that they had the right to vote, but not to hold office. The Ku Klux Klan threatened reprisals against blacks who voted in the 1868 elections. As a result

[24] Benson, "War Book," 699.
[25] *Augusta Chronicle*, 7 May 1867; Cashin, *Story of Augusta*, 134–35.

the troops returned, the expelled black members were reseated, and former Confederates expelled. Only then, in the January 1870 session did the Republicans gain political control of the state.

Before the return of military rule, Augusta held its mayoral election in 1868. Henry F. Russell stood against Foster Blodgett. The city celebrated the election of Russell with fireworks and bonfires. State Republican rule remained fragile and lasted only until the elections of 1870 returned Democrats to the majority. Rufus Bullock and Foster Blodgett fled the state. Bullock was later reconciled with most Georgians, but Blodgett remained a tragic figure, broken in reputation, fortune, and health.[26]

The emergence of "Lost Cause" rhetoric can be seen as a reaction against the radical Republican's second reconstruction of the South. Father Abram Ryan, the famous "poet priest of the Confederacy" preached and promoted the Lost Cause. Assigned to the Most Holy Trinity Church in Augusta from 1867 until 1870, he published a newspaper called the *Banner of the South* and wrote a column titled "The Lost Cause." His theatrical flourishes of oratory attracted crowds to his lectures. Five hundred flocked to hear him on 1 July 1867. He denounced the imposed military rule and declared passionately that "misery of oppression and desolation of tyranny is complete." More influential than his lectures or editorials were his poems, "The Sword of Lee" and "The Conquered Banner." The latter was put to doleful music and sung throughout the South. Generations of schoolboys, including this writer's generation, memorized the poems.[27]

Berry Benson admired "The Conquered Banner," copied it in his journal, and tried his own hand at a reconstruction poem: "Too

---

[26] *Augusta Chronicle*, 13 December 1868.

[27] Ibid., 1 July 1867; Cashin, *Story of Augusta*, 138–39; Special Collections, Reese Library, Augusta State University, Augusta GA, has an original set of *The Banner of the South*, 21 March 1868–13 March 1869. For more on Fr. Ryan, see David O'Connell, *Furl that Banner: The Life of Abram J. Ryan, Poet-Priest of the South* (Macon GA: Mercer University Press, 2006.

long have we pleaded for pity / Receiving instead your sneers / Too long have our hands remained idle / Too long have our mouths felt the bridle / Too long have our eyes filled with tears." The poem went on for several more stanzas. In writing the piece, Berry admitted that it sounded more bitter than he really felt.[28] Berry went to work as a clerk for the new mayor, Henry Russell.

Father Ryan, among the first to make the Lost Cause a crusade, soon found allies among the women of Augusta. In 1868 the ladies decided to atone for their recent diminished enthusiasm for the war effort. The Ladies Hospital and Relief Association changed the name of their organization to The Ladies Memorial Association and pledged to adorn the graves of the Confederate dead and to raise a monument to honor them. They collected $3,000 and contributed the money to a fund begun by St. James Methodist Church for the purpose of erecting a "cenotaph" or obelisk in the median of Greene Street in front of the church.[29]

The Lost Cause gained inspiration from the visit to Augusta of the embodiment of the Cause, General Robert E. Lee. Mayor J. V. H. Allen and other dignitaries met the hero at the depot and escorted him to the Planters Hotel. On 31 March, Lee graciously received long lines of admirers. Crowds gathered at the depot to see him off the next day. One twelve-year-old never forgot his sense of awe as he gazed up at the face of Lee. The boy grew up to be President Woodrow Wilson. Lee's death five months later plunged the city into mourning; the Cause was now truly lost. White and black Augustans wended their way in procession down black-draped Broad Street to the City Hall where Major Joseph Cumming read a resolution reciting Lee's virtues.[30] Berry Benson expressed in a private poem the sentiment that many felt:

---

[28] Benson, "War Book," 699–700.

[29] "Ladies Memorial Association Minute Book, 1872–1883," ms. 83-65-03, Special Collections, Reese Library, Augusta State University, Augusta GA.

[30] *Augusta Chronicle*, 13, 15, 16 October 1870.

Lee is dead!
Pass it down the lines—Lee is dead!
Dead, with all this weight of love upon him!
Dead, with the kisses of soldiers falling upon him,
And the kisses of soldiers' wives,
And of soldiers' daughters,
And the face of the whole world set toward him,
And bending o'er him.
Dead—oh, dead!—Pass it down the lines—Lee is dead![31]

Augustans, like many Southerners, began to reinvent the past to the point of glorification as they celebrated the Lost Cause. In time, memories of a city born and bred in commerce would be obscured by an imagined land of plantations peopled by genteel ladies and gentlemen. The sudden popularity of mock medieval jousts offers an example. Men dressed as "Bayard," "Lochinvar," and even "Lost Cause," competed for the hand of their sweetheart who would then be crowned "Queen of Love and Beauty" at the evening ball. Nineteen "knights" took part in the 1871 joust with 20,000 people watching. Each had to make cuts at a two posts with a saber, one on the right and one on the left. Then the contestant had to spear two rings at full gallop at a distance of 375 feet in twelve seconds. A writer in the *Constitutionalist* scoffed at the pretensions to nobility on the part of some who worked as fish peddlers and clerks. In a pre-tourney address, Colonel H. D. Capers told the knights not to worry about that. Even clerks could still "nobly illustrate a principle."[32] That happy phrase explains much about the oratory, monument building, and editorials of the day. Veterans of the war took it upon themselves to "nobly illustrate a principle" by their example.

---

[31] Collected poems of Berry and Jeanie Benson, Benson Family Papers, in private collection of Arthur Dupre, Newark NJ.
[32] Cashin, *Story of Augusta*, 145–46.

In 1872 Colonel George W. Rains, the genius who built and operated the great Confederate Powderworks, asked the city council of Augusta to preserve the lofty chimney of the works as a memorial. "Would it be asking too much from the City of Augusta that...at least the noble obelisk be allowed to remain forever as a fitting monument to the dead heroes who sleep on the unnumbered battlefields of the South?"[33] The Council agreed and the chimney still stands a century and a half later, the only extant structure built by the Confederate States of America.

If the Powderworks chimney was Augusta's first war memorial, the St. James cenotaph was second. Major Joseph B. Cumming delivered a stirring address at the dedication on 31 December 1873.[34] With the completion of that work, the Ladies Memorial Association concentrated on an even larger monument, eventually raising the impressive sum of $20,934 by holding bazaars, raffles, balls, and lectures. Interestingly, at their 14 October 1874 meeting, the association received an offer from the Colored Cotton States Minstrels to put on a benefit performance. The Ladies gladly accepted and the show proved a great success.[35]

The Ladies deferred to tradition and did their business work through committees of men who reported back to a Ladies meeting. Men went off to inspect marble factories. Men advertised for designs. Men conducted a referendum to determine the location of the monument. The Ladies had originally intended to erect the monument in the city cemetery, but the men wanted it in a more public place. They conducted a public vote and the preferred site was on Broad Street, the city's main thoroughfare, near McIntosh (7th) Street. The Ladies accepted that advice. The design committee recommended the model submitted by the firm of Van Gunden and Young of Philadelphia, showing three generals around the base and

---

[33] *Augusta Chronicle*, 5 November 1872.
[34] *Augusta Chronicle*, 1 January 1874.
[35] "Ladies Memorial Association Minute Book."

an anonymous enlisted man on top. Local marble worker Theodore Markwalter won the contract to build the monument.[36]

On 1 July 1875 the public saw the model for the first time. The statues standing on the base of the monument represented Lee for the Confederacy, Stonewall Jackson for Virginia, Thomas R. R. Cobb for Georgia, and native son W. H. T. Walker for Augusta. The place of honor atop the shaft held the statue of the enlisted soldier. The design committee sent photographs of the four generals to the sculptors in Italy. The committee, composed of three of the city's most distinguished citizens, Colonel George W. Rains, Major Joseph B. Cumming, and Dr. Lewis D. Ford, asked Berry Benson to pose for the statue of the enlisted man. The fact that Berry still owned his unsurrendered rifle argued in his behalf, but he would never had been chosen out of the hundreds of veterans in the city unless his courage and character were beyond reproach. It would not do to have a lesser man pose for the apotheosis of southern manhood.[37]

The local newspaper reported, "A photograph of Mr. Berry G. Benson, a gallant Confederate soldier who has preserved his suit of grey was sent on to Italy as a model for the statue." When the statue arrived, and Markwalter's workers hoisted it to its place, a reporter for the *St. Louis Christian Advocate* wrote this description, "On the top stands a figure of a Confederate private, with his rifle, knapsack, canteen, slouch cap, and baggy pants, all too familiar to us. The figure was taken from a young Confederate soldier in Augusta, a private, Mr. Berry Benson."[38] Berry might have winced at being reduced to the rank of private, but he was deeply touched by the implicit recognition of his service as a soldier. He later wrote to the newspaper, "I am certainly proud, naturally and properly proud—of

---

[36] Ibid; *Augusta Chronicle*, 10, 20 December 1874 and 24 April 1875.
[37] "Ladies Memorial Association Minute Book."
[38] *Augusta Chronicle*, 10 July 1878.

having been chosen to represent the private Confederate soldier whose figure was to crown the monument."[39]

The Elmira, New York, *Daily Advertiser* of 8 August 1878, carried an article titled, "A Confederate Monument with a Local Reminiscence." The article described the "splendid monument" being erected in Augusta. It noted that an image of "Mr. Berry G. Benson, a gallant Confederate soldier" was used to carve the crowning statue. It also explained the local significance: "Mr. Benson was a prisoner at Elmira during the war, and was among the number who successfully tunneled his way out of the prison camp during the Fall of 1864, and made good his escape. He is a man of considerable intelligence and a prominent citizen of Augusta."[40] Elmira seemed to claim Berry as a local personage of whom the city was proud.

The Columbia, South Carolina, *Register* cited the Elmira article and elaborated upon it, "Nearly every soldier in Jackson's Corps, Hill's Division, and especially of McGowan's Brigade, knew Sergt. B. G. Benson.... Mr. Benson was the most daring and successful scout of the Army of Northern Virginia and a true account of his extraordinary exploits would make a brilliant page in Southern history."[41] Berry's fame increased in proportion to the popularity of the Lost Cause; both achieved the status of legend.

The accolade that must have meant most to Berry was a brief letter from an Elmira prison-mate and fellow escapee, John Fox Maull. Berry felt closest to his family, his Elmira buddies, Company H, 1st South Carolina Volunteers, and McGowan's Brigade in that order. On 13 June 1877, Maull wrote Berry, "Accept my congratulations upon the choice of the Ladies of Augusta. I know

---

[39] Transcription of undated newspaper article, "War Book," p. 706; "Card from Berry Benson," *Augusta Chronicle*, 19 March 1879.

[40] Cited in Benson, "War Book," 706.

[41] *Augusta Morning News*, 19 April 1878; Benson, "War Book," 707.

that they could not have a truer or nobler son of the South than yourself."[42]

As the interest and excitement regarding the completion of the monument mounted, the Confederate veterans, as if pleased and flattered with the attention they had not received at the end of the war, formed an association. On 4 May 1878, the Confederate Survivors' Association met in the hall of the Richmond Hussars. General Goode Bryan occupied the chair, and Colonel Charles C. Jones, Jr., read a prepared constitution. The chairman asked all those wishing to join to step forward. Seventy-nine, probably everyone in the hall, responded. General Bryan called for elections. The men chose General Clement A. Evans as their president, Colonel Jones, General Marcellus Stovall, and Captain P. E. Eve as vice-presidents. They elected Captain George P. Butler as treasurer and Berry Benson as secretary, the only non-commissioned officer to be honored by this rank-conscious group. In a notice to the local newspapers, Berry invited other veterans to join the organization. Berry placed his treasured rifle, his haversack, and his canteen—the same he had worn as a model for the statue—in the hall used by the survivors. In return, General Evans gave Berry a part of the Confederate flag that flew over Fort Sumter.[43]

General Evans, with the immense collective prestige of the Confederate Survivors' Association behind him, requested the Ladies Memorial Association to delay the dedication of the monument until 26 April 1879, the next Confederate Memorial Day. The Ladies politely refused; they preferred to dedicate the memorial as soon as it was finished and set the dedication for 31 October 1878. There followed a "public meeting of the military" on 9 October that formally requested the postponement of the dedication. The Ladies replied that the dedication would take place on 31 October. The

---

[42] Berry Benson Papers, ms. 2636, Southern Historical Collection, University of North Carolina, Chapel Hill.

[43] *Augusta Chronicle*, 4, 10 May 1878.

Ladies might be celebrating the heroism of their men, but that did not mean they had to defer to them.[44]

Stores closed and 10,000 people jammed into Broad Street—as near to the great monument as they could—by noon of 31 October. Governor Alfred Colquitt arrived on schedule at the depot, and the Washington Artillery escorted him to Broad Street where the parade of sixteen carriages and hundreds of veterans waited in line. Mrs. Thomas J. Jackson, Stonewall's widow, rode with the governor as guest of honor. From a platform in front of the monument General Clement Evans, president of the Confederate Survivors Organization, delivered the opening prayer. Colonel Charles C. Jones, Jr., delivered the address. Jones, a master of florid oratory, recited the virtues of the great generals whose images graced the lower monument. He saved his choicest encomiums for the Confederate enlisted man:

> And now, above Brigadier General, Major General, Lieutenant General and full General, yes, upon the very summit of this imposing cenotaph, see the manly form of the private soldier of the Confederate army, the eloquent embodiment of the spirit and prowess alike of the county and state, and of all the sleeping hosts who, in the crusade for freedom, gave their lives to country. With a pathos entirely its own does this statue appeal to our hearts and rivet our attention, for who is there in this vast concourse who does not recognize in this calm marble the symbol of some father, son, husband, brother, friend....[45]

Many of the listeners no doubt recognized Berry Benson in both Jones's description and in the sculpture itself.

A stanza from a tribute to Lee written by Philip Stanhope Worsley absolved the Confederacy from any stigma of blame for the

---

[44] "Ladies Memorial Association Minute Book."
[45] *Augusta Chronicle*, 1 November 1878.

war. Carved into stone on the face of the monument, the words defined the Lost Cause: "No nation rose so white and fair, none fell so pure of crime."[46]

---

[46] Cashin, *Story of Augusta*, 113.

CHAPTER 14

The Promise of the New South

*"I was a mighty good Confederate and I am just as good
a Union man now."*

If Berry Benson became a symbol of the imagined world of the Lost
Cause by virtue of his image atop the Confederate Monument, he
could not live, work, and raise a family in that world.
Unreconstructed rebels like Robert Toombs might grouse about the
new order of things and refuse to compromise with corporations, but
most Southerners, and definitely most Augustans, were too pragmatic
for that. Patrick Walsh, editor of the *Augusta Chronicle*, had an
answer for Toombs. The new generation would not be true to their
ancestry, he argued, if they did not show the strength and spirit to
meet challenges under new conditions.[1] They could venerate the Old
South while striding manfully into the New South. The distinction
caused some later generations of Georgians to believe that the Old
South scorned money-making, while the New South was overly
concerned about it. Actually, money-making had always been a
favorite occupation of Augustans, and probably most Georgians. In
fact, the leaders of society before the war were the same after the war,
and they had always been businessmen and women.

Colonel George W. Rains, the genius of the Confederate
Powderworks, first suggested enlarging the Augusta Canal as early as
1868, in order to provide water power for larger factories. Nothing
could be done until after the turmoil of military occupation. It fell to
Charles Estes, elected mayor in 1870, to undertake the daunting task.
Estes had worked as an engineer on the Erie Canal before coming to

---

[1] *Augusta Chronicle*, 28 April 1889.

Augusta. He hired another Erie engineer, Charles Olmstead, to give
an estimate of the cost. Olmstead conceived a plan that allowed the
continued use of the canal while widening was going on, and
estimated a cost of only $371,610. (Before it was finished in 1875 it
had cost three times that amount.) Estes pushed through the
financing; the city bought the confiscated Confederate Powderworks
property from the federal government, and the work on canal
enlargement began.[2]

Interesting to this narrative is that the work included clearing
the bed of Rae's Creek to form a lake (later called Lake Olmstead)
that would feed into the canal. Berry Benson worked at clearing the
creek bed. It was one of many ways he would be caught up in the
progressive New South. Even before the completion of the
enlargement in 1875, new factories grew up. The Russell and
Simmons opened on 1 January 1874. Berry's commanding officer in
the Savannah campaign, Major George T. Jackson, built the
enormous Enterprise Mill in 1876. The crown jewel of factories, the
crenellated Sibley Mill, began operations in 1881, followed by its
neighbor the John P. King Mill in 1884. The depressed cotton prices
caused thousands of farm families to flee the countryside to the city
and settle in "mill villages," enclaves within the city.[3]

The business of the New South revolved around cotton.
Country stores gave credit to farmers in return for payment in
cotton. Georgia's "Lien Law" required the loan to be paid in cotton
and no other crop. Wagons brought the cotton to gins to be baled.
Farmers stored their cotton in warehouses owned by the larger

---

[2] Edward J. Cashin, *The Story of Augusta* (Augusta GA: Richmond County Board
of Education, 1980) 149; *Augusta Chronicle*, 2 November 1875.

[3] Berry Benson, Autobiographical Sketch, Berry and Charles Benson Papers, ms.
83-37, Special Collections, Reese Library, Augusta State University, Augusta GA;
henceforth cited as Benson, Autobiographical Sketch. The enlargement of the canal
and the rise of factories is treated in Edward J. Cashin, *The Brightest Arm of the
Savannah: The Augusta Canal, 1845–2000* (Augusta GA: Augusta Canal Authority,
2002) chapters 8 and 9.

merchants. Brokers bought the cotton with loans from banks, classified it according to value, and sold it to the mills. The workers who had grown cotton, now worked as "hands" at the looms and spindles, under an "overseer." Workers deferred to the paternalistic president of the mill. The system provided a New South version of the Old South plantation.

Berry Benson adapted easily to this world of cotton. After the abbreviated stints at teaching and clerking for Mayor Gardiner, Berry worked for Thomas Metcalf—one of the richest, if not the richest man in Augusta. Berry traveled to Georgia's growing southwest towns of Albany and Americus, buying cotton for Metcalf. Then Mayor Henry Russell hired him to work for his cotton firm. Berry started with Russell in October 1866 for a hundred dollars a month. He learned the art of "classing" cotton, distinguishing the length of fiber and the quality of the sample. A skilled classer could pull a tuft of cotton from a bale, in a second stretch the fiber and ascertain whether it was an inch, an inch and a thirty-second, or an inch and a sixteenth. Profits depended upon a sixteenth of an inch. Berry learned how to determine the grade and the vocabulary to describe it: good middling, strict middling, middling, strict low middling, low middling, strict good ordinary, or ordinary. There were a bewildering twenty-five possible "color" grades and eight "leaf" grades. The mills used different grades depending upon the type of textile product and paid a set price to the broker, who repaid the bank. Cotton merchants had to be clairvoyants to estimate the future price of cotton because they contracted to buy it before they sold it.[4]

Berry worked hard for Henry Russell, serving his apprenticeship in the cotton business. His salary increased from $1200 the first year to $2,500 in 1869. With a steady job and an increasing salary, he could marry the love of his life, Jeanie Oliver. The Olivers attended First Christian Church in a building erected by Emily Tubman, and

---

[4] Benson, Autobiographical Sketch; Barry Whitney, a veteran of the cotton business, explained the complexities of cotton grading to me.

Berry married Jeanie in that church on 6 February 1868, three days before his twenty-fifth birthday. Jeanie was twenty-eight. The pastor of the church, Reverend James S. Lamar, performed the wedding ceremony. Jeanie prized a portrait of the minister given her as a wedding present by Blackwood, and hung it in her bedroom. Jeanie had long known Reverend Lamar's nine-year-old son, Joseph, and Berry came to know and like him as well. The boy, Joseph R. Lamar, would become in time an associate justice of the United States Supreme Court.[5]

Berry and Jeanie were kindred spirits sharing the same interests—good literature, poetry, music, the beauty of the outdoors. Both had sensitive souls; Berry's sensitivity embraced life, Jeanie's worried about it. Berry's love of adventure inclined him to travel frequently; Jeanie seemed content to remain at home and mother her growing family. While Berry reflected upon his war years as a glorious drama, Jeanie remembered them as tragic. Berry coped with the federal occupation; Jeanie expressed her fears in an 1866 New Year's poem: "What hours of mingled hope and fear / Lie hidden in thy folded days? / My spirit looks with anxious gaze / Unto thy future O New Year!" She loved Berry and trusted him implicitly. Yet, in her poems a note of melancholy sounded now and again. The early deaths of her parents and her sister greatly affected her. Berry and she spent evenings writing poetry and reading their work to each other. A glimpse at them affords all the insight an outsider needs into their personal relationship. Jeanie wrote a piece titled "A Qui?": "At the clasp of thy hand, with an exquisite start / How the pulses of memory quiver! / All the hope of my life, all the love of my heart / Sweep back with the rush of the river." Berry replied in a poem of the same title:

---

[5] Benson, Autobiographical Sketch; Susan Williams Benson, ed., *Berry Benson's Civil War Book: Memoirs of a Confederate Scout and Sharpshooter* (Athens: University of Georgia Press, 1962) x.

Love amidst the crowd of life's memories,
Past and gone so long, yet ever freshly remembered,
Remembered fresher even than the deeds of yesterday's battle,
Or mother's parting kiss, or father's welcome home,
Or the first triumph at school, or war's first victory,
Fresher and stronger than remembrance of defeat
And of flight and of terrible pursuit,—
Than memory of sickness unto death, or a dear friend's illness;
Or the sight of his dead face in the coffin;
Fresher and stronger than any memory,
Love amidst the crowd of all life's memories,
And above them,
Today, sweetheart, I remember the one kiss you gave me.[6]

Berry loved to listen to Jeanie play the piano. On occasion, while transcribing his war diary, he had to pause, noting in his journal "Jeanie Oliver is playing the Natalie Waltz." And, "Now it's the Henrietta Waltz and I must stop again."[7]

The family grew during the next decade: Ida Jane, Arthur, Pauline, Olive, Charles, and Dorothy Lewis—all born between 1868 and 1879. In 1873 Berry decided that he had learned enough about the cotton business to leave Henry Russell's firm and strike out on his own. He formed a partnership with his friend Robert "Hoody" Hitt, leased an office, and hung out the new shingle, "Benson and Hitt." He celebrated his success as a businessman by buying a house

---

[6] Collected poems of Berry and Jeanie Benson, Benson Family Papers, in private collection of Arthur Dupre, Newark NJ.

[7] Berry Benson, "The War Book, Reminiscences of Berry Greenwood Benson, CSA," (Typescript prepared by Charles G. Benson, Ida Jane ["Jeanie"] Benson, and Olive Benson), Special Collections, Reese Library, Augusta State University, Augusta GA; hereafter cited as "War Book"), 369. A copy of the typescript is also held by the Southern Historical Collection at the University of North Carolina, Chapel Hill, in its Berry Benson Papers, ms. 2636. The original manuscript diary (ms. 326) is located in the Hargrett Rare Book & Manuscript Library at the University of Georgia in Athens.

on Bay Street and renting a summer residence in Summerville on the sand hills west of Augusta.[8]

Berry described his house at 318 Bay Street as an eight-room frame building, with a vegetable garden, flower garden, and grape arbor. The house faced the river, with an unobstructed view of the Carolina hills. Berry, a good carpenter, built a workshop in the back yard, and later a brick "conservatory" for his children to practice their music lessons.[9]

The cotton business required constant travel to make contacts with sellers and buyers. In 1877 he went to Waco, Texas. He saw clearly that the future of cotton business lay in the Texas fields, as the older cotton bottoms in the southeast burned out. Perhaps he would relocate his family to Texas. His commitment to Hoody Hitt kept him in Augusta until 1880 when Hitt moved to Alabama. Now Berry was able to seek his own fortune wherever it might lie.[10]

The investigation of business prospects in New York led to a bizarre adventure. His insatiable wanderlust got the better of him. He learned that a steamer named *The City of Alexandria* was scheduled to leave New York for Mexico on the following day. He did not have enough ready cash to pay passenger rates, but convinced the purser that he could help with the accounts. He wrote a narrative of his adventure intended for publication, titled "Afloat and Afoot," giving the purser the name "Harry Alexander." The man's real name was Emile DesClarets, and he wrote a glowing reference for Berry after the voyage, attesting to the fact that Berry had been "of great assistance in writing, discharging freight, and a willingness to do any other duty."[11]

---

[8] Benson, Autobiographical Sketch.
[9] *Augusta Chronicle*, 18 September 1898.
[10] Benson, Autobiographical Sketch.
[11] Emile DesClarets to Berry Benson, 3 April 1880, Benson Family Papers, in private collection of Arthur Dupre, Newark NJ.

Berry's story reads like a travelogue including his impressions of Havana and Vera Cruz, and of his long walk from Vera Cruz to Mexico City.[12] He liked to write home at every town that had a post office. In the village of Huatusco he found the post office closed and looked in vain for a foreigner who spoke any of his languages, English, French, or even German. He finally found the postmaster in a gambling house, and got his stamps. When he later returned to Augusta, a friend told him that his sister lived in Huatusco and would have been glad to welcome Berry.[13]

Though New York offered possibilities, Berry decided to move to Texas. A portion of a journal provides insight into family life at that time. Ida Jane, fourteen years of age in 1882, wrote most of the entries; Jeanie Oliver added a few notes, as did Berry and twelve-year-old Arthur. There are details of houseguests, records of the books Jeanie read to the children, and outside activities such as climbing Shultz Hill for a view of Augusta and walks to Brook's Pond. On 18 October 1882 Jeanie Oliver described taking the children, including three-year-old Dorothy Lewis, on "our usual long walk" across the Fifth Street Bridge into Hamburg. She gathered flowers and put them in the mantelpiece vase that Berry had given her on their first Christmas.

Berry, still planning the move to Texas, and contemplating his new role as farmer, wrote copious notes about agriculture and livestock in the journal. Blackwood and his family intended to accompany Berry to Texas. So did Jeanie Oliver's brother, Henry, who lived in Berzilia, Georgia, K. A. McKinnie of Troy, Alabama, and S. G. Rook of Laurens, South Carolina. Obviously, Berry's

---

[12] Berry's journal is in the Benson Papers, ms. 2636, Southern Historical Collection, University of North Carolina, Chapel Hill. Henceforth, cited as Benson Papers, Chapel Hill.

[13] Berry Benson to Henry D. Whitfield, 22 February 1913, Benson Family Papers, in private collection of Arthur Dupre, Newark NJ.

enthusiasm for the venture had affected them all; they were all bound for Texas.[14]

Skipping ahead to June 1883, as the move to Texas neared, the family journal continued to record the minutiae that formed the warp and woof of life. In passing, they mentioned a cook named Margaret. White Southern housewives considered it essential to have the help of black cooks. Berry cultivated a garden and had become interested in the insects that populated the garden, examining them with a magnifying glass. No one seemed overly worried about the big move.

Ida inherited her parents' facility in writing; she wrote about sewing, reading, visiting, shopping, and her piano lessons. She went to visit friends in Hephzibah, but got homesick and returned. Jeanie Oliver entered a note that Charlie and Lewis were banging on tin pans, "to the disgust of the neighbors, no doubt." She watched cheerful wrens building a nest on the piazza post, "Success to them!"

On 31 July 1883, excitement showed in Ida's note that Papa had come home unexpectedly. "He is going to take us out to Texas as soon as possible. He brought us candy and grapes." Preparations for the big trip involved packing six large dry goods boxes with books (the Bensons could not do without books), and another box with pictures. They packed up their furniture for shipment by rail, including Jeanie's piano. Many friends, sorry to see them go, came to the depot to say goodbye the morning of 17 August 1883 as they left on the 7:40 train. The train stopped at Belair where Blackwood's family boarded. They ate their packed lunch on the train. On the way Ida marveled at the sight of Stone Mountain, "the only mountain I ever saw."

They changed cars in Montgomery, Alabama, at 9:00 P.M. Ida remarked that the depot was lighted with electric lights, a recent marvel. Near Mobile the bridge had washed out, so they had to take a ferry across the Alabama River and board another train on the far

---

[14] Berry Benson to J. N. Victor, 16 February 1883, Benson Papers, Chapel Hill.

side. In Mobile Ida heard French spoken for the first time. During the next day the train followed the coast with beautiful views of the Gulf of Mexico. They missed their connections and had to spend the night in New Orleans. Berry made it fun. He divided the families into two parties. He took the first group on a tour of the French Market, then for a ride on the trolley, and did the same for the second group.

The next day a ferry carried their train across the Mississippi River. They arrived without incident in Austin, Texas. Berry and Blackwood chartered conveyances to take their baggage to a rental house. When their furniture arrived, they rented a large farmhouse. Berry bought two horses and a wagon and began building a house on his own property. By November they moved into the new house. Though the house was unfinished, they invited neighbors over for socials. Ida noted that she made friends in the neighborhood and that she went to as many dances as she could, "it didn't take me long to learn the steps." Berry continued to work on the house all through the winter. By March 1884, Ida reported that "now it is fixed up pretty comfortably." Berry then left for an eight-week trip to Mexico with a business friend. They went by steamer to Havana, then Vera Cruz. They traveled by coach to Mexico City, and returned overland to El Paso, San Antonio, and Austin.

Jeanie Oliver continued the same emphasis on reading and music with her children. Ida took the initiative of starting a reading club with other young people. They enlivened the readings by singing to Ida's piano playing. The soirees broke up around midnight. The Bensons weren't the first Georgians to move to Texas and transplant their customs and traditions. Late suppers and musical evenings were not unusual. The family journal does not hint of any dissatisfaction with their Texas sojourn, but late in 1885 they moved back to Augusta. Very likely Berry had decided not to follow a farmer's life. Blackwood's family stayed in Texas, and Blackwood sold Berry's property. Augusta offered better prospects for business, and more importantly, it was home. Fortunately, they still owned the large frame house on Bay Street.[15]

Charles Benson, age seven when the family moved back to Augusta, later wrote reminiscences about the Augusta of his boyhood and drew a map of the neighborhood. He knew everybody on his block and also the adjoining blocks. On the map he drew the "old field" east of the house where they played ball, along the side of their property the row of sycamores they liked to climb, the pomegranate tree with disappointing fruit. In the days before rigid segregation, black families lived in their neighborhood and in most Augusta neighborhoods. The Ladevezes, just behind them on Reynolds Street, owned an exclusive art and music store in the heart of town that Jeanne and Olive patronized.[16]

Berry enjoyed the tedious business of accounting, and soon found enough demand for his services in the local mills to earn a good salary. He became an accountant and an auditor instead of a cotton broker. From the "front end" of the cotton business, the supply side, he moved to the "back end," the totaling of receipts. For recreation, he continued his hikes in the countryside with his younger children, and for intellectual variety he worked on his war journal, wrote poems, and experimented with a new form of composition, short moral lessons he called "Outlines."[17] He had great hopes for his war journal.

While in Texas he had sounded out the Century Publishing Company, explaining who he was, and what his journal was about: "I was a mighty good Confederate and I am just as good a Union man now. I haven't any apologies to make, but think now the war ended

---

[15] Benson Family Journal, ms. 83-37, Special Collections, Reece Library, Augusta State University, Augusta GA.

[16] Charles Benson, "Ancient Days in Augusta," in Berry and Charles Benson Papers, ms. 83-37, Special Collections, Reese Library, Augusta State University, Augusta GA.

[17] Arthur Dupre has posted Berry Benson's "Outlines" at http://www.tcnj.edu/~dupre/benson.htm.

the best way for the South." He added, "Since the war a family has grown up about my knees and they love to hear me talk about the war." He suggested that they might break down the journal into chapters for their magazine, under the title "Rifle, Haversack, and Canteen," the three souvenirs he brought home from the war. Although Century later published several of Berry's articles, they declined to have anything to do with the war journal.[18]

Berry also inquired of the prestigious firm of Houghton, Mifflin, and Company. The company spokesperson answered less than tactfully that they did not care much for Southern writers who had a "tendency...to embroider their work with high-flown sentiment," as opposed to the "harder-hearted public taste in the North." With that slight encouragement, they agreed to look at the manuscript.[19] Nothing came of that either. Actually, Berry's prose was better suited to twentieth-century readers than those of the Victorian era. He wrote simply and cleanly, with sentiment, but without bombast or artificiality. An authority on the subject of good writing has recently declared unequivocally, "Berry Benson was a superb writer."[20] An abbreviated version of his journal, edited by his daughter-in-law Susan Williams Benson and published by the University of Georgia Press in 1962 under the title *Berry Benson's Civil War Book*, was well received.

Ironically, Blackwood succeeded where Berry did not by putting his war reminiscences into a novel entitled *Who Goes There? The Story of a Spy in the Civil War*. He invented a Union soldier named Jones Berwick who lost his memory in a battle and assumed the identity of a Confederate soldier in Gregg's Brigade, 1st South Carolina

---

[18] Berry Benson to Century Publishing Company, 15 February 1883, Benson Papers, Chapel Hill.

[19] Houghton, Mifflin, and Company to Berry Benson, 21 June 1883, Benson Papers, Chapel Hill.

[20] Jim Garvey, "Berry Benson in Peacetime," *Augusta Richmond County History* 33/1 (Spring 2002): 32. Dr. Garvey is professor of literature at Augusta State University.

Volunteers, Company H. The names and events came straight out of Blackwood's diary: the "deaf as a post" General Gregg; Colonel D. H. "Old Headquarters" Hamilton; the gallant Captain William Haskell; Captains Barnwell and Shooter; Sergeant Mackay; Privates Bail, Bellot, and Box; they all appear in their actual roles. Blackwood's penchant for accuracy enables the reader to infer Blackwood's opinions from the conversations in the novel. He agrees with Captain Haskell who is quoted as saying that the South's only hope of European support was to initiate a policy of gradual emancipation. "Our system does not give enough opportunity for a slave to develop and to make a future for himself," said Haskell.[21] The novel's literary device requires the fictitious Jones Berwick to recover his memory and reveal Confederate plans.

Though Blackwood's prose would seem melodramatic to modern readers, the critics of his day raved about it. The Chicago *Evening Post* exclaimed, "Unquestionably this production ranks with the very best stories that have been written about the great rebellion." The *Springfield Republican* called it "Beyond question the best story of the Civil War that has appeared in recent years." The *New York Tribune* described it as "touched especially with that air of reality which one gets from the recitals of an eye witness as from nothing else." The reason for the "air of reality," of course, is that Blackwood simply related his own experiences.[22]

Berry might have felt slighted that his own factual account of the war had been rejected and Blackwood's romanticized version had drawn such praise. Instead, he was delighted. He congratulated Blackwood, "To say that I am proud of your performance and of you is to speak very mildly." Blackwood confided that he had completed the draft of a second novel, *A Friend with the Countersign*, with a

---

[21] Blackwood K. Benson, *Who Goes There? The Story of a Spy in the Civil War* (New York: Macmillan, 1900) 402.
[22] The rave reviews of *Who Goes There?* are found in the appendix of B. K.'s novel *Old Squire* (New York: Macmillan, 1908).

similar theme. He hoped that veterans of the Union army would not discover that the author was an ex-Confederate, but Berry told him not to worry. Blackwood's third Civil War novel, *Old Squire*, featured a black servant of a Confederate soldier. Neither of the latter books achieved the success of the first.[23]

The *Augusta Chronicle* readily published Berry's short accounts of battles and incidents of the war. *Century Magazine* accepted several of his pithy moral lessons called "outlines," short pieces that cause the reader to stop and think, for example: "A man played at make believe. He drew a circle upon the ground and said: This is a magic circle: everything inside it is a miracle. He did not know that everything outside of it is a miracle also." The outlines reveal Berry's love of nature and the depth of his sensitivity: "A child brought me a pebble, round and smooth and white. What a wonderful thing! He said. Wonderful? I said. There are a millions and millions of things like that. Then, said he, There are millions and millions of wonderful things." Though not a churchgoer, Berry displayed a deeply spiritual quality: "God came to my door and begged. I railed at him, bidding him go and work." And another: "I heard a man say: God is great, infinitely great: let me show you what He is like. And he began to paint. And he painted outlines and limitations to represent Infinity. He painted with words." Berry realized that he was painting profound truths in mere outlines. He did not share the views of the biblical fundamentalists: "I came with God to a place where the heathen were. And they bowed themselves down to images of wood and stone, and worshiped them. And I looked to see God slay them in wrath. And he smote them not, but brought rain upon their fields and bounteous crops. And I said to God, Why hast thou not slain these wicked men? But God said, These are not wicked, they are searching after Me. They will find Me." Berry's great-grandson

---

[23] Berry Benson to B. K. Benson, 17 November 1900; B. K. to Berry, 22, 27 November 1900, 28 October 1902, Benson Papers, Chapel Hill..

Arthur Dupre has collected the complete set of "outlines" and posted them on the internet, under the heading "Berry Benson."

Some of Jeanie Oliver's poems were published in the New Orleans *Times Democrat*, and other newspapers.

Ida Jane's forte lay in her musical ability. After returning to Augusta from Texas, she preferred to be called Jeanie. She asked her father for a violin, and he advertised for one in the local newspaper. "When I first began to study, the violin was a very common one and my ear was very sensitive to bad tones—they made me shudder," she recalled. She studied for four years under Professor John Wiegand of Augusta. Then she read about Maud Powell and nothing would do but to go to New York and meet the artist. Maud was a child prodigy with the violin. She challenged the male-dominated world of professional musicians. In 1885 at the age of eighteen, she walked uninvited into the rehearsal hall of the New York Philharmonic and boldly asked for an audition from Theodore Thomas, America's premier conductor. She played and he hired her on the spot.

Thomas arranged for Maud to perform a solo at the Chicago World Exposition in 1893 and in that year she delivered a paper to the Women's Musical Congress in which she urged young women to make the violin a career. The challenge presented a formidable barrier to beginners like Jeanie Benson. There were only five professional orchestras in the United States, and solo concerts at the time were limited to men. Nevertheless, Maud Powell's example had lighted a fire in Jeanie's ambition. She felt she had to go to New York and study with Maud Powell. She remembered, "I begged for two years before I was allowed to go north, and was a happy girl the day Papa gave his consent." Jeanie called upon the virtuoso the day after arriving in New York.

Maud Powell took an immediate liking to Jeanie, told her she had "absolute pitch" and loaned her one of her violins; Jeanie called it "a splendid fiddle." Powell introduced Jeanie to the right people, one of whom was Richard Arnold, concert master of the New York

Philharmonic. Arnold agreed to coach Jeanie. As she became more proficient, a dealer gave her the use of a rare "Lorenzo Guadagnini" violin that she later bought. She studied for two years under the guidance of Leopold Lichtenberg, whom she called "the greatest genius the violin world has ever known." At last in 1898 Jeanie began her professional career with the New York Metropolitan Concert Company, a touring quintet.[24]

One by one, the other children found their niches in life. Arthur's talent lay in drawing. At the age of twelve he did some artwork for a printer. However, he decided that he could not make a living in art, so became a teller at the Georgia Railroad Bank. Olive, the quiet sister, claimed the family piano, became proficient at it, and took in students. She attracted the attention of the *Augusta Chronicle* on 16 December 1897 when she returned from New York (where she had been studying piano for the previous three months) to spend the holidays with her parents. Frances Thompson, niece of the Benson sisters, remembers that Olive had several suitors, but that in every case, they were attracted to the more dynamic Jeanie (or the more dynamic Jeanie attracted them).[25]

Pauline's frail health kept her at home, and her love of books led her to become a librarian. Charlie, having heard war stories from Berry all his life, finished college, joined the army during the Spanish-American War, and saw service in the Philippines. Lewis, the youngest, disappointed her parents by eloping at the age of sixteen with a man named Carlos Williams and setting up housekeeping in Washington, DC. The couple had five children—Edith, Margaret, Kate, Berry, and Jeanie—then Carlos Williams abandoned them. Lewis and her children became Berry's responsibility.[26]

---

[24] *Augusta Chronicle*, 18 September 1898. Karen A. Shaffer's sketch, "Maud Powell, A Pioneer's Legacy," may be found at http://www.maudpowell.org/pages/MPpioneer.htm.

[25] *Augusta Chronicle*, 16 December 1917.

[26] Benson Family Papers, in private collection of Frances Thompson, Starkville MS.

In 1897 Berry's familiarity with numbers paid off, literally. After several years of auditing books and catching mistakes, he invented a fool-proof way of detecting errors. According to a newspaper reporter, "It was not worked out slowly step by step, but flashed upon him full grown in the fraction of a second." He obtained the endorsement of E. H. Beach, editor of the accountant's journal, *The Bookkeeper*, and patented his idea under the title of "Benson's Automatic Monitor: The Zero System of Detecting and Correcting Errors." He charged a hundred dollars for a copy of his pamphlet explaining the system. The *Augusta Chronicle* heralded the discovery as a "Mathematical Marvel" and reported that within the year hundreds of letters of commendation had been received from all over the country and that Berry had to hire assistants to supply the demand for the booklet of instructions. Berry had clients in every state of the Union and parts of Canada.[27]

The increased income helped pay for Jeanie's music career, for piano lessons for Olive, and for Lewis and her children. Berry went to Washington, DC, in February 1900, partly to open an office for the sale of his Zero System, and partly to provide a home for Lewis and her family. He bought a house at 341 Bryant Street, and invited Jeanie and Olive to live there, as well as the Williamses.[28]

Earlier, Berry delayed his departure for Washington because of the illness of Jeanie Oliver. Jeanie, suffering from what Berry believed was typhoid fever, insisted on coming home from the hospital and urged Berry to go on to Washington. The children needed him, and Arthur and Pauline would take care of her. Berry's father, Mat, also still lived at their house on 318 Bay Street. Berry stopped in Asheville

---

[27] *Augusta Chronicle*, 8 January, 9 September, 9 October 1899; Berry Benson, *Benson's Automatic Monitor: Zero System of Detecting and Arresting Errors* (Augusta GA: *Augusta Chronicle* Job Printing Company, 1897). A copy is held by the Library of Congress.

[28] Benson Family Papers, in private collection of Frances Thompson, Starkville MS.

to visit a client on 16 February 1900, then continued on to Washington. While setting up an office and looking for a house, he worried about Jeanie. On 21 March he wrote, "Dear Sweetheart," urging Jeanie to "lie down or get up, sit still, or walk about, read or write, or do nothing." He was sending her some books that he bought at Brentanos. "I love you too much not to feel anxious.... With this kiss for a last word, I am with a heart full of love, Your Husband." He enclosed a flower to serve as a kiss.[29]

By return mail, he received a letter from Arthur; Jeanie was failing. "Last night I opened the window and let her see the boat go by, and she enjoyed it as much as a circus. Then I read to her out of the life of General Lee, and she fell asleep."[30] Unfortunately, she grew weaker. A newspaper account stated that she suffered from "nervous prostration" aggravated by "acute indigestion." Berry hurried back from Washington to be with her, accompanied by Jeanie and Lewis. Jeanie Oliver died on 22 April 1900 at the age of sixty. She was buried the next day from ʾFirst Christian Church. Reverend James S. Lamar, who had witnessed her marriage, presided at her funeral.

A generous obituary in the *Augusta Chronicle* praised her for her life of gentleness and self-sacrifice, and for her "cultural, artistic, and poetic" qualities. She was "the idolized center of the affectionate group" whose death "breaks a family circle of the closest intimacy, love, and confidence."[31]

---

[29] Berry Benson to Jeanie Benson, 21 March 1900, Benson Family Papers, in private collection of Frances Thompson, Starkville MS. When I opened the faded and fragile letter, a dried flower fell out.

[30] Arthur Benson to Berry Benson, 23 March 1900, Benson Family Papers, in private collection of Arthur Dupre, Newark NJ.

[31] *Augusta Chronicle*, 23 April 1900.

CHAPTER 15

New Causes, New Campaigns

"If a mob in Atlanta, incited by the ravings of the Jeffersonian,
*should murder Frank, may God, in his sorely-tried pity, have
mercy on Tom Watson's soul."*

While earning a living and raising a family, Berry Benson remained a
campaigner for causes he believed in, whether popular or not. In
1898 Augusta's "respectable people" opposed labor unions as Yankee
infiltrations, and suspected striking workers of radical if not anarchic
tendencies. Berry Benson supported the cause of the strikers.

A depression beginning in 1884 had taken some of the sheen off
the golden promises of the New South. During the war, women had
made up most of the work force in the mills. Men, returning from
the battlefield or coming in from the country, took most of the jobs
in the newer mills. They liked the sound of the name "Knights of
Labor" and many joined that union. If clerks and cobblers could
dress up as knights and engage in pretend jousts, workers could take
pride in being knights of sorts, even if they had to work in factories.
When in 1886, the mills cut wages, workers in the Algernon Mill
went out on strike.[1]

In retaliation, the area mill owners agreed to a general lock-out
that lasted through the summer and into the fall. Eight thousand
workers remained idle and unpaid, subsisting on emergency relief
from the central funds of the Knights of Labor. On 13 September,
the management of the Augusta Factory posted a notice that "as a

---

[1] Leeann Whites, "Paternalism and Protest in Augusta's Cotton Mills: What's
Gender Got to Do with It?" in Edward Cashin and Glenn Eskew, eds., *Paternalism in
a Southern City: Race, Religion, and Gender in Augusta, Georgia* (Athens: University of
Georgia Press, 2001) 77–79.

gesture of good will" the work day would be lowered from eleven and a half hours to eleven hours. Any worker continuing to strike would be evicted from company housing. Defeated, the operatives went back to work, and the Knights of Labor faced bankruptcy.[2]

During the next decade working conditions worsened. Annual wages in the John P. King Mill declined from $216 in 1880 to $181 in 1898. Local wages lagged behind the average Southern industrial average of $452.[3] Not surprisingly, Augusta experienced an increase in prostitution. In 1897 the women of the Christian Union Mission appeared before the city council and described "houses of shame, dives of damnable sin, suffering, debauchery and prostitution that exist openly without effort of concealment contrary to the city code." The members of the council were moved to the extent of donating $5.00 each to the Christian Union Mission.[4] Revivalist Sam Jones preached a mission in the mill district and thundered against liquor: "Democratic soak and whiskey soak are running Augusta in her hellbound course; Augusta needs cleaning up, but you are afraid to speak."[5]

In 1898 the Textile Union of America began a recruiting drive among the mill workers. The mill managers played into the hands of the disaffected by announcing a ten percent cut in wages as of 21 November 1898. Workers in the Sibley Mill walked out and paraded down Broad Street. There they were joined by Enterprise Mill operatives, and together they marched to the Confederate Monument to listen to union organizer E. P. Cranfill urge them to unite. The mills not affected by the walk-out announced a general

---

[2] The *Augusta Chronicle* covered the strike closely; see issues of 13, 22 June; 7, 10, 27 July; 15 September; and 5 November 1886.

[3] Richard Henry German, "The Queen City of the Savannah: Augusta, Georgia, during the Urban Progressive Era, 1890–1917" (Ph.D. diss., Florida State University, 1973) 84.

[4] Augusta City Council Minutes, 6 April, 2 August 1897, in *Council Minute Book*, 2 January 1893 to 27 December 1897, Augusta Municipal Archives, Augusta Richmond County Municipal Building, Augusta GA.

[5] *Augusta Chronicle*, 13 May 1897.

lockout to begin on Christmas Eve if the Sibley and Enterprise workers stayed out.[6]

Berry Benson, as though from his perch on the monument, could see both sides of the dispute. He socialized with managers in the routine auditing of factory accounts, and he saw first-hand the conditions of the working men, women, and children. The lockout began on Christmas Eve, and on that day Berry Benson inserted a notice in the *Augusta Chronicle*. He noted that General Gobin, commandant of the U.S. Army Camp McKenzie outside Augusta, had donated 500 loaves of bread to the women of the West End, the mill district, and Berry saluted him for his having the generous "heart of a soldier." He argued that the workers' cause "is not their battle only that they are fighting, it is your battle and mine, and of every one of us—it is the battle of humanity. It is the battle of the mill presidents, the same as any, for not one knows, nor can he have the slightest assurance, that children or grandchildren of his may not in a little time be working in these mills for the pittance they now refuse to give."[7]

Neither side gave in. On 6 January 1899, Charles Estes, president of the King Mill, applied the ultimate weapon. Strikers would be evicted from company housing to make way for non-union workers. Two days later, Berry Benson published a notice to the bookkeepers of Augusta: "From this date to the end of the mill strike (or lockout) all money received by me from the bookkeepers of Augusta in payment for the Zero system will be sent as a donation from the purchaser and in his name to the suffering women and children of the mills." He signed the notice, "In His Name, Berry Benson." As always, Jeanie Oliver Benson shared her husband's compassion for the unfortunate, and she joined the Women's Aid

---

[6] Edward J. Cashin, *The Brightest Arm of the Savannah*, 184.
[7] *Augusta Chronicle*, 24 December 1898.

Society of the First Christian Church to solicit food for the families of the unemployed.[8]

Spokesmen for the mills argued that they sympathized with the workers, but even with the ten percent cut in wages, they claimed that they were still paying six percent more than mills in the Horse Creek Valley of South Carolina, across the river from Augusta. The workers' representatives questioned that claim, so the mills challenged the union to hire someone to examine the books of all the mills. If the claim turned out to be wrong, the mills would compensate the union for their expenses up to five hundred dollars. Berry Benson considered that offer unfair. He wrote a strong letter to the editor of the *Chronicle*, stating that the owners had the information in their books. He knew that because he had looked in those books. Why not simply open the ledgers to the workers' representatives? Why ask them to go to the expense of hiring someone to go around examining books, when the workers did not have any money in the first place?[9]

He revealed information that must have dismayed the mill owners. The ten percent cut in wages would allow the mills to increase their profit margin by only one-sixteenth of a cent per yard of cloth. Furthermore, he knew of a mill that charged one-eighth of a cent more than the mills involved in the lockout, and that mill showed a profit. "Facts are hard things to get over," Berry wrote, "and the bald, bare, unretreating fact stares us in the face that nearby mill operatives are working cheerfully and contentedly, and producing goods that pay the investors good enough profits not to cut in two the skimp wages of hardworking women and children." He published his challenge to the mills twice more and asked the people of Augusta to keep count of how many times it went unanswered.[10]

---

[8] Ibid., 8, 22 January 1899.
[9] Ibid., 16, 18 January 1899.
[10] Ibid., 16 January 1899.

Not content with waiting for an answer, Berry resorted to an ingenious strategy to bring pressure on the mills to end the strike. His acquaintance with mills across the region gave him access to the managers of those mills. He inquired from the Fulton Bag and Cotton Mills of Atlanta if they could use some of the striking workers from Augusta. Berry showed a reporter the letter he received in response, dated 21 January 1899. The Atlanta mill could use 42 operatives immediately, and 380 in February. Berry told the reporter that he had been in contact with another mill that planned to start a night run and could take on even more than the Atlanta mill. He had already made arrangements with the Georgia Railroad for transportation of the first group to Atlanta.[11]

The *Augusta Chronicle* suggested that the exodus of workers would adversely affect the merchants and shopkeepers of the city, and that they might want to bring influence to bear on the mill owners to end the strike. The paper called Berry "perhaps the most ardent sympathizer the strikers have."[12]

Again, as in 1886, the mills' ultimate weapon, eviction, doomed the workers' unity of purpose. Three days after the enforcement of eviction, workers at the King, Sibley, Iasetta, and Langley Mills returned to work. The die-hards set up a tent city in Harrisburg called "Camp Eviction," but gradually even their numbers dwindled.[13]

On 24 January, P. W. Greene, president of the Textile Union of America, arrived in Augusta to negotiate on behalf of the workers. He declined to speak to reporters, but he did speak to Berry Benson, John T. Pugh (chairman of the Relief Committee), and a delegation of labor leaders. Together the group proceeded to a meeting with the representatives of the mills. Thus Berry found himself in a summit meeting with the leaders of capital and labor. The meeting produced

---

[11] Ibid., 23 January 1899.
[12] Ibid., 25 January 1899.
[13] German, "The Queen City of Savannah," 115.

a set of "Articles of Peace:" 1. Workers agreed to a wage scale six percent higher than wages of competing mills in South Carolina. 2. Coal would be sold to employees by the mills at wholesale price. 3. Strikers would be rehired without penalty. 4. Workers could join the union if they chose. Except for the lower price of coal, the articles amounted to a continuation of the status quo, and therefore a victory for the mills. The union movement never really recovered from the defeats of 1886 and 1898.[14]

Berry remained interested in the welfare of the mill families. The long workdays and low wages left no time for reading and no money for books. Many adults could not read anyhow but yearned to know about life outside their cramped existence. The Richmond County Board of Education opened the Fifth Ward School in the Harrisburg mill district. Superintendent of Schools Lawton B. Evans wrote, "It seemed to me pathetic when I saw a little child nine or ten years of age on the porch Sunday morning reading out of a third or fourth grade reader to a mother and father."[15] Berry organized the "Trades Union Lyceum," a series of lectures intended for the adult workers. Berry made it clear in his public announcement that the purpose of the lyceum was to further education, not to promote unionism. He gave the first lecture, "A Journey Through the Stars," on 14 December 1899. It is to be hoped that even if the workers could not comprehend his astronomy, they appreciated his good intentions.[16]

Berry undertook another project that he hoped would benefit poor black families as well as whites. On his frequent hikes with his children, he had noticed the proliferation of mushrooms in the countryside. In 1892 he sent several specimens to a Professor Peck, a

---

[14] Ibid., 116.
[15] Lawton B. Evans, *Memoirs*, cited in Edward J. Cashin, *The Quest: A History of Public Education in Richmond County* (Augusta: Richmond County Board of Education, 1985) 28.
[16] *Augusta Chronicle*, 10, 12 October 1899.

New York botanist, and to Dr. Taylor of the United States Department of Agriculture, explaining his idea that mushrooms might supply a nourishing and inexpensive source of food. Professor Peck agreed that the specimens he received were beneficial and encouraged Berry to take further steps. Berry secured the cooperation of Dr. Edward Forster of Boston in distinguishing healthy and poisonous varieties. Berry identified nineteen nutritious and safe varieties, but needed to do more research before he could do more.[17] (Berry's method of identification might have been less than professional. His granddaughter repeats the story that he would feed the cat a piece of mushroom; if it didn't die, he took a bite.)

As it happened, America's first billionaire, John D. Rockefeller, liked to winter in Augusta. Never shy, Berry hand-delivered a message to the oil tycoon. He prefaced his written request by noting that Rockefeller had been a bookkeeper, as was Berry, and therefore a "member of the guild." He told of his sympathy with the scanty fare of poor families he saw in the country, writing, "I feel ashamed of myself that I fare better than they." He admitted that some of his friends said that "improvidence and lack of thrift" caused their condition. Even if that were so, "I pity them for their ignorance and improvidence." Knowing that Rockefeller was a devout Baptist as well as a one-time bookkeeper, Berry appealed to religion, writing, "They are our dear Father's children and they are in need."[18] His purpose in writing was not to ask for money, either for himself or for others, but for enough funds to order a number of expensive books on the science of mytology, to allow him to complete his study of the subject of fungi. Extant letters do not reveal whether he got the books; however, Berry's granddaughter, Frances Benson Thompson of Starkville, Mississippi, recalled that the prestigious *National*

---

[17] Dr. Edward Forster to Berry Benson, 25 April 1894, Benson Papers, ms. 2636, Southern Historical Collection, University of North Carolina, Chapel Hill.

[18] Berry Benson to [John D. Rockefeller], n.d., Benson Family Papers, in private collection of Arthur Dupre, Newark NJ.

Geographic magazine published an article of Berry's on the subject of mushrooms.

Berry's concern for the poor families near Augusta might have touched a sensitive nerve in the philanthropist. Rockefeller invited Thomas Loyless, editor of the *Augusta Chronicle*, to accompany him on automobile rides to small towns in Georgia and South Carolina.[19] He noticed the debilitating effects of hookworm in children and adults. The infestation caused iron deficiency, fatigue, and increased susceptibility to other diseases. In 1909 he established the Rockefeller Sanitary Commission for the Eradication of Hookworm Disease, and gave it a million dollars to wage a five-year campaign against hookworm. As a result, hookworm disease was virtually eliminated in the southern United States.

Berry relished puzzles of all kinds. He occasionally published mathematical problems in the local newspapers. He had heard that the French called their secret code the "chiffre indéchiffrable," the undecipherable cipher. Somehow, perhaps through his friend Congressman James C. C. Black, he obtained a cryptogram in that code. On 26 October 1896, he wrote to Secretary of War Daniel S. Lamont that he had succeeded in solving the cipher. Lamont was interested enough to instruct the editor of the United States *Army and Navy Journal* to send several coded messages to Berry to see if he could work them out. Berry easily translated all four cryptograms, and in the process corrected several mistakes the expert had made. One of the codes looked like this:

"Dgxyjbuejugegfbsobmvjppnyhnbbbecntuktkavraaphlikmkciimongcl yflwniumbtmdry"

---

[19] Information about Loyless riding about the countryside with Rockefeller was provided by Loyless's daughter, the late Margaret Loyless Mell.

Berry translated it: "Old man Plunkett said that he was even with the world, for he owed about as much as he did not owe." Berry probably appreciated the cryptographer's sense of humor.[20]

Administrations changed. Grover Cleveland gave way to William McKinley, and Congressman Black was replaced by William H. Fleming, another friend of Benson's. When Congress declared war on Spain, Berry returned to the subject of secret codes. In a letter of 7 May 1898, he reminded Fleming that he liked to do puzzles, and that he had solved the secret French code. Now, perhaps, he might be useful in working out the Spanish codes. Fleming referred Berry's offer to the War Department and later chided the clerk for not responding to Berry quickly enough. The clerk grudgingly replied that the War Department did not want to change codes. That was not the point, Berry stated in a letter of 18 December 1899 to Secretary Elihu Root. He intended to volunteer his services in the interpretation of foreign codes. The War Department continued to be obtuse. On 2 January 1900, the chief signal officer replied, "The War Department has no need of purchasing or investigating ciphers of this kind." The bureaucrats could not disabuse themselves of the idea that this character named Berry Benson was trying to sell them something.[21]

He did not give up his interest in deciphering, or the patriotic impulse that led him to offer his services. When the United States declared war on Germany in April 1917, Berry contacted his friend Joseph Derry, Woodrow Wilson's old teacher, and asked him to tell President Wilson about Berry's ability to work out codes.[22] Berry reminisced about Derry's old school on the corner of McIntosh (7th)

---

[20] Berry Benson to Daniel S. Lamont, 26 October 1896, Benson Papers, Chapel Hill.

[21] Berry Benson to William H. Fleming, 7 May 1898, Benson Family Papers, in private collection of Arthur Dupre, Newark NJ; William H. Fleming to Berry Benson, 15 July 1898; Chief Signal Officer to Berry Benson, 2 January 1900, Benson Papers, Chapel Hill.

[22] Berry Benson to Joseph Derry, 25 May 1917, Benson Papers, Chapel Hill.

and Bay, then in the process of being torn down to make way for the massive levee flanking the Savannah River. In fact, Berry's beloved Bay Street residence met the same fate. Berry decided to move across the river to North Augusta, South Carolina.

Berry's intellectual energy overflowed in other ways. An unusual penchant he indulged in consisted of perusing and correcting dictionaries. An adult public spelling bee in which he participated prompted his interest. He and a Professor Parks were the last two standing after several rounds. Berry spelled his last word "conjurer;" Parks spelled it "conjuror." The judge declared Parks the winner, citing Webster's Unabridged Dictionary. Berry conceded politely, but said he thought that the dictionary had it wrong. Thus, he began his search through the dictionary, and eventually turned up thirty-seven errors. The publisher thanked Berry and incorporated the corrections in future editions of the dictionary. Berry then took up the correction of Funk and Wagnall's Dictionary.[23]

Of all of the civilian causes and campaigns Berry Benson engaged in, the one that obsessed him most, as he told his brother Blackwood, was the case of Leo Frank. That case became a national *cause célèbre*, one that horrified Georgians at the time and that has haunted them ever since. The historian C. Vann Woodward wrote that "the Frank case for a time rivalled the European war as a subject of national attention." The name of Berry Benson appeared in newspapers across the country in arguments for Leo Frank's innocence.[24]

On 26 April 1913, a Saturday, a young factory worker named Mary Phagan went to the National Pencil Factory in Atlanta to obtain her weekly wages of $1.20. She did not come home. The next day her body was found in the grimy basement of the factory. Largely

---

[23] Jim Garvey, "Berry Benson in Peacetime," *Augusta Richmond County History* 33/1 (Spring 2002): 34.

[24] C. Vann Woodward, *Tom Watson, Agrarian Rebel* (New York: Oxford University Press, 1963) 436.

on the testimony of the black handyman, Jim Conley, the Jewish manager of the factory, Leo Frank, was found guilty after a trial of twenty-five days and sentenced to death by the presiding judge, L. S. Roan. A crowd outside cheered the verdict.

Berry Benson took an initial interest in the case because Conley's lawyer, William Manning Smith, was Charles Benson's boyhood companion. Berry had befriended the young Augustan when Smith's father died in 1889 and had followed his progress with approval. William Smith's daughter Mary Lou told writer Steve Oney in 1987 that Berry was her father's "guardian" and that the children called him "Uncle Berry." Berry respected Smith because of his integrity, because of his fondness for the Lost Cause of the Confederacy, and for a penchant he shared with Berry: the habit of looking out for the underdog. Smith delivered a remarkable address on Confederate Memorial Day address at Augusta's Magnolia Cemetery on 26 April 1912. He contended that the South's most serious problem at the end of the Civil War was the plight of the ten million freed slaves, "the wards of the Southland." He called upon his listeners to concern themselves with this problem: "I have faith in the broad-minded, sane, and conservative spirit of our people in the handling of this problem and believe will be solved by Southern white men with as heroic a devotion to principle as that of their fathers who fought in the cause from which the present negro problem had its birth."[25]

Smith spoke in the context of an ugly recent trend in race relations. From the end of the war until 1900, race relations in Augusta had been fluid. Blacks voted, sat without distinction on street-cars, lived and worked in neighborhoods throughout the city, and participated in community leadership. As register of the treasury, Judson Lyons was the highest ranking black in the McKinley

---

[25] Steve Oney, *And the Dead Shall Rise: The Murder of Mary Phagan and the Lynching of Leo Frank* (New York: Pantheon Books, 2003) 151. Steve Oney's book is the definitive history of this sad affair.

administration. Many others such as John Hope, president of Morehouse College; the preacher Charles T. Walker, called "the black Spurgeon" for his eloquence; and Channing Tobias, a member of the executive council of the YMCA., grew up in a comparatively congenial climate.

A profound change followed the failure of the Populist Party to enlist black voters in their fight against the Democratic establishment. Under the leadership of one-term congressman Thomas E. Watson of Thomson, the former Populists formed a tight-knit, ward-based group within the Democratic Party and successfully campaigned for the state-wide adoption of the white primary in 1900. In that year, Augusta began to segregate in every aspect of life when leaders enacted an ordinance segregating the races in public conveyances. In 1906 Tom Watson campaigned for the election of Hoke Smith in return for his promise to disfranchise blacks. During the campaign, white hooligans ran riot through Atlanta's black neighborhood, killing ten blacks, injuring thirty-five, smashing windows, and wrecking trolleys.

In that worsening racial climate, William M. Smith determined to devote his services as an attorney to the defense of blacks accused of crime. He defended Jim Conley so well that Conley, who freely admitted helping Leo Frank dispose of the girl's dead body, was sentenced to only a year on the chain gang on 24 February 1914.

Berry Benson followed the conflicting newspaper reports of the trial with an open mind. A seemingly insignificant statement by Conley attracted his attention. Conley changed his testimony several times, but finally told this story:

In addition to his job as sweeper, Conley was paid by Frank to watch out when Frank had assignations with young women. Conley said that Frank was not like other men, that he had seen Frank kneeling in front of a woman who had her skirt up, and that he had hired him to stand guard when he was with Mary Phagan. Frank then whistled for him, and told him that Mary had refused his advances, that he had hit her and that she lay dead. Conley and Frank carried the body to the elevator and left it in the basement. Then they returned to Frank's office where Frank dictated notes to Conley supposedly written by Mary and throwing suspicion on Newt Lee, the night watchman. While they were in the office, Corinthia Hall and Emma Clark came to see Frank, and Jim hid in the wardrobe. He remembered the names as "Quincy" Hall and Emma Hart. When the women left, Frank pulled out two hundred dollars in rolled-up bills to pay Conley, but then took it back.[26]

Conley's testimony regarding Frank's alleged perversion both horrified and titillated Atlantans. Conley's most graphic descriptions never made it to the press, but the jury heard it all, as did the crowd in the courtroom, and it created such an angry murmur that Judge Roan ordered the women and children to leave the courtroom. The part that piqued Berry's interest was the statement that Frank had a roll of bills amounting to two hundred dollars. He knew that no business manager would have kept such a sum on a weekend. Undoubtedly, many other fair-minded Georgians had misgivings about the validity of Conley's testimony, but Berry Benson was different in that he did something about it. He loved working out puzzles, and this case puzzled him. Besides, his ingrained sense of fair play compelled him.

On 19 May 1914, he went to Atlanta and stayed at the home of his friend William M. Smith. Mary Lou Smith remembered that her mother worried about what to cook for "Uncle Berry," knowing that he was a vegetarian. She also remembered that Uncle Berry got up at an unusually early hour. She thought it was because he lived in "the

---

[26] Berry Benson, "Five Arguments in the Frank Case" (Augusta GA: n.p., 1915). The copy used here was from the Library of Congress.

country." Berry said no, it was that his pet St. Bernard mix, Caesar, insisted on getting in bed with him.[27]

Before Berry arrived in Atlanta, things had not gone well for Leo Frank. On 31 October 1913, Judge Roan denied a motion for a new trial and set the execution date for 17 April 1914. Frank's lawyers then appealed to the Georgia Supreme Court for a new trial. The appeal was denied on 17 February. On 6 April the attorneys filed a motion in the Fulton County Superior Court to set aside the guilty verdict. The execution date was postponed until 22 January 1915. The Fulton County Court denied the motion to set aside the verdict on 6 June, but that motion was still pending when Berry Benson asked William Smith to take him to see Jim Conley. At the time, Berry later recalled, Smith believed Conley's story.

The appeals and delays irritated Tom Watson terribly, if his newspaper the *Jeffersonian* indicated his true feelings. Headlines of the 19 March issue referred to Frank as "THAT FOUL DEGENERATE WHO MURDERED LITTLE MARY PHAGAN," and went on to accuse Frank's defenders of being paid by rich northern Jews. Sales of the *Jeffersonian* climbed dramatically, as did the anger of its readers. So Berry Benson knew when he went to Atlanta with doubts about Frank's guilt that he could be accused of being in the pay of northern Jews.[28]

Smith first took Berry to see Conley, then serving out his one year sentence in prison. Berry asked Conley for a sample of his handwriting, and Conley obliged. No danger lay in that for Conley, for all along he had said that he wrote the notes dictated by Frank. Berry was convinced that the notes contained words that a Brooklynite like Frank would not have known. Berry asked Conley,

---

[27] Mary Lou Smith Allen (William Smith's daughter), interview by Steve Oney, 22 June 1987, from personal communication from Steve Oney to author, 8 September 2004.

[28] Oney, *And the Dead Shall Rise*, 426; Woodward, *Tom Watson, Agrarian Rebel*, 437–38.

"Jim, if Mr. Frank took out two hundred dollars and took it back, how did you know it was two hundred dollars?" Conley was not to be caught that easily. "Because he told me it was two hundred dollars," he answered.[29]

From the jail the two went to the National Pencil Factory and met Herbert Schiff, Frank's personal assistant and a firm believer in Frank's innocence. He had testified during the trial that he worked with Frank on most Saturdays, and that there had never been women in the office. Further, he showed the financial paperwork Frank had done on the fateful day, contending that it would have taken Frank three and a half hours to complete, so he would have had no time to murder the girl and dispose of the body. Berry asked Smith to check the books to see how much cash Frank had on hand that Saturday. The books showed about twenty-six dollars. Frank's personal bank account indicated habitual withdrawals in small sums, usually five dollars. As he had suspected, Conley had to have lied about Frank having two hundred dollars.[30]

Schiff took them to the basement on the elevator Conley said he and Frank used. The elevator hit bottom. "Did it always hit bottom?" Berry wondered. Schiff explained that there was a cable that could have arrested the descent, but that the cable had rusted from lack of use, so, yes, it always hit bottom. Berry knew that the fact was of momentous importance. Conley had testified that he had defecated that morning under the elevator shaft. The police report on the crime scene mentioned that they found the feces intact. So, the elevator could not have been used! The girl's body must have been pushed through the trap door. Berry concluded that Conley was "the damndest liar in Georgia." Berry noticed a bloody hand print on a post and urged Schiff to get a copy of it. Later, at Schiff's urging, an

---

[29] Benson, "Five Arguments."
[30] *Augusta Chronicle*, 14 May, 19 June 1914.

investigator named "Colonel" Perry Fyffe actually disengaged a piece
of the wood with the print on it.[31]

Berry and Smith then called on the mother of Mary Phagan. As
considerately as they could, they learned from the grief-stricken
woman Mary's actions on the fatal morning. The girl helped her
mother with housework until about 11:30, and then she ate lunch.
She left to catch the streetcar at 11:45. According to the streetcar
conductor, the car arrived near the pencil factory at 12:07. Berry
learned from Schiff that a normal walk from the car stop at Marietta
and Forsyth Streets took three minutes and forty-five seconds.
Walking to Frank's office would take another forty seconds. The
arithmetic corroborated Frank's testimony that Mary came to his
office at 12:15 and left immediately—and that he did not see her
again.[32]

According to Conley, the murder had taken place about thirty
minutes before two women entered Frank's office to use the
telephone. Frank made him hide from the women in the wardrobe.
However, the women testified that they went to Frank's office at
11:35, used the phone, and left at 11:45. Miss Hattie Hall, Frank's
stenographer was there at the time, and she did not leave until 12:02.
Berry concluded that either Conley lied, or these three women and
Mary Phagan's mother lied.[33]

When he returned to Augusta, he published an article in the
Augusta Chronicle titled "Where was Mary Phagan?" With biting
irony he asked, "How could Mary Phagan be at home and alive, and
at the factory, being killed at 11:05?" He ridiculed Prosecutor Hugh
Dorsey who called Conley "Old Jim" and portrayed him as one of the
harmless "darkies" of the Old South. For Berry, the case came down

[31] Berry Benson to Herbert Schiff, 14 December 1914; Schiff to Benson, 18
December 1914, Leo Frank Papers, Atlanta History Center, Atlanta GA. Hereafter
cited as Leo Frank Papers.
[32] *Augusta Chronicle*, 18 June 1914; Schiff to Benson, 18 December 1914, Leo
Frank Papers.
[33] *Augusta Chronicle*, 18 June 1914.

to a mathematical certainty: only two people could have killed Mary Phagan, Frank or Conley. Conley's lies convicted him.

Before leaving Atlanta and the Smiths, Berry called on Judge Ben Hill and presented his arguments on behalf of Frank. The judge told him that he could not order a new trial without new evidence. Indeed, Judge Hill turned down Frank's bid for a new trial on 6 June. Frank's lawyers immediately appealed to the Georgia Supreme Court. On 14 October, the Court refused to grant a new trial, and on 14 November denied the motion to set aside the guilty verdict. Frank then appealed to the United States Circuit Court, presided over by Supreme Court Justice Joseph R. Lamar.[34]

Berry had written to Leo Frank on 15 September 1914, stating that he had been in touch with Perry Fyffe, the investigator. He understood that Fyffe had managed to get a piece of the basement door with the bloody handprint, but that he had not heard from him as yet. Berry thought that the print might be the new evidence they were looking for.[35]

He wrote again on 3 December after learning that Judge Lamar would hear Frank's appeal for a new trial. "Of one thing you may be sure," Berry wrote, "that Judge Lamar, whatever he may do or advise, will be perfectly honest. He and I are warm personal friends." However, Berry cautioned Frank not to expect too much, "These justices are bound within the limits of technical decision as to legal proceeding, and however their sympathies may lie, are bound by construction of law and by precedent." Even so, Berry had not given up hope that Frank would be vindicated.[36]

After Berry Benson's visit in May, William Smith felt with growing dread that he had helped perpetrate a terrible injustice.

---

[34] Benson, "Five Arguments."

[35] Berry Benson to Leo Frank, 14 September 1914, Leo Frank Papers. I am grateful to Steve Oney for bringing the Benson letters in the Frank Papers to my attention.

[36] Benson to Frank, 3 December 1914, Leo Frank Papers.

Perry Fyffe added to his qualms. The bloody print on the basement door did not match Frank's hand. Fyffe showed him another clue he had not thought of: the murder note, supposedly dictated by Frank in his office, read "that negro...down here did this." If it had been written upstairs, it would have said "down there." Smith gathered all the evidence from the trial, some of which he had missed. He and his wife painstakingly examined every shred of testimony, with a vanishing hope of verifying Conley's story. Still friendly with Hugh Dorsey, the prosecutor, Smith explained his misgivings. Dorsey told him it was too late to reverse the verdict. In search of new evidence, Smith went to see Conley in his jail cell. He wanted to see if Conley's prints matched the piece of blood-stained wood Perry Fyffe had obtained. Conley refused to give an imprint.[37]

Finally Smith wrote his opinion in a hundred-page manuscript that began with an acknowledgment of his debt to Berry Benson. "As a child I have played in the Benson home, and learned to know him as the great and good man that he is." Benson's doubts first set Smith to do his own investigation. Benson's arguments "were among too many things that caused me to actually take up a student analysis this case, and which has forced upon me the only conclusion possible—the death of Mary Phagan is not at the door of Frank, but of the negro Conley, alone."[38]

The news of Smith's change of heart caused a minor sensation. Word began to leak out that Smith had changed his mind about Conley's guilt. When a reporter asked him about it, Smith explained his doubts, and the next morning the *Atlanta Journal*'s headlines read "Frank Not Guilty Believes Conley's Lawyer." The next day the *New York Times* announced "Conley, not Frank, Called the Slayer." A special report to the 8 October *New York Times* stated that Smith handed reporters an analysis of the murder notes made by Berry

---

[37] Oney, *And the Dead Shall Rise*, 430–35.
[38] William Smith, introduction to unpublished manuscript, copy supplied to author by Steve Oney.

Benson, "one of the leading handwriting experts of Georgia." The *Times* article quoted Benson as stating that "there is not a white man, North or South, who could have dictated the notes with their typical negro lingo."[39]

Tom Watson turned his wrath upon Smith, mocking him in the 8 October *Jeffersonian* and ending with a threat, "Let W. M. Smith be careful!" The warning from Watson brought dozens of letters threatening Smith with bodily harm and even death. He sent his family to the country for their protection. He bravely defied Watson and his other detractors in a notice to the *Atlanta Georgian*, "Though I am condemned by every citizen of this town, county, and state as a traitor, I intend to stick by my guns, figuratively and literally." He would go armed in the future and he said to any lynch mob, "As the Sage of McDuffie does to me, Be Careful!" Watson retaliated by calling Smith "a braying donkey" and accused him of taking "Jew money." Lawyers in Atlanta rebuked Smith for betraying his client—even after the case had been closed. Smith's stand for Leo Frank meant a virtual end to his law career in Atlanta. Conditions in Georgia had become emotionally incendiary and verged upon physical violence.[40]

Justice Lamar presented a type of gift to Leo Frank on 28 December 1914, ruling that Frank's absence from the courtroom when the judge read the verdict might involve a violation of his constitutional rights. The Supreme Court met to decide the issue on 25 February 1915. Frank's lawyers argued that an angry mob outside the court intimidated the jury. Judge Roan had cautioned Frank not to appear because he feared mob violence if Frank were acquitted. The jurors feared for their own safety if they acquitted Frank. Frank's absence from the courtroom when the verdict was read and the threat of violence were reasons for setting aside the verdict. The nine justices deliberated with magisterial slowness and on 19 April ruled

---

[39] *New York Times*, 8 October 1914.
[40] Oney, *And the Dead Shall Rise*, 438–41.

that, with all its defects, the trial met constitutional requirements. On 10 May Judge Ben Hill again set Frank's execution date; this time for 22 June 1915.[41]

Berry Benson's name appeared in newspapers across the country as a result of attorney Henry Alexander's circulation of Berry's analysis of the murder notes. John Owens, editor of the *Baltimore Sun*, wrote to congratulate Berry on his arguments, all of which were "sound and clear." In particular he "was struck with your statements concerning the fecal matter in the shaft." Berry collected favorable comments from the *Duluth Herald, Rochester Democrat, Pittsburgh Dispatch, Houston Chronicle, Jacksonville Times-Union,* and *Springfield Republican* and mailed them to Frank. He also included one ominous clipping from Tom Watson's *Jeffersonian* that read, "Now is the time to have a vigilance committee appoint its own sentries to watch that desperate criminal."[42]

Berry seemed not to worry about his own safety or his standing in the community. As Tom Watson's threats grew in intensity, so did Berry's efforts on Frank's behalf. On 16 December 1914, he informed Frank that he was preparing "a good strong article" for the *Augusta Chronicle*. The article appeared in the 21 December issue. Ostensibly, Berry's letter was in response to a written inquiry from five prominent Augustans as to why Berry thought that Frank was innocent. (Berry later confided to Frank, "Of course, I engineered the request of my five friends.") He began by asking them not to follow the example of others who said in regard to defendants in other jury trials, "Oh hell, the jury convicted them, didn't they?" as if juries had never been wrong. He recited the discrepancy between Conley's statement that Frank had two hundred dollars in bills and the books showing that he had only twenty-six dollars in the office. In detail he explained how Conley put the time of the murder at 11:30 A.M. when Mary Phagan was still at home, and how several

---

[41] Ibid., 460, 467.
[42] Benson to Frank, 3, 10 December 1914, Leo Frank Papers.

witnesses placed Frank in his office during that time. He cited the incontrovertible fact that Conley went to the basement earlier that morning and "there deposited on the ground certain offensive matter which delicacy forbids to name." If Frank and Conley had brought the girl's body down on the elevator, as Conley testified, the "offensive matter" would have been crushed beneath the elevator car. He finished by saying that he could give other reasons, "but if these will not convince you, neither would the rest—not even if told by an angel from heaven."[43]

On the day the article appeared, Berry sent a copy to Leo Frank. He explained that his first version had been more forceful, but that he had to tone it down to suit the publisher, Tom Loyless. The publisher who also acted as editor at first objected to any mention of "the shit in the shaft" as the reporters privately referred to it. "I had to argue mightily to get the excrement argument in at all; he did not want to permit any reference to so indelicate a subject," Berry wrote, tongue-in-cheek. It was all right to talk about perversion and murder, but not about toilet matters. Incredibly, Berry's reference to the feces marked the first time that argument appeared in print in Georgia. A well-known "muckraking" journalist named C. P. Connolly, working in part from William Smith's notes, also mentioned the unsavory subject in a two-part article in *Colliers* weekly magazine on 17 and 23 December.[44]

Tom Loyless thought that he was bending over backward to be fair and impartial in reporting the case. Like most Georgians, he believed that Frank must be guilty simply because the jury said so. However, Loyless admitted that he harbored a reasonable doubt and would not want to put a man to death. Because of that reservation, he had permitted Berry's article, and had even "dared" (the word was his) to broach the subject in his editorial. The fact that it required

---

[43] Benson to Frank, 16 December 1914, Leo Frank Papers; *Augusta Chronicle*, 21 December 1914.

[44] Benson to Frank, 21 December 1914, Leo Frank Papers.

"daring" to discuss the case indicated that freedom of expression in Georgia was being squeezed by threats of mob violence.[45]

On the other hand, editorial protests of the death sentence ran rampant throughout the rest of the country. Tom Watson declared that the outpouring of support for Frank in the northern press amounted to an attack on Georgia. In the 25 March *Jeffersonian* he warned, "If Frank's rich connections keep on lying about this case SOMETHING BAD WILL HAPPEN!"[46]

Indeed, the Frank case had become a national issue. As Steve Oney described in his definitive study of the case, "And so somewhere in America on every day of May 1915 someone was either circulating a petition asking that the Georgia authorities commute Frank's death sentence, making a speech demanding the same, or from the pulpits of both temples and church praying for divine intervention."[47]

Of the few voices raised in Georgia in defense of Frank, none was more vigorous than that of Berry Benson. On 25 May he wrote Frank that he had prepared a booklet called "Five Arguments in the Frank Case" and was printing a thousand copies in the first run. He intended to mail copies to every state governor, to many United States senators, to preachers, and to most of the principal newspapers in the South. He would also send a copy to each of the jurors who sat in judgment of Frank, with a personal letter asking them to reconsider. He had telegraphed his brother Blackwood in Austin, Texas, "who is a man of some prominence there," to influence the Texas legislature to make a plea for commutation.[48]

Berry began his "Five Arguments" with a comment aimed at Tom Watson. He had not received a cent from Frank or his

---

[45] *Augusta Chronicle*, 16 December 1914.
[46] Woodward, *Tom Watson, Agrarian Rebel*, 439.
[47] Oney, *And the Dead Shall Rise*, 476.
[48] Benson to Frank, 25 May 1915, Leo Frank Papers. Whether Blackwood Benson's influence had anything to do with it or not, the Texas legislature did go on record as recommending commutation for Frank.

supporters and was paying for the publication out of his own pocket. He wrote, "I make this statement to anticipate the low jibe of any vicious or crazy person, or any person both crazy and vicious, who may say that I am in the pay of Jews." He repeated the arguments he had used in the 19 June and 21 December issues of the *Augusta Chronicle* regarding the notes written in the black southern dialect, and the discrepancy in the time sequence of Conley's account and Mary Phagan's actual activities. His third argument was the familiar one about the excrement in the elevator shaft.

The last two were points he had not made before in print. The prosecution had made much of the testimony of a factory worker named Monteen Stover who stated that she had gone to Frank's office at precisely 12:05 P.M. on that Saturday and had not seen him there. She left at 12:10 P.M. The prosecution argued that Frank was not in his office because he was out killing Mary Phagan. Berry did not attack the accuracy of the statement or the character of the witness. In fact, Monteen Stover, like many of the prosecution witnesses, had a very shady reputation. (She would later be convicted of luring married men to hotel rooms and then blackmailing them.) Berry's argument was simply that the statement was irrelevant. It could be demonstrated that Mary Phagan did not reach the office until after 12:10 P.M., so it did not matter what Frank might have been doing in Stover's five-minute interval. Finally, he took issue with Conley's statement that Frank had a pre-arranged tryst with the girl. That implied Mary's complicity in lewd behavior. Conley was the only person who had thus impugned Mary's character.[49]

In preparation for an appeal for clemency before the Georgia Prison Commission on 31 May, Frank hired a Georgia lawyer of impeccable reputation, William Schley Howard. Howard gathered all the evidence he could in the short time available, including William

---

[49] Benson, "Five Arguments."

Smith's study of the case. Berry Benson wrote Frank, "Mr. Howard came to see me and we had a two-hour talk." Berry doubted that Frank would get satisfaction from the Prison Commission, but held out hope that the appeal would be granted if it came before Governor John Slaton.[50] The problem was time. Frank's execution was set for 22 June, and the governor's term ended on 26 June. The incoming governor, Nathaniel Harris, had been supported in the election by Tom Watson and likely would not want to cross that powerful political figure.

Schley Howard presented a powerful case for clemency on 31 May to the Prison Commission. He played his trump card, a letter from Judge Roan who had presided over the trial, saying that he favored commutation because of his grave doubts about Frank's guilt. Howard went on to use the familiar arguments in defense of Frank and presented a parade of witnesses attesting to Frank's good character.[51]

Howard's opponent before the commission was prosecutor Hugh Dorsey, but a greater foe spoke only editorially from his home in Thomson. In the 27 May issue of the *Jeffersonian* he warned the commission as well as the governor that any commutation would cause "the bloodiest riot ever known in the history of the South." As if to enforce Watson's position, a thousand people gathered in Marietta and protested commutation. A delegation representing the Marietta protesters called on the commission on 1 June and, among other things, declared Judge Roan's letter a forgery. During the following week, as the commissioners deliberated, the protests grew louder and the crowds larger. On 6 June 2,500 people gathered at the state capitol and demanded Frank's death.[52]

---

[50] Benson to Frank, 25 May 1915, Leo Frank Papers.
[51] Oney, *And the Dead Shall Rise*, 481–84.
[52] Ibid., 480, 487.

Ironically, Jim Conley was freed during the same week after serving ten months of his twelve-month sentence. He was treated as something of a hero.

On 9 June, the commission denied Frank's appeal by a vote of two to one. The verdict disappointed and emboldened *Chronicle* editor Tom Loyless. He blamed Tom Watson's "poison pen" for intimidating two of the commissioners who had earlier expressed doubt about Frank's guilt. He reminded readers of how Watson had tried to persuade then-governor Hoke Smith to pardon Arthur Glover, a friend of Watson's who had ruthlessly murdered a factory girl in Augusta's Sibley mill—in plain sight of her fellow workers.[53]

In the same 10 June issue, Berry Benson called attention to Tom Watson's latest editorial in which Watson cited Monteen Stover's testimony that she had entered Frank's office at 12:10 P.M. and had left at 12:15 P.M. and had not seen Frank. Watson repeated Hugh Dorsey's statement in court that Stover's testimony was vital to the case. If Stover was there then, she was there while Mary Phagan was in the factory. However, Berry showed that Watson had deliberately misquoted from the actual testimony. The court record made it clear that Stover had said she arrived at 12:05 and left at 12:10. That would have been before Mary Phagan's arrival, and therefore beside the point.[54]

"I have caught Tom Watson in a manifest untruth," Berry wrote to his brother Blackwood. On 11 June, Berry inserted another notice in the *Chronicle*. In case some of his friends thought that he "had lost his spectacles" and had mistaken the court records, he printed the testimony given by Stover verbatim and in large type, the same passage misquoted by Watson. He baited Watson, saying that Conley lied to save his own life. Berry asked, "Whose life is the *Jeffersonian* trying to save?" He concluded with a statement that, in such an inflamed emotional atmosphere, required more than ordinary

---

[53] *Augusta Chronicle*, 10 June 1915.
[54] Ibid.

courage: "If a mob in Atlanta, incited by the ravings of the *Jeffersonian*, should murder Frank, may God, in his sorely-tried pity, have mercy on Tom Watson's soul."[55]

Whether he liked it or not, the burden of decision now fell on Governor John Slaton. At the tension-filled hearing before the governor on 12 June, Schley Howard led with the excrement argument and the other fallacies in Conley's story. He then listed the prosecution's points apart from the Conley testimony, and found them easy to reconcile with Frank's innocence. Prosecutor Dorsey argued that those circumstantial pieces of evidence were indeed enough to convict Frank. However, he put most emphasis on the fact that the jury had decided and if the governor began to set aside jury verdicts, "it would be an incentive to lawlessness in our state, the consequences of which no man can calculate." The ever-present delegation from Marietta warned the governor that commutation would be "a dangerous blow at our institutions and our civilization."[56]

Slaton made a personal visit to the pencil factory and toured through Frank's office, the metal room where the girl allegedly struck her head, and the grimy basement. Slaton operated the elevator time and time again. It always hit bottom. William Smith twice called upon the governor privately at Slaton's Buckhead residence and reviewed his collected evidence. Berry Benson exerted subtle influence of his own. On 15 June he mailed the governor a copy of the recently published book containing Berry's account of his escape from Elmira Prison. He thought that reading it "might relieve the tedium of a hard-working hour." He urged the governor to read about Berry's adventures "and learn something about the man who is so zealously and so honestly defending Leo Frank." The harassed governor would not likely have had time to read about the Civil War,

---

[55] Berry Benson to Blackwood Benson, 14 August 1915, Benson Papers, Chapel Hill; *Augusta Chronicle*, 11 June 1915.

[56] Oney, *And the Dead Shall Rise*, 490.

but it might help Frank's cause if the governor knew that a Confederate hero believed in his innocence.[57]

Tom Watson could also be subtle. He sent a spokesman to Slaton to say that if the governor let Frank die that Watson would be his friend; Slaton would then become senator and "master of Georgia politics for twenty years to come."[58]

On 21 June, the day before Frank's scheduled execution, Governor Slaton commuted Frank's sentence to life in prison. Anticipating violence, he ordered Frank to be taken to the prison in Milledgeville late on the same night. Berry Benson telegraphed his congratulations to Frank on 22 June. Frank responded in a letter dated the same day. After thanking Berry, he continued, "In a few days I will be adjusted to my present surroundings and will have regained my equilibrium.... I see they are cutting up a little in Atlanta, but that will subside, and the reaction will set in in due time, intelligent public opinion in Georgia has been with me." That hope proved sadly wrong.[59]

The news of the commutation broke like a thunderclap upon Atlanta on the morning of 22 June. A crowd gathered, growing larger and angrier as the day wore on. In the evening four thousand people marched the six miles from the capitol to Buckhead and confronted the National Guard surrounding the governor's residence. The crowd pelted the troops with rocks and was in turn driven back by bayonets. In Marietta, protestors hung an effigy of Slaton bearing the caption "King of the Jews and Traitor Governor of Georgia."

Watson's *Jeffersonian* screamed its outrage, "Our grand old Empire State HAS BEEN RAPED! We have been violated and WE ARE ASHAMED! We have been betrayed! The breath of some leprous monster has passed over us, and we feel like crying out in

---

[57] Berry Benson to Gov. John Slaton, 15 June 1915, John M. Slaton Papers, Georgia Archives, Morrow GA. I am indebted to Julie Turner for finding this letter.

[58] Slaton to Tom Loyless, in *Augusta Chronicle*, 25 November 1915.

[59] Frank to Benson, in *Augusta Chronicle*, 25 June 1915.

horror and despair UNCLEAN, UNCLEAN!" Slaton was not safe in Georgia, and Frank was not safe in prison. Slaton could, and did, leave the state—but Frank could not leave the penitentiary. On 18 July a demented fellow inmate named William Creen slashed Frank's throat with a butcher's knife. Quick work by prison doctors saved Frank's life. In a cruel thrust Tom Watson wrote that he hoped the knife was kosher. His editorial of 12 August warned, "The next Jew who does what Frank did is going to get exactly the same thing that we give to negro rapists."[60]

Frank did not know that 17 August would be the last day of his life. He was unusually optimistic that day. William Smith had sent him a box of Berry Benson's "Five Arguments" and Frank wrote a friend that he was doing "missionary work with them in Milledgeville.... Bill wanted them given away."

That night twenty-five men riding in a caravan of seven cars drove from Marietta to Milledgeville and took Frank out of the jail with only token opposition from the guards. They drove back to Marietta, Mary Phagan's town, and there at Frey's cotton gin they lynched Leo Frank. At Hickory Hill in Thomson, Tom Watson waited up for the news. At 2:00 A.M. the phone rang; the voice at the other end said that the deed was done. Watson congratulated the lynchers in the next issue of the *Jeffersonian*, which proclaimed that "lynch law was the voice of the people and therefore the voice of God."[61]

The lynching was the last straw for editor Tom Loyless. Angry and exasperated, he used *Jeffersonian*-size type in the headlines of the 12 September issue, "SLATON OR WATSON—WHICH?" Which of them represented Georgia to the world? Loyless devoted four pages of his paper to a condemnation of Tom Watson and a vindication of Slaton, and therefore of Frank. He used Berry Benson's arguments and very likely his advice. As the only

---

[60] *The Jeffersonian*, 24 June, 12 August 1915.
[61] Woodward, *Tom Watson, Agrarian Rebel*, 444–45.

newspaperman man in Georgia to denounce the lynching, Loyless paid a price for his brave stand. The *Chronicle* lost subscribers and advertisers. Loyless received threatening letters, such as one that read, "Yes, we are with Tom Watson and when he calls for help we are coming, 50,000 strong, and soon more of Frank's kind will swing. Hurrah for our noble Tom Watson!"[62]

The year 1915 represented one of the darkest periods in Georgia's history. When Tom Loyless asked who spoke for Georgia, it seemed that Tom Watson did. When the *Jeffersonian* called for a revival of the Ku Klux Klan, thirty-four men signed a petition to Georgia's secretary of state for a charter for the new Klan. Fifteen of them climbed Stone Mountain, and on its summit set afire a wooden cross as if announcing that they would enforce Tom Watson's message.

But historians who have written about the Frank case—there have been more than twenty books, numerous articles, and several stage plays—have acknowledged that Georgia spoke with voices other than Watson's. John Slaton's memory is honored; so is that of Tom Loyless. Steve Oney's classic study of the case recognizes the courage of William M. Smith. Berry Benson also deserves to be remembered as one who fought for justice and decency with the same courage he displayed at Manassas and Spotsylvania. The man who best expressed this thought was John Owens, editor of the *Baltimore Sun*, in a letter to Benson: "I am sure that your work for Frank is a labor of justice and mercy, and I believe that you and others in the South who have raised your heads above the clamor, the insane,

---

[62] *Augusta Chronicle*, 12 September, 7 October 1915.

unreasoning clamor, will one day be rewarded by general recognition of your work, as well as by the immediate reward of your own consciences."[63]

---

[63] Benson to Frank, 3 December 1914, Leo Frank Papers. An echo of the passions raised by the Frank case occurred in 1982 when eighty-five-year-old Alonzo Mann revealed a secret he had harbored for seventy years. He told a reporter for the Nashville *Tennessean* that as a fifteen-year-old office boy he had gone to the Pencil Factory on that fatal Saturday and had seen Conley carrying the limp body of Mary Phagan through the corridor. Conley warned the boy that he would kill him if he revealed what he had seen. Alonzo told his mother who advised him to keep quiet. After the story came out in the 7 March 1982 issue of the *Tennessean*, lawyers representing the Anti-Defamation League filed a petition with the Georgia Board of Pardons and Paroles for a posthumous pardon for Leo Frank. Tom Watson Brown, great-grandson of Tom Watson, filed a vigorous objection, giving a detailed history of the trial, and emphasizing the testimony of witnesses who accused Frank of sexual improprieties. (I am grateful to my cousin Harry Cashin for a copy of Tom Watson Brown's brief. Harry is a former partner of Brown and a prominent Georgia attorney in his own right.) Others objected to re-opening the case. The main characters were dead. The trial evidence had disappeared. The board decided that it did not have enough new evidence to issue a pardon. Later, it issued a statement that the State of Georgia had not done due justice to Frank by its failure to protect him in jail. Frank's defenders would have to be satisfied with that rather evident fact. For the Mann episode and other late developments in the Frank case, see Oney, *And the Dead Shall Rise*, 644–49.

CHAPTER 16

The Confederate's Burden

"The Soldier's heart is always in the right place"

Berry Benson and Tom Watson personified different eras in Southern history. Berry's confrontation with Watson represented more than an isolated, unfortunate incident. Confederate veterans who had controlled politics since the war were being shunted aside by men who had grown into maturity after the war. Confederate leaders typically exhorted their listeners to lead nobler lives. But Watson in Georgia, Cole Blease in South Carolina, James Vardaman in Mississippi, and Sidney Catts in Florida appealed to the fears and prejudices of their followers.

The war left an indelible imprint on Berry Benson's character. The exigencies of war had continually tested him. Facing enemy fire demanded courage. Survival depended upon cooperation with his comrades. The intimacy of camp life required honesty. To win the respect of officers and men, he had to be reliable and worthy of their trust. He and his fellows were bound by a common code of duty and honor. They believed in a natural hierarchy of character, and they recognized and respected those who deserved to be at the top.

There were disreputable men in the Confederate army, slackers, thieves, and cowards. Berry did not regard them as "true soldiers," nor did he identify with them. He admired men like the Haskell brothers, particularly the chivalric Captain William Haskell, by whose side he had fought and with whom he had discussed Roman poets. Though all veterans were comrades, he felt a special bond with those with whom he shared the dangers and deprivations of prison life.

Berry expressed himself in his writing. His war journal is a celebration of things positive, written to inspire the next generation to worthy conduct. His poems and frequent newspaper contributions served the same purpose. He was not a ceremonial orator. Though his image spoke eloquently from atop the Confederate Monument on Broad Street, others delivered orations at its base. While all veterans professed to be brothers, everyone expected officers to do the talking. The premier orator for the great 1878 dedication of the Broad Street monument and for nineteen successive Confederate Memorial Days was Colonel Charles Colcock Jones, Jr. He put into words the sentiments felt by most of his listeners. Berry and his colleagues must have applauded when Colonel Jones urged the members of the Confederate Survivors Association at their 26 April 1879 meeting to "be devoted to the traditions and the impulses of a Confederate past, and observant of all that is just, pure, and of good report."[1]

The distinguished historian C. Vann Woodward singled out Colonel Jones in his classic biography, *Tom Watson, Agrarian Rebel*, as representative of a type, and quoted extensively from the colonel's 1887 address. However, Woodward did not do the colonel justice in writing, "His elaborate rhetoric and ecclesiastical tone belong to the man and his day, and were doubtless smiled at in the bustling 'eighties."[2] People living during "the bustling 'eighties" expected speeches in the grand style and would have been disappointed with less. Besides, no one dared smile condescendingly at the colonel or his message.

In his address to the 1881 gathering of the Confederate Survivors Association, Jones explained the purpose of the organization: We "associate ourselves together not as a potential

---

[1] Charles C. Jones, Jr., *An Address Delivered Before the Confederate Survivors' Association, April 26, 1879* (Augusta GA: Jewitt and Shaver, 1879), Confederate Survivors' Association Collection, Reese Library, Augusta State University, Augusta GA. Location hereafter cited as CSA Collection.

[2] C. Vann Woodward, *Tom Watson, Agrarian Rebel* (New York: Oxford University Press, 1963) 424–25.

factor in the politics of the hour, not as enemies of the new order of affairs, not as the supporters of antagonisms born of disappointment and hate, not as dreary mourners over the dead past, oblivious of the duties which appertain to the present and to the future, but as comrades—allied by memories which embrace all that was brave in purpose, self-denying in action, patriotic in impulse, and chivalric in arms."[3] He spoke for them all.

Berry Benson was a founding member of the Confederate Survivors Association in 1878, the year of the dedication of the great monument, and as secretary, was one of its officers. He processed applications for membership, placed notices in newspapers, and kept the records. When he and his family moved to Texas Berry reluctantly submitted his resignation. Addressing Berry as "Friend and Comrade," Colonel Jones replied graciously that "truly did we lament the necessity which compelled you to tender your resignation as Secretary of the Association." He praised Berry for filling his job "so acceptably, so zealously, and with such ability" and continued, "Sadly we will miss you. You are still one of us wherever you may be."[4] The freely-given respect of one's comrades is one of the highest compliments to a soldier. The duty to live up to the standards set by the war was a Confederate soldier's burden.

The code applied regardless of the rightness or wrongness of the reason for war. Once in combat, the soldier does his best. Major Joseph B. Cumming, second only to Colonel Jones as a commemorative orator, struggled to articulate this battle-induced compulsion. He addressed the reunion of the 5th Georgia Regiment:

> Do I not voice the feeling of every Confederate heart when I say that that period of my life is the one with which I am most nearly satisfied. If ever I was unselfish, it was then. If ever I was capable of self-denial, it was then. If ever I was able

---

[3] Jones, *An Address Delivered Before the Confederate Survivors' Association, April 26, 1881* (Augusta GA: M. M. Hill & Co., 1881), CSA Collection.
[4] Jones to Berry Benson, 5 February 1884, CSA Collection.

to trample on self-indulgence, it was then. If ever I was strong to make sacrifices, even unto death, it was in those days. And if I were called upon to say on the peril of my soul when it lived its highest life, when it was least faithless to true manhood, when it was most loyal to the best part of man's nature, I would answer "In those days when I followed yon bullet-pierced flag through its shifting fortunes of victory and defeat."[5]

On each Confederate Memorial Day, and at each reunion, orators reminded the diminishing band of brothers of their collective burden, stressing the obligation to exhibit proper conduct in their own lives, to instill their ideals in their children. The fact that some veterans failed to live up to the code caused others to be more diligent. Berry's commanding officer in the Battle of Savannah, Major George T. Jackson, nearly bankrupted the Enterprise Mill by his embezzlement. Major J. C. C. Black, a man of personally impeccable character, looked the other way when his political allies bought black votes in his successful bid for Congress. Berry Benson looked up an old comrade in Washington, DC, Eccles Cuthbert, "a happy-go-lucky fellow whom I liked." He found a little old gentleman with a long white beard, bleary eyes, and the strong odor of drink. He showed a spark of recognition, then averted his eyes. "I felt that the Cuthbert I had known was dead," said Berry.[6] Those who failed to bear the Confederate's burden might as well be dead, as far as their comrades were concerned.

The responsibility of acting as a role model sometimes led to exaggerated behavior. Major Cumming became almost a caricature of a Confederate officer. He liked to vault upon his horse from the rear. Once he addressed a group of students in Latin, though none of

[5] Joseph B. Cumming, "Remarks at the Reunion of the Survivors of the Fifth Regiment at Augusta," 30 August 1883, CSA Collection.
[6] Berry Benson to Jeanie Benson, 4 March 1900, Benson Family Papers, in private collection of Frances Thompson, Starkville MS.

them knew the language. He admonished his grandson not to sell lemonade because "We are not tradesmen," although his own grandfather had been a merchant and banker.[7]

Berry Benson's behavior could sometimes be peculiar. He kept his old uniform and wore it in veterans' parades until holes developed in unseemly places. He proudly carried his unsurrendered rifle even though no other veteran in the parades carried a gun. Because he frequently went barefoot during the war, he trekked barefoot through Mexico. He posed modestly as a model for the figure on the monument and assumed an heroic stance for a promotional poster in his seventies. Shocked by the language of his Yankee guards, he would not permit so much as a slang expression in his household. Convinced that a gentleman should strive for self-improvement, he compulsively devoted his life to learning all he could.

Confederate veterans preserved the antebellum paternalistic attitude toward blacks. In his 1887 address to the Confederate Survivors Association in Augusta, General and Governor John B. Gordon reminded his listeners of the loyalty of black men and women who worked on plantations while the white men went off to war. He expressed satisfaction at the "harmonious race relations" of his day.[8] Compared to conditions after the turn of the century, race relations were benign. There was a generally understood de facto segregation, but it was unwritten. When ten black men attempted to get a drink at the bar of Hensen's, the best restaurant in Augusta, the owner, Lexius Hensen, told them that they could not. Interestingly, Lexius Hensen happened to be black. The Ladevezes, who were among several black families in Berry Benson's neighborhood, owned the town's best art and music store where Jeanne Oliver and her daughters shopped. One of the professional photographers on Broad

---

[7] Conversation with Joseph B. Cumming, grandson of Maj. Cumming.

[8] John B. Gordon, *An Address Delivered Before the Confederate Survivors' Association, April 26, 1887* (Augusta GA: Chronicle Publishing Co., 1887), CSA Collection.

Street was Robert E. Williams, also black. Blacks lived in every part of the city and on the same streets as whites; they traveled on the same streetcars without distinction of seating; they went to the same revivals and public celebrations. They staged a huge parade on Emancipation Day, 1 January. They turned out in large numbers to greet President Grant and Frederick Douglass when they visited the town.

A remarkable group of black leaders grew to maturity in post-war Augusta. Channing Tobias, one of these men and an executive of the national YMCA., recalled, "There was something in that atmosphere. I cannot say just what it was. John Hope and I used to talk about it at times...it was possible for a Negro in the Augusta of John Hope's boyhood to aspire to the heights and to receive encouragement from white people in so doing." John Hope's biographer wrote that Augusta could boast "one of the most stimulating Negro communities in the South."[9] Major Cumming loaned the young John Hope money to attend Brown University; Hope went on to become president of Atlanta's Morehouse College. At a time when the state did not support high schools for whites, the Richmond County Board of Education opened Ware High School for black boys and girls in 1880.

Historians do not agree on why the racial climate changed, only that it declined drastically. One theory is that those who joined the Populist Party in the 1890s and appealed to black voters to join them in defeating the Democrats, turned against black voters for their failure to leave the Democratic Party. Former Populists formed a closely organized, ward-based association within the Democratic Party, and campaigned against the custom of buying black votes by advocating disenfranchisement of black voters. Another reason might have been that the old Confederate leaders were being replaced by new politicians who did not carry the burden of expected and

<hr>

[9] Cashin, *Old Springfield*, 66–68.

acceptable political behavior. It is impossible to think of Colonel Jones, or Major Cumming, as speaking about blacks as Tom Watson did when he wrote, "In the South we have to lynch him occasionally, and flog him, now and then, to keep him from blaspheming the Almighty, by his conduct, on account of his smell, and his color."[10] Watson promised his support to the gubernatorial candidate who favored disenfranchisement of blacks in 1906 and had a sufficient following of former Populists to elect Hoke Smith. Having found discrimination a useful tool, Watson kept his constituency loyal by appealing to fear of Catholics, Jews, foreigners, and "outsiders." The KKK represented his politics, and Watson called himself "King of the Ku Kluxers."

In his biography of Tom Watson, Vann Woodward wondered about the worsening political climate and blamed it on the "impersonal forces of economics and race and historical heritage." He calls Watson's life in particular, "in many ways the tragedy of a class, and mor especially, the tragedy of a section."[11] But the demagogues did not speak for all Southerners, though all Southerners shared the same conditions, and Watson did not speak for all Georgians, though all Georgians shared the same environment and heritage. When Thomas Dixon's drama *The Clansman* was performed in Augusta, with hooded riders on the stage, Major Joseph B. Cumming denounced it as "not only nasty but fiendish and cowardly, because it seeks to incite more violence against a helpless segment of our society."[12] Berry Benson reminded readers of the *Augusta Chronicle* that those who stand by when they could prevent injustice, share in the injustice.

The publication of *The Elmira Prison Camp* in 1913, the year of Mary Phagan's murder, reminded its readers of the values of an

---

[10] Woodward, *Tom Watson, Agrarian Rebel*, 432.

[11] Woodward, preface to *Tom Watson, Agrarian Rebel*, 2nd ed. (Savannah GA: The Beehive Press, 1973) x.

[12] *Augusta Chronicle*, 22 October 1905.

earlier day. It enabled Berry and his comrades to relive the war. Berry contributed a chapter to the book and recruited his friends to write their own experiences. Some of these friends, such as Joe Womack, he had kept in touch with since the war days; others he was able to locate later. Womack, whom Berry had had to leave behind when he escaped from Elmira, later was able to escape after forging a commandant's name to a pass (on Berry's advice). Womack had written an account of his imprisonment and escape for publication and told Berry, "You will find yourself figuring in the picture to some considerable extent." The two kept up a correspondence for the rest of their lives.[13] When Clay Holmes, a former Union soldier and a resident of Elmira, wrote Berry that he intended publishing a history of the prison camp, Berry secured Womack's story for the book.

John Fox Maull, a fellow tunneler, located Berry on 7 June 1877. Later, Maull wrote again to congratulate Berry on being chosen as a model for the statue on the Confederate Monument, writing, "I know that they could not have a truer or nobler son of the South than yourself." Maull and Berry agreed to write each other every 6 October, the anniversary of their escape, and they did so. By 1898 they had celebrated twenty such anniversaries.

Cecrops "Cyclops" Malone joined the literary celebrations. He told of his escape through enemy territory with J. P. Pretegnat. Unfortunately, Pretegnat died at Rio Grande City, Texas, in 1874. Berry contacted Pretegnat's widow and in 1899, she began writing. In that year, Washington Traweek, the group's leader, began corresponding with Berry, Maull, Malone, and Mrs. Pretegnat. And after John Fox Maull died on 22 September 1902, his wife, Annie, wrote to the others on every anniversary.[14]

---

[13] Berry Benson to Robert Adams, 23 May 1866; Joseph Womack to Benson, 13 August 1969, Benson Papers, ms. 2636, Southern Historical Collection, University of North Carolina, Chapel Hill.

[14] Maull to Benson, 7 June 1877; Malone to Benson, 6 October 1897, 7 October 1907, Benson Papers, Chapel Hill.

Ingraham Hasell, Berry's lieutenant at the end of the war, kept in close touch with Berry from his Charleston home. Ben Powell, the sharpshooter, came to visit Berry in 1913 and reminisce about their prowls about enemy lines. Ben was seventy-two then, with long, silky white hair.[15]

In his search for other comrades, Berry located Elmira survivors William Templin, George "Hickory" Jackson, and John Purifoy. The three of them met with Berry and Wash Traweek at Annie Maull's house in Montgomery, Alabama, on 4 February 1912. Illness kept Cecrops Malone away from that reunion. Berry found J. P. Crawford through one of Crawford's relatives, and wrote to Traweek that Crawford had hardly enough money to live on. Berry suggested that those who could afford to do so might contribute to a fund for the relief of needy comrades. "Parson" Scruggs, the "sick sergeant" who brought soup to keep up the strength of the diggers (in his separate tent; Berry got none) and who escaped with them, kept up a correspondence with Berry. "The story of Scruggs was known only to myself," Berry informed a friend.[16]

So, when Clay Holmes asked for Berry's help in compiling his story of Elmira, he received, in addition to Berry's account, the accounts of Wash Traweek, John Fox Maull, Parson Scruggs, Cyclops Malone, "Hickory" Jackson, and Joe Womack. Holmes recognized Berry's contribution in enlisting his friends. In the editing, Berry found Holmes to be overly cautious. Berry had used

---

[15] Berry Benson, "The War Book, Reminiscences of Berry Greenwood Benson, CSA," (Typescript prepared by Charles G. Benson, Ida Jane ["Jeanie"] Benson, and Olive Benson), Special Collections, Reese Library, Augusta State University, Augusta GA; hereafter cited as "War Book"), 694. A copy of the typescript is also held by the Southern Historical Collection at the University of North Carolina, Chapel Hill, in its Berry Benson Papers, ms. 2636. The original manuscript diary (ms. 326) is located in the Hargrett Rare Book & Manuscript Library at the University of Georgia in Athens.

[16] Berry Benson to John Purifoy, 27 January 1912; Purifoy to Benson, 21 February 1912; Benson to Traweek, 8 May 1912, all found in the Benson Papers, Chapel Hill; Holmes, *The Elmira Prison Camp*, 200.

the expression, "I'll be dammed." Holmes changed it to "He uttered an emphatic surprise." Holmes explained that children might read the book, and he wanted only "a high class" work. Therefore, he deleted references to harsh words, rats, stinking water, and other unpleasantness.[17]

In the publication process, Berry learned that one of the contributors was a man he had considered a friend while in prison, Melvin M. Conklin. Holmes revealed that Conklin was really a mole, a Yankee spy sent amongst the prisoners to discover escape plots. It was he who informed on Traweek and was responsible for his arrest. Berry hastened to tell Traweek about the informer. Oddly, after Berry had written Traweek, Conklin himself wrote a friendly letter to Berry, hoping to meet him at the Gettysburg reunion in July 1913. Berry replied that he would not be going to the reunion, and that if he had known Conklin was a spy, his life "would not have been worth five cents." However, Berry held no grudge, and hoped to meet Conklin if he ever got to Elmira. He asked Conklin to do him the favor of placing flowers on the grave of Benjamin Bogan, a friend who had died in prison and was buried in Elmira. Conklin did so for the next seven years until he became too frail.[18]

Berry wrote to Annie Maull to thank her for sending her husband's story, written shortly before his death, to Clay Holmes. He passed along Holmes's comment that Maull's account would be the first of the prisoners' narratives, the "foundation" for the others. Berry urged Mrs. Maull to be prepared to accept some kind of present from Holmes if he should send something. He did not tell her that he had suggested to Holmes to send the widow the hundred-

---

[17] Holmes, *The Elmira Prison Camp*, 158; Berry Benson to Traweek, 8 May 1912; Holmes to Benson, 10 May 1912, Benson Papers, Chapel Hill.

[18] Melvin Conklin to Berry Benson, 8 February 1912; Benson to Conklin, 10 February 1912, Benson Papers, Chapel Hill; *Augusta Chronicle*, 15 June 1920.

dollar stipend offered to the contributors, or that he had told Holmes not to mention that Berry had anything to do with it.[19]

The book was a literary success, handsomely printed by G. P. Putnam, and generously illustrated. Berry was pleased and proud of the book, but miffed at Holmes for sending him only one copy. He sent it back, thanking Holmes for the "loan." He had to buy books to send to friends and others that he wanted to impress. He informed Blackwood that he had sent copies to President Wilson, "who you know is an Augusta boy"; Theodore Roosevelt, "who I have always admired" (and who so resembled Berry in his love of life); Supreme Court justice Joseph R. Lamar, "who is a warm friend of mine"; and one to Blackwood. He sent a book to the relatives of the Gibson ladies who had offered him hospitality during his escape and fed him with all they had, chestnuts and milk. He sent another to Governor John Slaton in the hope of influencing his decision in the commutation of Leo Frank's sentence. His message was clear: A true Confederate had to stand up against injustice.[20]

The Elmira book further cemented ties already formed. The survivors agreed to observe a simple ceremony every anniversary of their escape. The would drink a glass of water (in deference to Berry's boyhood pledge not to touch liquor) to the health of the living, and write a letter of greeting to each other.[21]

The motivation to do the right thing led Berry to intervene in the 1898 textile strike in Augusta. "The soldier's heart is always in the right place," he wrote to the editor of the *Augusta Chronicle*; "Rough as he may ride in war, heavy blows as he may strike with his mailed hand in battle, his heart ever leaps in response to an appeal for pity,

---

[19] Berry Benson to Clay Holmes, 21 January 1913; Benson to Annie Maull, 22 January 1913, Benson Family Papers, in private collection of Arthur Dupre, Newark NJ.

[20] Berry Benson to Blackwood Benson, 6 December 1912, Benson Family Papers, in private collection of Arthur Dupre, Newark NJ; Berry Benson to Gov. John Slaton, 15 June 1915, John M. Slaton Papers, Georgia Archives, Morrow GA.

[21] *Augusta Chronicle*, 15 October 1914.

whether it be from a beaten and kneeling foe, or from the outstretched hands of oppressed womanhood and childhood."[22] If one used the language of chivalry, one had to act chivalrously.

At the time of the Leo Frank episode, Berry enjoyed the respect and admiration of his townspeople. Like the lad in Hawthorne's story whose virtues made him resemble the noble stone face on the mountain, Berry had become recognized as "the Man on the Monument." It was no longer the anonymous enlisted man standing atop the shaft; it was Berry Benson.

A Confederate soldier's burden included the obligation to pass along the old virtues to younger generations. A 1913 newspaper notice called attention to "an interesting event." Mr. Berry Benson would read a portion of his war journal at the North Augusta School. The announcement explained that the younger generation did not know all they should about the Civil War, "and the old generation who bore the heat and burden of the day are rapidly passing away."[23]

As the grey line of Confederate veterans grew thinner, parades and reunions took on greater importance. Another war loomed in 1917, and parades became patriotic celebrations. The *Augusta Chronicle* made public note of Berry Benson's seventy-fourth birthday on 9 February of that year, describing him as "widely traveled, an omnivorous reader, and always thirsting for an increase in knowledge." Berry marched as usual in Augusta's Memorial Day parade; however, the big event of the year was the veterans' parade in Washington in June, and he intended to be part of it.[24]

Berry thought that the parade might present an opportunity for a signal of reconciliation between North and South. He wrote to Jimmy Dumars of Elmira, New York, to join him in Washington and stay at the Washington home of daughters Jeanie, Olive, and Lewis. Jimmy Dumars was the twelve-year-old son of a Union officer at the

[22] Ibid., 24 December 1898.
[23] Ibid., 10 January 1913.
[24] *Augusta Chronicle*, 9 October 1916, 25 May, 6 June 1917.

Elmira Prison Camp who had the run of the place and whom Berry befriended. Berry urged Dumars to bring former guard Melvin Conklin with him. One of the staff of the *Augusta Chronicle*, D. C. Stebbins, happened to have been in the Union army, and by a quirk of coincidence, had also been a guard at Elmira Prison at the time Berry escaped. He had joked about arresting Berry on Augusta's streets. Berry invited Stebbins to be his guest in Washington. When they reached Washington, Berry's comrades made a show of arresting Stebbins and confining him to "Camp Benson."[25]

The parade on 5 June was a grand affair, attended by President Woodrow Wilson and a galaxy of dignitaries. As usual, Berry carried his gun, the only soldier to do so. He wore his old uniform, torn at the knees, and for verisimilitude, no underwear. A rolled blanket, a canteen, and a rusty tin cup added to the authenticity. Nearly all the other marchers wore new grey uniforms. The organizers placed Berry at the head of the Georgia battalion, ten paces behind the mounted commander, and ten paces ahead of the next man. Berry was in his glory, and the crowd loved the sight of him; "I was cheered and handclapped all the way," he wrote to Blackwood. When the line of march reached the presidential party at the reviewing stand, the veterans broke rank and rushed to shake President Wilson's hand. Berry watched, amused. Then he looked to his left and saw three newsreel cameras aimed at him. "Come closer," one of the men called. Obligingly, Berry approached while the cranks on the cameras ground away. The police restored order and the march resumed, but the pause made Berry a celebrity. His picture was shown in theaters all over the country as the consummate image of the Confederate soldier. Nothing could have pleased him more.[26]

---

[25] Ibid., 3, 6, 28 June 1917.
[26] Berry Benson to Charles B. Griffin, 2 July 1917, Benson Family Papers, in private collection of Arthur Dupre, Newark NJ; Berry to Blackwood Benson, 1 July 1917, Benson Papers, Chapel Hill; *Augusta Chronicle*, 28 June 1917.

When Ken Burns produced his marvelous documentary of the Civil War in 1990, he included the segment of the 1917 film featuring Berry Benson, and interspersed quotes from Berry's war journal throughout.[27]

Before leaving Washington, Berry and his son Charlie, then a civil engineer in the Department of the Interior, traveled to nearby Point Lookout and the site of the prison. They found only a plowed field, but the visit whetted Berry's nostalgia. Returning by train to Augusta, he reported to his office at the King Mill still wearing his old uniform, explaining that he had to catch up on his bookkeeping. He tossed his gun aside and went to work.

"Been home?" he was asked.

"No, I'll go at six o'clock."

"Had dinner?"

"Ate on the train," Berry replied.[28]

Back from his brief encounter with the president, Berry felt the need to send him advice. Beginning with a reminder that he had sent Wilson the Elmira book, he continued, "The whole war, Mr. Wilson, is for good, its purpose is to bring freedom and democracy to the world, and thrift and sobriety and organization for the public welfare. And it is to stop war. It is your duty when the war is ended, to see to that. I mean you. You will be in power—see to it." To emphasize the importance of the message, Berry had it witnessed by five fellow accountants. (One of whom, Thomas J. O'Leary, then acting president of King Mill in the wartime absence of Landon Thomas, was the grandfather of this writer.) Whether Berry knew Wilson as a boy as well as he knew Joseph R. Lamar, Wilson's friend and neighbor, he certainly sounded as though he did. In the same letter, Berry suggested a method of dealing with German submarines. If our

---

[27] Ken Burns's epic documentary appeared on public television in 1990 (Ken Burns, *The Civil War* [Florentine Films Production in association with WETA-TV, Public Broadcasting System, 1990]).

[28] *Augusta Chronicle*, 17 June 1917.

merchant ships were coated with a mirror-like substance, they would reflect only water and be hidden from the U-boats. The method was never tried, but it might have worked.[29]

Berry searched for ways to make himself useful to the war effort. When the YMCA advertised for accountants to volunteer to go to Europe, he immediately sent his name in, but he was not chosen. He wrote the lyrics to a patriotic song, "Johnny Over the Sea," and hummed the tune to Jeanie who set it to music. He published it and sent proceeds to charity.[30]

Berry found a cause near to his heart when he read about the plight of French children whose fathers had been killed in the war; some had been abandoned. He found ways to "adopt" five of these orphans. In addition, he solicited help from prominent Augustans and arranged for the care of 160 children in all. Berry treasured the photographs and letters he received from his "grandchildren." Jusserand, the French ambassador to the United States, wrote a personal letter of thanks to Berry for his work in caring for orphans.[31]

In the process of exchanging dollars for francs, he noticed an opportunity for chicanery. Francs sold for a fixed price in the United States, but about half that amount in France. Concerned, he wrote Postmaster General Burleson on 4 November 1919, that the system was an open invitation to fraud. Burleson answered in a typically bureaucratic way, by informing Berry that the exchange rate was fixed, and he could do nothing about it. In reply, Berry wanted to know why the weather bureau could make daily changes in its prognostications and the post office could not. He explained that by buying cheap francs in France and exchanging them in this country he could make a fortune; "the only deterrent is that I decline to be dishonest." Burleson refused to be budged, assuring Berry that there

---

[29] Berry Benson to President Woodrow Wilson, 26 July 1917, Benson Family Papers, in private collection of Arthur Dupre, Newark NJ.

[30] *Augusta Chronicle*, 5 September 1918, 29 June 1919.

[31] Ibid., 16 January, 4 September 1919.

was no chance of peculation. By now, Berry had become exasperated. His letter to the postmaster general of 13 February 1920 notes, "Your gate is wide open, and there are men smarter than I am who can see it, and who haven't as much conscience as I have. Shut the gate and shut it quick."[32]

In fact, an Italian immigrant with a prison record had already walked through the gate. In August 1919, Carlos "Charles" Ponzi wrote to a man in Spain who returned a postal coupon worth about one cent in Spain. When Ponzi exchanged the coupon at the American post-office, he found that each was worth six cents. He realized that he could buy a hundred dollars worth of stamps in Spain and exchange them for six hundred dollars in the United States. On 26 December 1919 (after Berry had warned Postmaster General Burleson about such things), Ponzi formed a company called the Security Exchange Company, promising huge returns on investments. Thousands of people invested in Ponzi's company. By the summer of 1920, Ponzi had taken in an estimated eight million dollars.[33]

On 30 July 1920, Berry Benson sent an urgent telegram to Massachusetts attorney general Joseph Pelletier urging him to shut Ponzi down. "These intelligent postmasters know almost as much as rabbits. Ponzi and his tribe buy foreign postal money orders on America which American bankers exchange on Europe. Shut the door and shut it quick."[34] In fact, Pelletier had managed to persuade Ponzi to stop accepting investments (averaging $200,000 a day) as of 26 July while he looked at Ponzi's books. The announcement started a run on Ponzi's bank, but Ponzi put up a bold front, returning dollar

---

[32] Berry Benson to Postmaster General Burleson, 4 November 1919; Burleson to Benson, 8 November 1919; Benson to Burleson, 5 February 1920; Burleson to Benson, 11 February 1920; Benson to Burleson, 13 February 1920. All of above are in Benson Papers, Chapel Hill.

[33] *Augusta Chronicle*, 8 August 1920.

[34] Berry Benson to Atty. Gen. Pelletier, 30 July 1920, Benson Papers, Chapel Hill.

for dollar, and gradually stemmed the panic. However, the end came for him on 10 August 1920, when the auditors announced that Ponzi was bankrupt. Ultimately, Ponzi was sentenced to five years in federal prison for using the mails to defraud. The postmaster general found that it was possible, after all, to change to a policy of flexible exchange rates.

In the midst of the furor over the Ponzi fraud, the *Augusta Chronicle* of 8 August gave Berry Benson credit for exposing the scheme in a front page headline that read, "Sergt. Berry Benson of Augusta Exposed Exchange Speculation," and added in smaller type, "Warned Postmaster General Month Before Ponzi Began Operations that Millions Could be Made at Expense of Government." The article reviewed Berry's fruitless exchange of letters with the postmaster general.[35]

Berry stepped vigorously into the decade of the 1920s, intellectually as well as physically. His extant letters reveal only shreds of evidence about his personal philosophy and spiritual inclinations. He had carried his mother's Bible throughout the war and found comfort in its message. He might have pondered the Apostle Paul's statement that "creation itself will be set free from its bondage to decay and obtain the glorious liberty of the children of God."[36] As a young man he would have read Thoreau and Emerson and been influenced by the idea of a divinity pervading all of nature. As he matured, his beliefs were affected by the intellectual currents swirling about the early years of the twentieth century. Thinkers like William James, Alfred North Whitehead, and John Dewey held that the world was not fixed and static but in the process of becoming. He would not have known about a contemporary Jesuit priest and anthropologist named Teillard de Chardin who wrote that the world was caught up in an evolutionary spiral that would lead to a brotherhood of man and

---

[35] *Augusta Chronicle*, 8 August 1920.
[36] Romans 8:21.

union with God, but he probably would have agreed with Teillard. He wrote to his daughter Jeanie, "We see that the world in all its ways is moving onward and upward—human affairs are but part of this great onward movement—death is merely an incident in the midst of life."[37] Berry remained open to the belief that because energy cannot be destroyed, a being's energy system could reappear in another form.

Late in life he learned of a system of belief called "theosophy" that held that God is infinite energy and that matter, being made up of energy, shares in divinity. He wrote to Sir Arthur Conan Doyle, the creator of Sherlock Holmes and a theosophist, that he had long been a theosophist before he ever heard the term.[38] Some of the finer points of theosophy anticipated the "string" theory that the ultimate stuff of the universe is vibrating particles of energy. Berry loved to work out puzzles, and the riddle of the universe was the greatest puzzle of them all.

Evidence of Berry Benson's sustained intellectual vigor was his continuing practice of monitoring dictionaries. On 28 April 1922, he wrote to Funk and Wagnall's Company with corrections to several items. One such was the word entered as "Tugurium," Berry asked if it should not be "Tegurium, from the Latin Tegere, to cover." Not many men of seventy-nine—or of any age—have the energy or the will to proof-read dictionaries. In a response to a 1922 letter he wrote to the Merriam Company, publishers of Webster's Dictionary, he received a query from Curtis Rowley, president of the company: "Your name signed to a letter that recently received attention from our editorial department brings up memories of bygone days and I have wondered as to whether you are, or are not, the gentleman of that name I have in mind. I refer to the Elmira Confederate prison

[37] Berry Benson to Jeanie Benson, 28 February 1900, Benson Family Papers, in private collection of Frances Thompson, Starkville MS.
[38] Berry Benson to Arthur Conan Doyle, 28 November 1920, Benson Papers, Chapel Hill.

camp in the year of 1864, and the escape of ten prisoners by tunneling on the night of October 7 of that year."

Rowley then revealed that he had been a guard on duty the night of the escape. He remembered that he had caught a prisoner out of his tent that same evening and had let him go back to his tent instead of putting him under arrest. "Perhaps you are the man I challenged for being out of quarters?" He would "very much appreciate" a letter from Berry. Rowley, the president of the Merriam Company signed himself, "H. Curtis Rowley, Pvt., Co. C, New York Inf." The signature is interesting. At the time Rowley and his family lived in the elegant Queen Anne-style Wyndhurst House outside Springfield, Massachusetts, an 1843 mansion that Rowley had purchased in 1893. The expansive gardens were designed by Frederick Law Olmsted. The Rowleys' distinguished guests included President William McKinley who dined at Wyndhurst in 1899. Yet, the war had left its mark on Rowley's identity, as it had on Berry's, and one would always think of himself as Private Rowley and the other as Sergeant Benson. Berry returned a courteous letter saying yes he was indeed one of the tunnelers, but no he was not the man Rowley let go. He wished Rowley well.[39]

Berry remained as physically vigorous as he was mentally. His boyhood love of the outdoors never left him. He enjoyed leading Boy Scouts on overnight hikes. On 1 May 1921, the scribe for Troop One, based at Sacred Heart Church, wrote about a coming outing: "Ladies and gentlemen, let me introduce you to Mr. Berry Benson, the biggest sport that ever watched a campfire glow!" A week later the same reporter described the adventure. The boys walked from Sacred Heart across the Thirteenth Street bridge up Georgia Avenue to the Benson home where they set out on a fifteen-mile hike. They set up tents near a creek and cooked their supper. As darkness settled,

---

[39] Jim Garvey, "Berry Benson in Peacetime," *Augusta Richmond County History* 33/1 (Spring 2002): 34–35; *Augusta Chronicle*, 13 May 1922; Berry Benson to Curtis Rowley, 22 May 1922, Benson Papers, Chapel Hill.

Berry suggested they go snipe hunting. Each boy was stationed all alone with an open sack and a candle and Berry was supposed to chase snipes into their bags. Berry had great fun making scurrying noises in the darkness, but of course there were no snipes in the area and had probably never been any. When his candle gave out, one of the boys yelled for Mr. Berry, and he took pity on them and called off the hunt. Next morning, Berry was up first and took a swim in the river. The boys decided that the water was too cold to follow his example. At the age of seventy-eight, Berry was the liveliest scout of them all.[40]

When a reporter asked Jeanie Benson if Berry was up to the 1921 Memorial Day parade, she replied that he had just completed a fifteen-mile hike and she supposed he was good for it. Indeed, he did march in the parade that year, in the same tattered uniform that he had worn at Appomattox. The *Augusta Chronicle* reported, "The sergeant stepped proudly out in advance of the column as he might have done when he was going off to fight the Yankees."[41]

Of all Berry's parades, he probably enjoyed the last one most. Berry was invited to lead the Georgia Brigade in the 22 June 1922 Veterans Parade in Richmond, Virginia. While waiting to fall in behind the Florida Brigade, he was startled to hear a young lady call out, "Won't you come ride with us in our automobile?" Her car carried some other dignitary and was waiting to join the parade.

"Why, no," answered Berry. "I am ordered to march alone, in advance of the brigade, in this old war rig as you see, with my rifle." Impulsively, he added, "You'd better march along with me."

To his great surprise she replied, "Well, I will." She then stepped lightly from the car and came over to his side.

Berry tried not to act flustered and told the lady, "You may march with me one block." The drums started up, and they took their position at the head of the Georgia column. They enjoyed

---

[40] *Augusta Chronicle*, 1, 8 May 1921.
[41] Ibid., 27 May 1921.

themselves so much that Berry forgot about her marching only one block and said to her, "Here, slip your hand in my arm; we are going to march together the whole way."

The crowds lining the streets cheered to see the old soldier arm in arm with the pretty young lady. "There was never anything to equal this in Richmond before; even Marshal Foch when he came from France, did not get this cheering that you are getting," she said.

"That *you* are getting," Berry replied. He knew that the cheering was for both of them; he the symbol of the old order, and she the bright vision of the future. All along the line of march cameras clicked, women rushed out to take Berry's hand or pat him on the back, and now and then a rebel yell sounded shrilly. The years seemed to slip by, and Berry remembered women cheering A. P. Hill's Corps as they marched through Richmond tired and grimy from the Seven Days campaign.

The 23 June *Richmond Times-Dispatch* carried a description of the parade. A paragraph referred to Berry and his fair companion, "A touch of pathos was added by the sight of an aged and bent warrior, in full field equipment, including musket, rolled blanket and canteen, supported along the line by a young woman." Berry Benson would not be himself if he let that description go unanswered. He managed to strike a good-natured tone in his letter to the editor, "Pathetic, rats! Bent, fiddlesticks! Why I marched I protest in this review as straight and erect as ever I marched in the Valley turnpike behind Stonewall Jackson, one of his foot cavalry. Supported by a young woman—Why I could have picked the slim damsel up in my arms and carried her, too, had there been need to." Berry advised the offending reporter to bring his spectacles the next time Berry marched with his lady companion, "for my charming comrade of the march has promised me that in the next parade she will march with me again."[42]

---

[42] The *Richmond Times-Dispatch* article and Berry's response appeared in the *Augusta Chronicle*, 16 July 1922.

The Richmond review marked the last time Berry donned his uniform. But no dramatist or film director could have staged a more fitting last march for him. In his old battle garb, he marched like a clearer-eyed Don Quixote who had conquered his windmills and completed his quests, taking the plaudits of an admiring crowd—with his Dulcinea on his arm. He had borne the Confederate's burden gallantly, and could now face whatever transcendental adventure awaited.

Epilogue

Berry Benson died on New Year's Day 1923. He would have celebrated his eightieth birthday on 9 February. Until his last morning, he remained hearty and healthy. He had breakfast with daughters Jeanie and Olive as usual, but then began to feel ill. Jeanie called the doctor, who did what he could to ease the pain, but Berry grew worse. Early that evening the old soldier closed his eyes and died peacefully. A small group of surviving Confederate veterans acted as honorary pallbearers at his funeral the next day. Hundreds of mourners attended. The Ladies Memorial Association draped the Confederate Monument in black.[1]

Algernon Morgan wrote a tribute to Berry as a guest editorial in the *Augusta Chronicle* on 3 January. So many readers asked Morgan for a copy that he had the article printed. This writer can pen no better epitaph than his.

> I think I have never known a finer man, or a better than Berry Benson, and in making this statement I am carefully measuring the value of the meaning conveyed by the words I use. Above all things, he was a kindly hearted man; his whole being pulsed with a broad, universal sympathy for every living creature; he was the friend and brother of all men; he loved and was in turn loved by the little creatures of the woods, four-footed and winged; so kindly was he that he would walk out of the way rather than crush a worm or insect under his feet.

---

[1] Berry was survived by his children, Arthur, Jeanie, Olive, Charles, and Dorothy Lewis (then with the married name of Mrs. Eugene Rosen); by his brother Blackwood; and by his sisters Callie and Elizabeth (Mrs. C. C. Carey and Mrs. S. G. Rook).

When the World War left thousands of desolate orphans in France, Berry Benson's great heart responded to their cry of distress, and, quitting all other activities, he made a personal canvass from house to house of our wealthier citizens, until he had found protectors and benefactors for one hundred and sixty French orphans.

Not a wealthy man himself, though in comfortable circum-stances, I think that he and his family, inspired by his great sympathy, themselves took care of five of these little waifs of grim circumstance—these innocent victims of hate.

I think that Berry Benson had found content in this life in the simple things of our woods and fields. He was never happier than on a day spent in the woods, with his basket on his arm, gathering specimens of our native flora. The towering pines were his cathedrals; among them he was ever in a gentle and reverent mood; he truly found "books in the running brooks, sermons in stone, and good in everything."

He loved the splendor of the sunshine and the gloom of the storm; he gloried in the calm beauty of the eternal stars and the mystic majesty of the moon; nothing in all of Nature was too small to find its niche of affection in his great, kindly heart. He had no sordid, ignoble ambitions; his most ardent wish was to continuously develop his mind; if to be forever hungry and thirsty for knowledge is what makes a philosopher, then Berry Benson was a philosopher in its clearest definition.

His was a wonderfully, bright, incisive, alert mentality; spurred on by his keen desire to enlarge his store of information, he was always deeply interested in the new things, new theories, new discoveries of science. His was the distinctly literary mind, and he possessed to a brilliant degree the power of expression. He has written many beautiful sketches for the *Augusta Chronicle*, the *Century*, and *Scribner's* magazine; after sixty-five years of age he practically learned the French language, so that he could read the rich stores of its literature in the original tongue.

Bravest of the brave of the Confederate soldiers in the great Civil War, he did his duty in that war without any hatred of his enemies; he did not know what hatred means; he had blotted out of his heart all hatred, bitterness and discontent, so that he only had room left for love; no old Confederate had more friends than he among the old guard of the Grand Army of the Republic.

A good man, a kindly man, a gentle man; it can never be said of any man more truly than of him that "the world was his church, to do good was his religion." Emerson has said that there are as many religions as there are men. I only wish that more of us had the religion of Berry Benson.

So let us think and let us speak of Berry Benson. His active mind, his keen sympathies and his great heart are stilled, and our whole community is the poorer because of it. There was but one Berry Benson, and we shall not look upon his like again.

He found his greatest joy and content in the simple things of our woods and fields; let us hope that he has now found the Supreme—the Everlasting Content!

Long ago while writing his war journal, Berry anticipated his last moments and thought of the rifle he had proudly carried during and after the war:

I would fain, when I lie old and dying, feeling the chill of Death begin to creep over me, take its (rifle) barrel once more in my hand, and felt its slim trigger with my finger once again before I die. And I would that some old comrade, ere the listless few disperse from the fresh mound they have raised over the old man, should take the old weapon, and with none other accompaniment, three times load it and fire a parting salute to the spirit that shall no more mingle in war. No more the twisted blanket, no more the measured tramp of four marching abreast, no more the grease-soiled hip where swings the haversack, no more the hitching back of the canteen from its noisy clink on the shank of the bayonet. For the long campaign is over, the last drill and dress-parade, the last tattoo has beaten, and the soldier, old and weary and worn, lies down to his last sleep.[2]

[2] *Augusta Chronicle*, 3 January 1923; Berry Benson, "The War Book, Reminiscences of Berry Greenwood Benson, CSA," (Typescript prepared by Charles G. Benson, Ida Jane ["Jeanie"] Benson, and Olive Benson), Special Collections, Reese Library, Augusta State University, Augusta GA; hereafter cited as "War Book"), 41–42. A copy of the typescript is also held by the Southern Historical Collection at the University of North Carolina, Chapel Hill, in its Berry Benson Papers, ms. 2636. The original manuscript diary (ms. 326) is located in the Hargrett Rare Book & Manuscript Library at the University of Georgia in Athens.

Index

Benson, Berry Greenwood (1843–
1923): abstention from alcohol of,
7-8, 28, 246; and Confederate
flag's symbolism, viii; diaries and
War Journal of, ix, x; and slavery,
ix, 8, 51;
—Antebellum life of BB: birth and
parentage of, 1-2; childhood of,
2-4; childhood reading interests
of, 6-7; education of, 4-6, 8, 9;
employment as bookkeeper of, 9
—Civil War experiences of BB: acts
as assistant adjutant general, 87-
88; in attack on the Jones House,
Petersburg, 148-149; in the
Appomattox campaign, 149-163;
at Appomattox Court House, 161,
163-165; attitude toward
conscripts of, 88; Augusta
furlough of (1863), 66-70; avoids
execution of deserters, 146;
becomes sharpshooter, 90; books
read by (early 1864),87; captured
by Union pickets (May 1864),
104; captured by home guard
(June 1864), 107; and Company
H messmates, 21-22;
confrontation of Captain Haskell
by, 20-21; in the Chancellorsville
campaign, 60-64; as escapee from
Elmira Prison, 124-133; in First
Manassas campaign, 15; at
Blackwater River, 23; at Cedar
Mountain (train guard), 35;
Elmira Prison escape plots of,
111-121; at Fort Sumter, 13-14;
in the Fredericksburg campaign,
55-57; at Gaines' Mill, 26-30; at
Germantown, Maryland, 16; at
Goldsborough, N.C., 23; at
Hatcher's Run, 151-152; at
Laurel Hill, Virginia, 34; at
Manassas Junction, 37; at Old
Capitol Prison, 108-110; in the
Petersburg campaign, 143-149; at

Point Lookout Prison, 105-106;
cares for wounded Blackwood,
30; escapes from Point Lookout
prison, 106; fights at Second
Manassas, 38-40; follows
Gettysburg campaign through
newspapers and letters, 70-84;
offended by Union soldiers'
profanity, 104, 105; in the
Peninsula Campaign, 24-33; as
prisoner of war, 104-121; in the
Savannah campaign, 134-139; in
the Second Manassas Campaign,
34-42; in the Spotsylvania
campaign, 96-101; suggested for
independent command by
General Lee, 150, 150n.14; at
Sutherland's Station, 155-156;
travels homeward from
Appomattox, 167-168; in the
Wilderness campaign, 91-96;
joins Capt. William Haskell's
company, 17; log cabin in winter
camp built by, 88; on
reconnaissance after Spotsylvania,
103-104; on reconnaissance
during Peninsula Campaign, 25-
26; on reconnaissance with Capt.
Haskell, 24; in the Sharpsburg
Campaign, 43-49; visits Great
Dismal Swamp, 22-23; in winter
quarters (1862), 50-51; leaves
Blackwood for march to
Fredericksburg, 51-52; reacts to
Capt. Haskell's death, 80; reads
and shares Bible, 35; re-
enlistment for war of, 89; returns
to active duty (December 1863),
86-87; and skulker (April 1865),
154; spying adventure along the
Rapidan of, 90-91; stay with
Mosby's men,; travels to
Savannah under artillery fire
(December 1864), 135; visits
Blackwood in Richmond hospital,